REDUCING POVERTY, BUILDING PEACE

REDUCING POVERTY, BUILDING PEACE

Coralie Bryant and Christina Kappaz

Kumarian
Press, Inc.

Reducing Poverty, Building Peace

Published in 2005 in the United States of America by Kumarian Press, Inc., 1294 Blue Hills Avenue, Bloomfield, CT 06002 USA

The text of this book is set in Sabon 10/12
Production and design by Scribe, Inc.
Printed by McNaughton-Gunn, Inc.

∞:The paper used in this publication meets the minimum requirements of the American National Standard for Information Sciences—Permanence of Paper for printed Library Materials, ANSI Z39.48-1984

Library of Congress Cataloging-in-Publication Data

Bryant, Coralie.
    Reducing poverty, building peace / Coralie Bryant and Christina Kappaz.
      p. cm.
Includes bibliographical references.
    ISBN 1-56549-205-6 (pbk.: alk. paper)
1. Poverty. 2. Peacebuilding. I. Kappaz, Christina. II. Title.
    HC79.P6B69 2005
    362.5'6—dc22

2005006059

14 13 12 11 10 09 08 07 06 05   10 9 8 7 6 5 4 3 2 1   First Printing 2005

For Abigail, Eve, Isaiah, and Camila...
with the hope that their generation will know times
with less poverty and more peace

CONTENTS

ILLUSTRATIONS

FIGURES

PHOTOGRAPHS

TABLES

PREFACE AND ACKNOWLEDGMENTS

These are troubled times. And these are miraculous times. We live in a world full of people harmed or homeless due to wars, natural disasters, and poor governance. Millions of refugees and two billion very poor people are struggling each day to stay alive. Yet, simultaneously, these are also times of positive changes that improve lives. New lifesaving discoveries have been made. We know more about protecting our environment. More newborns arrive safely; more of their mothers survive. More of us live longer, are literate, and have access to more information than ever before in human history.

Our world is not "either-or," but rather "both-and." We live in an era that is both war-torn and full of promise; it is full of both new opportunities and serious challenges. We are more aware of the scale of poverty and better positioned to address it. We know more about violence and somewhat more about how to prevent it. Much of the world is changing, with boundaries moving, technological innovation spreading, and inventions underway. We are more secure (warnings are issued on everything from traffic snarls to pending hurricanes) and less secure (terrorist strikes are more likely and less predictable). Politically, more countries are democratic than ever before in human history. More local grassroots organizing is helping to build civil societies in transitional countries in the new and enlarging European Union, as well as throughout Africa, Asia, and Latin America. People the world over are coming together to work on development in their villages, communities, towns, and countries, as well as at the international level.

Much of the material in this book is derived from our years of practical experience working on development programs and projects. Coralie (Corky) was a senior staff member at the World Bank for 7 years. While there, her work included projects in Zambia and in Brazil, as well as work on the World Bank's policy paper on governance (1991). Prior to the World Bank, she worked in Uganda, Zambia, Botswana, Swaziland, Bangladesh, South Africa, and Lesotho. Christina, too, has worked with the World Bank and the Inter-American Development Bank and is currently a consultant with Millennia Consulting in Chicago. Her work has involved projects throughout Central and South America, Eastern Europe, and the Caribbean including

Mexico, Peru, Brazil, Panama, and Jamaica, among other countries, as well as working on domestic issues in Washington, D.C., New York, and Chicago. Throughout our decades of development work, we both have noticed the striking similarities, as well as important differences, in the conditions and problems that deepen poverty in north and south, east and west.

A recent shared seminal experience came in working with Marc Lindenberg on a consultative process with senior leaders of major international NGOs and writing up what was learned from that experience in *Going Global: Transforming International Relief and Development NGOs* between 1998 and 2002. (Tragically, Marc died in May 2002. We will always miss him.) To gather more data for that work, we interviewed, in France, England, and the United States, several senior leaders in Oxfam UK, CARE France, Save the Children UK, Médecins Sans Frontières, World Vision, Oxfam America, CARE International, CARE USA, Save the Children USA, and Plan International. We also talked with researchers and practitioners at the Overseas Development Institute UK, the Institute of Development Studies at the University of Sussex, and at the London School of Economics, especially the Center on Civil Society.

Throughout these interviews, we were struck by the distinction between European approaches to aspects of poverty—for example, policies promoting inclusion to address social exclusion—and differently conceived approaches to similar problems in the United States. We were also impressed at how far all these groups—on either side of the Atlantic—had come in conceiving of poverty not as a "North–South" problem, but rather as a nested group of problems with real similarities in different places. Many NGOs, we learned, had taken down the separation within their organizations between domestic programming and international programming. Staff, who knew how to work in India or Ecuador, also knew how to proceed in the poorest sections of Los Angeles or London. Of course, they knew how to contextualize their work—and they also knew well the similarities commonly found in any poor community in any country. Organizations that had done humanitarian work in Afghanistan or the Balkans or in Africa such as, among others, Mercy Corps, were among the first to respond to the terrorist attacks of September 11, 2001. Some staff, about to head to Afghanistan, headed instead to New York, ready yet again to deliver emergency humanitarian care.

We learned a great deal from the leaders and staff of these NGOs and hence want to thank the special people who taught us during those Senior NGO Leaders meetings over those 3 years. In the Oxfam network, David Bryer, Barbara Staunton, Ray Offenheiser, Susan Holcombe, Justine Forsythe, and Chris Roche. In the CARE network, Peter Bell, Kevin Henry, and Damien Desjonquieres. In the Save the Children network, Charles McCormick, Burkhard Gnaerig, Carolyn Miller, and Gary Shaye.

In the Plan network, John Greensmith, Subhadra Belbase, Martin McCann, and Sam McPherson. In the Médecins Sans Frontières network, Philippe Bibberson, Jean Herve-Bradol, James Orbinski, Odile Hardy, Bruce Mahin, and Francoise Saulnier. In Mercy Corps International, Neal Keny-Guyer and Nancy Lindborg. In the International Medical Corps, Nancy Aossey and Steve Tomlin. At the International Rescue Committee, Ronald Levy and Gerry Martone. Michael Edwards, who attended the first session at Bellagio was, as one would predict, especially adept at cutting through material to reach core insights. There are many, many more that we should name. May they forgive us for not wanting to wear out our readers' patience while we remain grateful for their help. We thank them all for their assistance in contributing to our understanding of the scale and scope of their work on poverty and humanitarian relief.

This NGO process led to current ongoing work, in particular research comparing and contrasting the theory and practice of NGOs in Europe, especially France, and the United States. For that ongoing work we want to thank Francois Rubio of Médecins du Monde and Philippe Leveque and Damien Desjonquieres of CARE France, Marc Levy of GRET, and Henri Rouille d'Orfeuil of Coordination Sud. Their insights into the similarities and differences on either side of the Atlantic, as well as within the European Union, added to our perspective.

This book also grows out of our work with many wonderful colleagues and students in the Economic and Political Development Program (EPD) at the School of International and Public Affairs, Columbia University. We both have found it exciting and rewarding to watch anywhere from sixty-five to eighty-five skilled young professionals enter into work on poverty reduction each year.

Before joining the faculty at Columbia University, Corky had, along with Steven Arnold, founded the International Development Program in the School of International Service at the American University in Washington, D.C. That program, led now for several years by David Hirschman, has become one of the preeminent programs in the United States. Both Steve and Corky thank him for his wonderful stewardship. Corky is delighted to now be helping L'Institut d'Études Politique (Sciences Po) in Paris as it builds its new professional master's degree with a concentration in international development. This important program in Sciences Po, with its own outstanding reputation, will contribute more skilled young professionals to this critically needed field.

We are convinced that Development Studies Programs, with a clear focus on participatory development to reduce poverty, matter. There are several such programs in the United States, the United Kingdom, France, Canada, Holland, Germany, India, Australia...and doubtless in other places. One of the signature aspects of the Economic and Political Development Program at

Columbia University is the Applied International Development Workshop that we expanded, with much faculty support, into a major part of the curriculum in the School of International and Public Affairs (SIPA). In this Applied International Development Workshop, students work *pro bono* on real projects for agencies or organizations (for example, UNICEF, Oxfam, TechnoServe, World Bank, UNDP, Open Society Institute/Soros Foundations Network, Rockefeller Foundation, ACCION International, Catholic Relief Services, Movimento Sem Terra, International Organization for Migration, and many local community organizations). As they are still full-time students, they only travel to do field research when breaks allow them the time and clients help support the costs. That SIPA is committed to the value of this work is indicated by Dean Lisa Anderson's support and commitment to the Workshop, for which we thank her. One aspect of this support is a modest travel fund, to which clients contribute. This Workshop is currently fielding ten to thirteen teams of seven to eight students each every year. We want to thank Fida Adely, now the SIPA Workshop Coordinator, for her creative and thorough work in making each Workshop experience special.

The students in the Applied International Development Workshop have had as much influence on our thinking as we may have had on theirs. And the outstanding students at Sciences Po have contributed more new perspectives. Sciences Po now has its own Workshop, or *Atelier de Developpement*. The extraordinary leadership of Francis Verillaud and Laurent Bigorgne has made this possible. Pascal Delisle of the Alliance Program has also supported this major curricular innovation. The faculty that assisted with this endeavor in Paris proved to be adept and committed, making the first group of eight projects highly worthwhile for both graduate education and the clients they served. None of this would have been possible without the foresight of Richard Descoings, Director of Sciences Po, whose vision for Sciences Po is inspiring. He is working with commitment on a difficult and sophisticated curricular change process that promises to provide excellent preparation for future international leaders.

Another source of input for this book has been the students who in three different iterations of the course Global Poverty and Policy Choice pushed, challenged, debated, and critiqued different parts of the arguments made within this book. Coming from all over the globe, they conveyed their realities from Kenya to Finland; Iran to Argentina. They debated, discussed, and added to every aspect of the different issues we discuss in this volume. As they cited their own first hand experience or knowledge, the course grew, and so did our understanding of the scope of the poverty problem.

There are also a host of scholar/practitioners who shared their thinking and experience along the decades of work. The Development Management Network, as well as the scholar/practitioner networks, and the

Bethesda Friends (Quaker) Meeting have been for decades, and remain, constant sources of insight. All these sources mean there really are too many to name, but some so special they cannot be omitted. They include, but are not limited to, Chick and Judy Nelson, Peter and Ellie Szanton, Jane Coe, Porter and Lisa Dawson, Joan Nelson, Richard Nelson, Jacob Meerman, Deborah Brautigam, Derick and Jennifer Brinkerhoff, Benjamin Crosby, Tom Timberg, Ted Thomas, Colin Bradford, Jo Marie Greisgraber, Norman Uphoff, Alfred Stepan, Ousmane Kane, Joseph Stiglitz, Elliot Sklar, Jeffrey Sachs, Eric Hershberg, Shubham Chaudhuri, Robin Lewis, Steve Arnold, Malgosia Madajewicz, Marcia Wright, Helena Cobban, Eluned Schweitzer, and Guy Stevens.

And, in England, Donal Cruise O'Brien at the School of African and Oriental Studies; Shula Marks, formerly at the Institute of Commonwealth Studies and SOAS; Merle Lipton and Michael Lipton at the University of Sussex; and Robert Chambers at the Institute of Development Studies have all been, more than they might even know, sources of inspiration. We were very grateful for important suggestions made by Timothy M. Shaw, Director of the Institute of Commonwealth Studies, School of Advanced Study, University of London, for some revisions and additions to the original manuscript. We also want readers to become aware of the useful annual reports on civil society available on the website of the Center for Civil Society at the London School of Economics.

Sharbanou Tadjbakhsh has been a friend and source of insight into Tadjikistan, Uzbekistan, Afghanistan, Mongolia, and Iran. Her first hand knowledge about the costs of transition in Central Asia was a special help. Ashok Gurung's shared insights into Tibetan and Nepalese development were enlightening. The work and insights of Louise G. White have often been seminal in our thinking. And also the clear-headed insights of Ivana Aleksic and Marta Schaaf, whose in-depth experience in the Balkans, concern for the Roma therein, and focus on the need for a more peaceful and socially just future were apparent in every conversation. Suzue Saito kept in touch from Mozambique, educating us on how to program a rights-based approach to reducing child poverty.

Terry Bergdall shared insights on participatory evaluation and his work applying an assets-based model to international development work. The Institute for Cultural Affairs shared their participatory consensus workshop method. Colleagues at Millennia Consulting, including Jim Troxel, Karen Snyder, Ken O'Hare, Wendy Siegel, Carmen Mendoza, and Brenda Bannor, contributed to Christina's learning on community development in the United States and effective participatory processes.

Many other friends and colleagues shared articles and insights, often over hours of passionate discussion on these topics, and some even reviewed early drafts. We are particularly grateful to Anna Lappé, Lucy Mair, Darcy Tromanhauser, and Tara Rangarajan.

In Washington, D.C., at the World Bank, Gregory Ingram, Alexandre Marc, Lucia Fort, Michael Bamberger, Paul Collier, Paul Isenman, Chukwuma Obidegwu, Geoffrey Lamb, Alex Shakow, Marianne Haug, Adyline Waafass Ofosu-Amaah, Paula Donelly-Roark, Mamadou Dia, Tia Duer, and Sarwar Lateef were always helpful when we had more questions to pursue. And at the Inter-American Development Bank, Jacqueline Mazza, Consuelo Ricart, Elizabeth Davidsen, Maria Elena Nawar, Bernardo Guillamon, and others provided opportunities to work on projects that provided an ongoing learning experience.

We are also grateful to participants in the Development Policy Roundtables we organized, one of which provided an opportunity for us to present the outline of this book and receive valuable feedback. Some sessions included L. David Brown, John Sewell, Jacqueline Mazza, Larry Cooley, Sakiko Fukoda-Parr, Crispin Gregoire, Virginia Hodgkinson, Jacob Meerman, Michael Morfit, Joan Nelson, Haven North, Jeanne North, Nancy Ruther, Louise G. White, and Julie Fisher. Encouraged to do so by Ted Thomas, we hope to have another Development Policy Roundtable in the near future.

Our editor, Sarah Polen, deserves an award for her brave struggle to render our dense prose less so. Krishna Sondhi at Kumarian Press deserves a medal as well—for waiting patiently for a manuscript often lost in the wilderness of other work. But our husbands had the most patience of all. Ralph Bryant and Mauricio Ardila were sounding boards for ideas, engaging partners in debating some of the tough issues grappled with in the book, and rescue heroes when computer systems failed. Best of all they helped us keep at it, even when that came with costs to them.

Several different teams in the Applied International Development Workshop contributed photographs, especially of undertaking participatory action research. The Theta team, for example, worked over spring break in 2002 with the Kampala and Katakiri Traditional Healers' Associations in the Luzira and Omodoi-Adulgulu Village communities and provided us with the pictures used in Chapter 5 and the photos of the Ugandan homes in Chapter 2. Felicia Price Nigel and Asaf Kastner were the principal photographers. Working with Felicia and Asaf on the Theta team were Sang Hoon Lee, Storm Jackson, Sushant Palakurthi Rao, and Naomi Lince. A team working in Ecuador for the International Institute for Rural Reconstruction over spring break in 2004 also granted us permission to use their picture of their participatory action research on an impact evaluation of an IIRR microcredit program. That picture is in Chapter 5 as well. On that team were Rachel Dubin, Johanna Barrero, Maria Cruz Barluenga-Badiola, Marisol Vigil, Susan Grove, and Erika Helms. The picture of the Roma home came from a team working with the Roma. On that team were Victoria Chia, Jan Meher, Suzue Saito, Eileen Simpson, and Luis Rodriguez. The photo was most likely taken by Jam Meher or Victoria Chia. We thank them all for their permission to use it here.

We used to talk about the presence of a third world inside the first, and a first world inside the third. Now even those terms are obsolete. We often ask ourselves and others in the development field: Are we not all "developing" countries? The fast-paced changes intrinsic to globalization have changed irrevocably the terms of debate over development and its role in reducing poverty. We believe we are all on journeys in development; just the places where we fall down or stumble vary. This book is finally our chance to talk about what we have learned thus far on this road. It is also about what can be done to build opportunities for a less poor and more peaceful world.

No one of all those who tried their best to guide, correct, or educate us are to be blamed for shortcomings or failures in logic or fact in this book. We alone accept responsibility for our errors.

Coralie Bryant
Chevy Chase, Maryland
Christina Kappaz
Chicago, Illinois

ACRONYMS

ABCD—Asset Based Community Development

AIDS—Acquired Immune Deficiency Syndrome

CIDA—Canadian International Development Agency

EU—European Union

GDP—Gross Domestic Product

GNP—Gross National Product

HDR—Human Development Report (published by UNDP)

HIPC—Heavily Indebted Poor Countries

HIV/AIDS—Human Immunodeficiency Virus/Acquired Immune Deficiency Syndrome

IDB—Inter-American Development Bank

IMF—International Monetary Fund

MDG—Millennium Development Goals

NGO—Nongovernmental Organization

ODA—Official Development Assistance

OECD—Organization for Economic Cooperation and Development

PRA—Participatory Rural Appraisal

PRSP—Poverty Reduction Strategy Paper

SAF—Social Action Fund

SARS—Severe Acute Respiratory Syndrome

SIDA—Swedish International Development Agency

SIF—Social Investment Fund

USAID—United States Agency for International Development

UN—United Nations

UNAIDS—Joint United Nations Programme on HIV/AIDS

UNDP—United Nations Development Program

UNICEF—United Nations Children's Fund

UNESCO—United Nations Educational, Scientific and Cultural Organization

WDR—World Development Report (published by the World Bank)

WTO—World Trade Organization

1

POVERTY: THE GLOBAL PROBLEM

"The task is to put to, and at least alleviate, evident and atrocious poverty. This is [the] distressing, but all too real, dominant problem, the starting point from which we have to begin."
— Fernand Braudel, *A History of Civilizations*, 1979

INTRODUCTION

Poverty—around the world, not just in "developing" countries—is also where we have to begin. In our opening quotation, Braudel was referring to India, but he could as readily have been talking about nations all across our world, where poverty remains a dominant feature. Poverty is now, along with security, a major international concern. In the early 1990s, many hoped the end of the Cold War, the dismantling of the Soviet Union, the unwinding of South Africa's apartheid, and the quickened pace of cross-border trade would mark the beginning of a new era of improved well-being. But that is not what has happened. Instead, for hundreds of millions, poverty and wars have laid waste to their lives.

Poverty, violence, and war interact with one another, creating intricate patterns of reinforcing stress. Most of the wars since the end of the Cold War have taken place where poverty is most severe. And they have worsened that poverty and taken far larger numbers of civilian lives, especially women and children, than earlier wars. Research on the relationships between poverty and peace, or economic causes of war, is producing empirical results that hold some promise for identifying plausible policies and programs that hold some potential for averting the conflicts that give rise to wars (Kaldor, 2001; Duffield, 2001; Stewart, 2002; Nafziger et al.,

1

2002; Collier, 2002, 2003). Of course, defining exactly what one means by peace and war is an issue when doing empirical research. For example, one can argue that poverty, especially when it results in premature death, is a form of silent violence. Watts' work on famine makes this case (Watts, 1983). We consider peace to be more than just the absence of war. Peace defines an environment that fosters well-being and provides security from physical, as well as emotional violence. And we contend that reducing poverty helps increase the opportunities for peace by reducing the occasions for conflict that can fuel war.

Let us introduce you to Azusa, a young girl in northern Uganda who has lived in an internally displaced persons camp for 10 of her 13 years. Or, Jonas, a demobilized teenage soldier in Sierra Leone who has no land, nor skills. Or, Nana, an elderly Sioux woman in North Dakota. Or, Rica Ruparelia, an immigrant who cleans houses near her tiny flat in Birmingham, England. Or, Jose, a crippled ex-guerrilla living in the slums of Bogotá, Colombia. Or, Alonso, an occasional fruit picker when he can slip across the Mexican/US border. Or, Vernon, an occasional clerk at McDonald's who lives 12 blocks from the White House. Or, Pierre, an unemployed laborer who lives in Beauvais, France.

These are a few of those caught in global poverty, some by war, some by economic factors, some by both. Each of them has different stories, country contexts, and opportunities but each also has similar problems, struggles, and fears. The one characteristic they share is the probability that, without some intervention or stroke of good fortune, their poverty will be replicated in the lives of their children. Some will struggle to migrate; others will subsist. But all are diminished by current circumstances, many of which are beyond their control.

We have heard the numbers—1.2 billion people out of the 6 billion on the globe live on less than $1 a day. Half of these extremely poor are children. If the floor is raised to $2, the proportion jumps from 20% to 50% of the world's population. The problem is not isolated in poor countries. Significant poverty also exists within wealthy nations. For example, in the United States, 32 million people (12% of the population) live below the US poverty line—a figure that makes the US poverty rate the highest of the nine major industrial powers and includes the largest share of children in poverty.[1]

Poverty has deepened or persisted in regions across the globe. Countries in the former Soviet Union are reported by the *UNDP 2002 Human Development Report* to have experienced negative growth after 1990. The economies of all five Central Asian countries shrank each year from 1990 to 1999, while experiencing startling increases in inequality.[2] The Balkans have yet to recover fully from the difficulties and, for some, bloodshed, that followed the breakup of the former Yugoslavia. Per capita incomes in many African countries have stagnated. The 1990s was also a dismal decade for Latin America in terms of growth and poverty reduction. Asia—especially East Asia—was lauded in the late 1980s for its growth, only to have the financial crisis of the 1990s set back much of the progress. With the serious downturn in Japan's economy in the past 5 years, the impressive Asian growth has been reduced, diminishing what had been one of the major poverty reduction success stories. The carnage in the war in Iraq has also laid waste to the country's economy.

Seized by the scale, scope, and implications of these widespread poverty problems, in September 2000, 189 member states of the United Nations adopted the Millennium Development Goals (MDGs) at a summit in New York. Signatory governments pledged to eight major goals, the first of which was to reduce extreme poverty and hunger in poor countries by half by 2015. Each of the eight goals was assigned targets and indicators to be monitored in order to judge progress made, or missed. Indeed, we will return to these goals in Chapter 6 below. One UN document produced during the summit on the Millennium Goals said, "If the 1980s were characterized as a 'lost decade' in development, the 1990s were a decade of broken promises" (UNDP, 2001). It remains to be seen how the first decade of the new millennium will be characterized. Thus far wars and rumors of more war, not growth and improved well-being, have dominated the beginning of our new millennium.

Among the broken promises in the 1990s was the steady decline in official development assistance. One of the key measures of development assistance is the percent of Gross National Product (GNP) a country commits to give as Official Development Assistance (ODA). The internationally agreed-upon goal is to have every major donor nation achieve a level of seventh-tenths of 1% of its GNP. Only Denmark, Sweden, Norway, and The Netherlands achieve that goal; the United States level has been one-tenth of 1% of GNP (OECD, 1999). ODA declined throughout the 1990s. It has increased recently, but the levels of U.S. net official development assistance at 16.25 billion in 2003 still means the United States ranks 22 among major donors (OECD, 2004).

Some governments have recently committed to increase their investments in official development assistance. In the United States, the Millennium Challenge Corporation has been established; this is a new agency promised by President Bush at the Monterrey Development Conference in 2002. However, none of the amounts currently appropriated are as high as had been promised. The US appropriation for fiscal year 2004, at $1.4 billion, is in fact only slightly higher than that which was appropriated in 2003. And the big picture to remember is that the total development assistance program of the United States is no more than a tiny fraction of the budget compared to the huge and ballooning amounts readily found for defense.

Another much lauded promise of the 1990s was the benefit of increased private capital flows. Indeed private sources do comprise the principle source of capital throughout the world. In 1999, private capital flows accounted for 80% of total resources flowing to developing countries each year, nearly double 1990 levels (UNDP, HDR 1999). But, once again, global data can be deceptive. An examination of flows by region reveals that private capital seldom gravitates to the neediest countries. In 1995, 80% of total private flows went to just twelve developing countries, while the forty-nine countries in sub-Saharan Africa received only 5%.

Yet—and here is the good news—in spite of all this there have been serious improvements in three of the major characteristics of poverty: life expectancies, infant mortality, and literacy have improved in many countries in Asia and Africa in the last two decades. Interestingly, programs in countries addressing these problems were able to succeed, sometimes in adverse macroeconomic environments. That is revealing about the potential of good projects and programs even under difficult circumstances.

Progress also has been achieved in other areas: more countries have significant numbers of community and local level associations, in short, more of a civil society. More countries now hold elections, tolerate some opposition (and therefore policy debate), and are coming to appreciate the role and importance of civil society in participatory development. Many are also opening up their economies in order to have more effective markets and export trade. Such moves, if coupled with pro-poor policies and attention to distribution, have the potential to reduce poverty.

Many argue that open markets and democracy are linked. But empirical work on the direction of the causality comes up with different findings. Putnam's research in Italy points to increases in local level associational activity leading to economic growth, a view that countered economists who generally argue the reverse. It is in fact an old debate whether democracy precedes economic growth or economic growth precedes democracy. (Consider Alexis de Tocqueville's *Democracy in America*; Adam Smith's *The Wealth of Nations*; Max Weber's *The Protestant Ethic and the Spirit of Capitalism*; Joseph Schumpeter's *Capitalism, Socialism and Democracy*, or Gunnar Myrdal's three-volume *Asian Drama*, among many others.)[3]

Other progress has come in recent decisions to increase official development assistance in Europe, the United States, and Canada, though it remains to be seen how well these commitments will be met and funds actually appropriated. Private giving in support of nongovernmental international relief and development organizations has held steady over the past decade. Much of this financing is funding programs and projects directed at reducing poverty, relief for internally displaced people or refugees, and postwar reconstruction.

WHY IS POVERTY A GLOBAL PROBLEM?

Why talk about *global* poverty? We mean by "global" that poverty is now both a common feature across nations and an interacting one among them. A focus on poverty is needed not just for what have been termed, often euphemistically, "developing" countries, but rather for all countries. Poverty anywhere has repercussions for other countries in ways that are substantially different today from earlier historical periods. Well, you might ask, hasn't poverty in one country always impacted other countries? Not to the same extent. Poverty in Spain in the eighteenth century was less likely to have an impact on England, or to worsen poverty in Thailand, Canada, or Japan. But today those countries are more interdependent (R. Bryant, 1980, 2003). China experiences an economic downturn during the SARS virus episode and stock markets in OECD countries shudder. Or the US dollar's value drops in currency markets and central bank reserves in dozens of countries are reduced in value.

We are more invested in one another's economies and more closely linked by financial capital flows, trade, and commerce. Information about events and issues flows rapidly across the electronic networks and influences decisions for multiple actors in multiple places. Larger numbers of people travel greater distances and do so more frequently. With economies more integrated, pension funds invested in corporations millions of miles away, illnesses that travel on jets, and electronic communication that shrinks space, economic downturns or sociopolitical problems that feed anger and anxieties are transmitted with speeds never seen before in history. Similarly our poverty problems interact with one another and can worsen one another's chances for improvement, in varied, complex, and often unpredictable ways.

Those older distinctions between "developed" and "developing" or "first" and "third" world are no longer descriptive or helpful. Countries' poverty problems share more commonalities than usually acknowledged. Yes, the contexts are different. That is true within countries, as well as across them. But the terms "developed" or "developing" do little to capture that difference. We admit that we still use these terms at times in this book because new language has not yet emerged. But we know that they are not accurate. Market failures happen across the world; policy problems are ubiquitous; and much of what development workers do in poor countries has been found to be useful in redressing poverty in the rich OECD countries too.

In rich countries? Yes. Some of what development practitioners do in countries like Uganda or Sri Lanka can be useful in an industrialized OECD country—though ironically, it may be more difficult. For example, participatory rural appraisal—a wonderfully helpful way to connect with people who are chronically poor so that they can both tell their stories and identify possible ways forward—is easier to do in villages in Africa than in the industrial slums of Paris or Bonn. The down-and-out neighborhoods of Montmartre in Paris, the slums of Berlin, or the tenements of Moscow are characterized by lower levels of trust and more criminality. Mutual trust, needed for participatory development, has been corroded by harsh urban experiences that eat away at hope. There is more mutual trust in less urbanized sub-Saharan Africa.

That said, interactions among development workers and various antipoverty programs now cross borders and lead to learning from one another, almost as seamlessly as in other private sector activities. Witness the work of the Grameen Bank, the famously effective microcredit lending program in Bangladesh that is also currently at work in poor neighborhoods in the United States, though US Grameen Bank workers find it more difficult than their counterparts' work in Bangladesh. Similarly, some of the largest and most effective nongovernmental organizations, for example, Save the Children UK and Oxfam Great Britain, have restructured their organizations to remove the separation between their domestic and international programming in order to move toward an integrated approach in all their work.

Oxfam Great Britain brought the Bangladeshi community organizers who had facilitated their microcredit program in Bangladesh to England to work with residents in housing estates to help develop microcredit programs. The English participants were initially resistant, doubting that people from a developed country needed help from someone from a developing country. However, Oxfam leaders simply responded, "Why presume that we have more of a right to work in their country than they do to work in ours? Why assume that learning can only happen in one direction?" (Lindenberg and Bryant, 2001, p. 110). As it happened, the exchanges of views and perspectives led to some important innovative thinking. One Bangladeshi organizer pointed out how the residents of the housing estates could improve trash collection—and do it in a manner that was income-generating for entrepreneurial residents of the public housing units. The project participants in turn helped him to think about appropriate roles for the state. Although they did organize themselves to take over local trash collection, they also questioned whether it was wise in the long run to fill in for the role of government rather than hold government accountable to perform its responsibilities.

New thinking is sorely needed about the similarities among poverty issues in rich and poor places and therefore about the potential of similar programs to effectively redress poverty; thinking that dispenses with the labels "developing" and "developed," which impede reflection and discovery. This is especially true as globalization has so markedly changed international political economy. Cross-border movements of capital, labor, refugees, and even terrorists means that we all now live in "developing" countries.

We are not the first to point out this reality. Indeed, Simon Maxwell, director of the Overseas Development Institute in London, raised the central question as early as 1997 at a seminal conference at the Institute of Development Studies at which he asked, "Do developed countries not need to modernize? Do they not face growing pains associated with structural change in their economies? Do they not struggle with market failure? If 'development studies' by induction is what students of development do, then many themes are relevant to both North and South: restructuring the state; poverty reduction and livelihood; political development and governance; gender inequality; social capital; agency and participation—the list goes on—and of course includes social exclusion" (Maxwell, 1998, p. 25).

In response to these changes, we do not propose yet another global fund or specialized agency with more bureaucracy than productivity. Rather we are arguing for serious thinking about the nature of poverty, its causes, its relationships to violence and war, and what has been learned about effectiveness in poverty reduction policies, programs, and projects. It makes sense to look at the interdependencies among poverty problems across the world. Actions in one place have consequences across space and political borders in surprising ways. While few of those connectors can be fully explored in this book, what we will explore is the learning about poverty that is happening across borders.

A more nuanced, sophisticated, and integrated approach is needed for learning across borders and for strengthening institutional capacities simultaneously at several levels for more effective poverty and conflict reduction. Significant changes are needed in international capacities to make progress on global poverty, although we accept that most of the immediate operational work will still need to be done at national and local levels.

Capacities for reducing poverty are needed internationally, nationally, and in communities around the world. Moreover, building this capacity is best done while drawing upon, listening to, and engaging with more widely participatory structures built by citizens. The challenge is not just more efficient governance, but more effective governance that is accountable to participation by people at the local level.

Most poverty research is either in-depth within a country, or comparative cross-national research, largely focused on measurement and comparisons of the scale and scope of poverty, sometimes with reference to the relationships between poverty and economic growth. Unsurprisingly, in those contexts poverty policies are largely cast as national policy choices, although there is sector work that gets some attention, for example on the differences between rural and urban poverty, or in agriculture, education, health, or private sector development.

We, however, are taking a different approach. While hoping to bring in as much of the relevant material as possible, our purpose in this book is to fly over a wide landscape, pointing out the major features, but not stopping for too long, lest we lose sight of the big picture. This big picture is that poverty is a global problem; that poverty, inequality, and social exclusion create circumstances that lead to, or abet, violence, even war; and that the argument that we do not know how to reduce poverty is no longer relevant, if it ever was, as much has been learned about effectiveness. Each of these propositions is contentious. We invite that debate, as it is the debate needed in our times.

Poverty is not about some remote or exotic "them"—it is also about *us*. That poverty within industrialized countries is currently researched separately from poverty elsewhere is a fundamental obstacle to addressing the problem. A little-known book by Harold Brookfield called *Interdependent Development* once pointed out the interdependencies among actions taken in rich countries and their consequences for poor countries, as well as the feedback loops among countries (Brookfield, 1975). More such research is needed—not just in trade and finance, but in environmental practices, migration, technological change, innovation, and institutional change. Multiple systems within each of these areas affect poverty globally.

Chronic poverty in rich countries has some especially destructive characteristics. Being poor in, for example, North America, carries more stigma, or sense of shame, than being poor in Malawi. Poor neighborhoods in dense urban settings—Birmingham, or Chicago, or Rome—are more dangerous than the rural villages of Malawi, India, or Thailand. When one is poor and surrounded by affluence, life provides constant reminders of low status/failure that slowly but surely can force an internalization of negative self images. Cynicism, anger, frustration levels are higher. Those development workers who have worked in, for example, both Calcutta and the South Bronx readily admit that trying to reduce poverty's impact on people's overall well-being is tougher in the South Bronx.

Amartya Sen calls attention to the ultimate way in which being poor in a rich country can be worse—notably in the markedly shorter life expectancies of African-American men in the United States in contrast to men in South Asia (Sen, 2000). Another difference is the widespread presumption in public opinion that poverty in rich countries is most often due to personal failure (ne'er-do-wells who are lazy, unable, and/or have addiction problems). That leads to the further presumption that single interventions are the answer—a drug clinic, a shelter program, or mandated work programs. When those are not successful, the issue is seen as hopeless and hence often gets dropped from the public agenda. Yet poverty in India,

Tibet, or Tajikistan is rarely seen either by those in rich countries, or by fellow citizens, as personal failure or soluble by a single intervention.

NEW OPPORTUNITIES

Yet there is room for hope. We live in times of unprecedented opportunity to do more, and do it more effectively. First note that, in terms of new opportunities, there are now more peace studies programs in which skills in conflict resolution and mediation are taught in at-risk communities. For example, the American Friends Service Committee has a "Help Increase Peace" program in inner city high schools with high levels of violence. Professional Peace Studies programs are in place at several universities. On the poverty and inequality front much has been learned from decades of experience with microcredit and microfinance, social funds, investments in health care, education, mediation, ways to facilitate pluralism, and institutional innovation and learning. And much more is known about the policy frameworks that make a difference. The next generation, those who are currently in graduate school, are turning to programs in conflict resolution, development, and humanitarian studies in large numbers. They are highly motivated, and, best of all, are better educated and skilled in what can work.

Poor people themselves also know more about their possible choices. They are more literate and more organized. Guatemalan coffee growers in the highlands drive in battered trucks to distant places to get an Internet connection to check on coffee prices. Small producers of soybeans in Indian villages get to places where they too can log on to check on the prices for soybean commodity futures on the Chicago Board of Trade.[4] And literally millions of these people know more about how to organize community programs and projects. The growth in local collective action, groups, associations, and organizations in the past two decades is higher than ever before seen in human history.

People are learning more about how to build upon assets, how to use participatory processes to identify problems and solve them, how to build capacity for local initiatives, and how to encourage institutional innovation. They have therefore more to bring to bear that can make a difference.

The Internet has facilitated much of this growth and change, easing, as it does, the transaction costs of building community networks across borders and making information more widely available so that citizens can hold governments accountable. These are all major changes in people's capacities to affect change.

Nongovernmental Organizations (NGOs) can also raise funds for useful projects more readily. There is also more competition among groups for such support. More competitiveness leads to more chances to build support for reducing poverty. Increasing attention is being paid to conflict mediation with roots in ethnic rivalries, political economies, or racial problems. Learning how to manage conflict builds opportunities for more peaceful outcomes, ameliorating the conditions that give rise to bloodshed. Creating opportunities for peace is at the core of development.

While we are in an era full of opportunities, it is also rife with threats. Hence it is all the more important to seize every opportunity to move effectively toward alleviating poverty. The political, technical, and scientific changes of the past two decades have opened up new avenues for research and development and for new policies, programs, and approaches. Social innovation is underway. Thousands of new NGOs and community-based organizations are active in making a difference. Ours is a time of discovery.

INTERNATIONAL ORGANIZATIONS AND POVERTY WORK

Increased economic and financial integration across borders has irrevocably changed the international system within which national governments determine policies. On many issues, power has moved from national governments upwards to international organizations and downwards to rapidly changing civil society and local governments. Caught in the middle, national governments now have fewer degrees of freedom as a result of the cumulative effects of social, financial, and environmental interdependence. While the United States government currently asserts its hegemony through unilateralism, that may prove to be short lived. Joseph Nye's book, *Paradox of American Power*, is aptly subtitled, "Why the World's Only Superpower Can't Go It Alone" (Nye, 2002). He documents the existing, widespread agreement on the wisdom of working cooperatively rather than unilaterally. (See, also, for example, Brainard, Graham, Purvis, Radelet, and Smith, 2003.)

If poverty is a global problem, what international organizations are addressing poverty in all countries in the world? The anomaly is that in fact few have this as part of their mission. Sound reasons exist for their limited mandate, yet it has unfortunate implications. The two major international organizations with a mandate to address poverty—the World Bank and the United Nations Development Program (UNDP)—face real constraints. The World Bank, governed by its Articles of Agreement and its Board of Executive Directors, is mandated to lend to poor and lower-middle income countries, *not* the entire world. What about the World Bank's ability to raise consciousness on certain issues, for example, policies taken by rich countries that adversely impact poor countries or, indeed, policies that even add to poverty within rich countries? Using the World Bank's bully pulpit for such a purpose would not be well received by the Board of the Bank, where power is solidly held by the Group of Seven industrial powers.

Interestingly, in sharp contrast, the other Bretton Woods organization—the International Monetary Fund—does work in all member countries and carries out, for example, consultations with rich countries on their macro-economic performance. The presumption appears to be that international finance requires international reach, but international development does not.

The United Nations Development Program has far fewer financial resources and is largely a grant making, not a lending, organization. While it does not implement programs in rich countries, it does include rich countries in its research programs and thus in its various data collections. The annual *Human Development Report*, for example, includes helpful comparative measures of performance of rich industrial countries on various development indicators. While this has sometimes been politically controversial (especially when a major power is embarrassed), it is important. Such data reports help increase the possibility of a more informed public that, if embarrassed by their country's performance, might bring pressure to bear on public policy decision-making.

Many poor countries have followed up with their own National Human Development Reports, detailing the poverty situation within their country. Would it not be equally useful to have a Human Development Report for France or Germany or the United Kingdom or Italy or Japan or Portugal or Spain or the United States? It would be revealing and provocative if these were available. But while there are pockets of poverty in all these countries, and social exclusion is part of the fabric of their societies, these aspects of underdevelopment get no international organizational analysis.

Neither the UNDP nor the World Bank nor the other multilateral development banks nor the specialized agencies of the United Nations (UNICEF, UNESCO, etc.) are mandated to program operational work in countries that are above certain income thresholds. That means, among other things, that if these international organizations devise new project modalities, they cannot be made useful by these organizations for people caught in chronic poverty within middle or upper income countries. It also means that some useful instruments—such as poverty reduction strategy papers (PRSPs) or public expenditure reviews[5]—are not required of countries above certain income levels.

It also means that cross-border learning among countries on who is doing what toward reducing poverty is largely driven by NGOs, private sector entities, or civil society, while public sector learning is constrained. But national policies are part of the poverty problem—both in wealthy countries and in poor countries. Publicly identifying those wealthy countries' national policies with damaging impacts is beyond the reach of the World Bank. Agricultural policies or trade policies are a case in point. Both the United States and the European Union members have agricultural subsidy policies (especially for cotton, sugar, and rice) that provide more support to large corporate farms than to small producers. That in turn deepens rural poverty from Mississippi to California and from Marseille to Dresden. It also reduces the access to markets badly needed by small producers in Latin America, Africa, and Asia.

This issue surfaces upon occasion in the WTO (for example in the "banana wars"), but not in other international organizations. Yet fulfilling the missions of these organizations—for example, the World Bank states "Our dream is a world free of poverty"—logically requires that they address these issues, even if the solutions cross the divide between developed and developing countries. If the Bank requires that African countries refrain from, or cancel, existing farm subsidies, why should the existence and impact of subsidies in Europe or the United States be ignored in Bank documents? (Of course the political logic for their silence is obvious given the power of the North American and European industrial powers on their decision-making.)

This brings us back to the central role being played by civil society—often acting across borders and making a difference. Increasing numbers of civil society organizations are beginning to work globally to call attention to poverty and the impoverishing impacts of war. It was civil society at work that brought nearly nine million people out on the streets in February 2003 to protest the war in Iraq. This protest was organized almost wholly via the Internet at very low cost.

It was also the hard work of several international NGOs over a period of 10 years that brought debt relief onto the international policy agenda. This example is especially important as it addressed a complex issue and involved people protesting *for* something, rather than *against* something. It is more difficult to build a movement for positive change, and although debt relief has a long way to go to reach fulfillment, it was securely put on the international policy agenda through extraordinary NGO collaborative work.

SUMMARY OVERVIEW OF WHAT IS AHEAD

This book's major arguments will be expanded upon in two parts. The first two chapters provide a summary overview of central poverty issues—its incidence, measurement, relation to social exclusion, inequality, and violence. We turn then in Chapter 3 to the special role played by institutional development and collective action. Included in those discussions are the relationships among reducing poverty and building opportunities for peace—for greater security.

The second part—Chapters 4, 5, and 6—turns to what has been learned through experience about what works and what can make a difference. Thus the policies, programs, projects, and people's roles that are effective in poverty reduction are broadly covered in these chapters. Much of this material comes from the world of development practice. We seek to highlight international development work by people working through community-based organizations or NGOs, through foundations, and sometimes through official development agencies that has worked and has made a difference.

These last three chapters look at how policies, programs, and projects impact upon one another and discuss the overwhelming importance of implementation—the orphan topic in most books on poverty. The current preoccupation in the development field with "results" is often more about new packaging than product improvement. We believe that improved implementation with its messy iterative problem solving work is central to getting results. Lastly, we will say a few words about the need for greater policy coherence and international institutional development—global governance—if poverty and war are to be reduced in the long run.

Primarily, we present a practical, not a theoretical, focus. We are not going to be talking about any quick fixes or panaceas. Rather we will talk about experience to date with participatory approaches so that people have a stake in their societies, about collective action, about innovative policy choices, and about NGO networks for policy advocacy, as well as program delivery.

BACK TO BASICS: WHO IS POOR? WHERE ARE THEY?

Trying to answer directly the question of who is poor highlights poverty's definitional challenges. As cited earlier, measured by income—and specifically defined as living on less than $1 a day—1.2 billion people out of the world's 6 billion people are poor. Definitions frame a problem and thereby shape the way the problem is perceived, measured, and to some extent, the choice of strategies to fight it. But subjectivity enters into any definition of poverty: Who defines what it means to be poor? When poor people are consulted about their own definition of poverty, they quickly turn to multiple interacting factors beyond income, beyond, in short, what outsiders identify as poverty.

Living in poverty means more than living without enough money. Poor people say it is about vulnerability, powerlessness, and ill-being. While characteristics of poverty, these forces are also causes of poverty that maintain the vicious circle. Poor people, speaking for themselves, can be heard in the wide-ranging *Voices of the Poor* by Deepa Narayan, Robert Chambers, and others (Narayan, Chambers, et al., 2000). They asked poor people to define and characterize their situations. The poor identified dozens of interacting factors in addition to lack of money or jobs. For example, they pointed to lack of access to seeds and technical help, overly long trips to work, ill-health, low levels of education, inadequate shelter, family stress, physical insecurity, and criminality, as well as disdain and rudeness from potential service providers, violence, exclusion, and racism. The various levels at which poverty impacts a poor family's prospects form webs of interacting problems reinforcing one another (Narayan, Chambers, et al., 2000).

In summary, two major findings emerge from the poor's own characterization of their situation. First, poverty is caused and perpetuated by multiple interactions of different aspects of ill-being. Second, any choice of intervention requires attention to the interdependence among these drivers. The effectiveness of a change is contingent upon context—for the person, the community, and the nation.

Poverty is not measured, however, in ways that capture this complex reality. It is still primarily measured in terms of income, or estimates of income, compared to the costs of an essential basket of goods. While the UNDP has made a significant contribution to poverty measurement by emphasizing nonincome factors in its Human Development Index and Human Poverty Index, even these indices are composites of standard measures such as life expectancy, literacy, and access to health care. Work on measuring vulnerability, exclusion, and other elements of ill-being is only beginning to emerge. Better definitions will eventually have significant implications for our understanding of, and approaches to, the problem. Nevertheless, some of those studying this issue point out that because most factors affecting poverty are interrelated, rough estimates based on traditional measurements tend to present a reasonable approximation of who is counted as poor in terms of aggregate data (Kanbur and Squire, 1999).

Household surveys, most generally done by the World Bank, are now considered to be the most accurate way to measure poverty data despite the inherent problems these suverys face. But there are not enough household-level surveys that are up to date for widespread use. Most commonly, national poverty measurement is done by developing a basket of goods needed for survival and then estimating, from income data, which income groups are able to purchase that basket. Sometimes countries establish a poverty line from their income data and, using statistical estimations, calculate how many people fall below that line. In short, while national poverty measurements have come a long way, much also remains to be done. Nor are rich countries very far ahead in measuring their own poverty problem. All too often we are working with data that simply extrapolates from older census data.

Although income-based definitions of poverty remain the mainstay indicator when people talk about who is poor, a focus on income alone has limitations. It too readily translates into a focus on national economic growth and an assumption that growth, if achieved, will lift everyone out of poverty by increasing income. But in reality chronic poverty persists even during high levels of national economic growth unless distributional programs are in place, including a progressive tax system. A progressive income tax system is one of the central requirements for reducing poverty.

But putting in place—and keeping in place—a progressive income tax is exceedingly hard to do politically in all countries (Rodrik, 1999).

An emphasis on income alone overlooks other substantial individual freedoms, which have merit in and of themselves and which can in turn contribute to more economic growth and poverty alleviation. In the 1980s attention turned to the "East Asian Miracle" and development practitioners began to acknowledge the importance of investing in social sectors in addition to focusing on the financial sector and industrial growth. For example, Japan's economic growth was based on social opportunities generated by, among other factors, investment in education, as well as land reform, both of which substantially improved access to assets.

But the most fundamental limitation of income-based definitions of poverty is that income is a means toward other objectives and not an end in itself. Therefore, measuring income is only useful to the extent that it measures an ability to purchase other things deemed important such as health care, education, food, and other commodities. Poverty clearly includes shortages or deficiencies in addition to income that may, in practice, be more disabling than income shortfalls. Or, in other words, while increases in income may, and often do, improve how people manage to cope with various shortages, it is possible that some shortages are more difficult to overcome than others and that looking at income poverty alone is inadequate for capturing the poverty story. Just how much of an income increase it would take to overcome lack of access to assets is the issue. If one is without shelter, land, or drinkable water, or is suffering from physical disabilities or disease, then increases in income would have to be at extremely high levels in order to enable one to overcome these shortfalls.

Because income poverty is the most widely used measurement, however, it is useful to look at trends in poverty alleviation based on income from 1987 to 2001. As shown in Table 1.1, when the data is broken down by region, it becomes clear that positive progress in poverty reduction has taken place almost exclusively in East Asia and China. While those countries dramatically reduced the numbers of poor, the total number of people living in poverty increased during this same period in Eastern Europe, Central Asia, Latin America, the Caribbean, South Asia, and sub-Saharan Africa, and declined only slightly in the Middle East and North Africa.

In an effort to provide a more in-depth current view of the percentage of people living below either $1 or $2 a day, some selected country figures are provided in Table 1.2. This table shows how sharply upwards the numbers go when the $2 cutoff is used. Notice also the increase in poverty between different time periods and the worsening situations in several countries.

Diversity in regional patterns can also be seen by looking at World Bank indicators that measure nonincome characteristics of poverty such as health and education. Gross primary enrollment rates improved globally

Table 1.1
Total Number of People Living on Less than $1 per Day (millions and %)

| Region | 1987 | | 1998 | | 2001* |
	Number	Share of Population	Number	Share of Population	Share of Population
East Asia and the Pacific	417.5	26.6%	278.3	15.3%	14.32%
(excluding China)	114.1	23.9%	65.1	11.3%	NA
Eastern Europe and Central Asia	1.1	0.2%	24.0	5.1%	3.46%
Latin America and Caribbean	63.7	15.3%	78.2	15.6%	9.91%
Middle East and North Africa	9.3	4.3%	5.5	1.9%	2.35%
South Asia	474.4	44.9%	522.0	40.0%	31.89%
Sub-Saharan Africa	217.2	46.6%	290.9	46.3%	46.38%
Total	1,183.2	28.3%	1,198.9	24.0%	

Source: Data for 1987, 1998 are derived from the World Bank World Development Report 2000 and based on household surveys and adjusted for 1993 Purchasing Power Parity.
*This last column is from the POVCAL database set up under Martin Ravallion's supervision and helpfully provides data for 2001. We thank Shubham Chaudhuri for his help in providing this update.

over the last 25 years but, as was the case with measures of income poverty, sharp regional differences exist with less progress in sub-Saharan Africa. In 1995, the illiteracy rate for the entire world was 25%. Illiteracy rates on a global scale have declined over the last 10 years, due almost exclusively to declines in East Asia. The number of illiterate people actually increased, however, by 17 million people in South Asia and 3 million in sub-Saharan Africa.

Infant mortality rates on average declined during the 1990s for all regions except Eastern Europe and Central Asia. However, in some individual countries such as Kenya and Zimbabwe, infant mortality rates increased. Despite improvements in infant mortality rates globally, the rate of change has been slower than expected and thus global targets for 2015 set in 1990 will not be achieved. Life expectancy on average for developing countries increased from 55 years in 1970 to 65 years in 1997, but this is still far behind the life expectancy of 78 years for people living in OECD countries.

In an attempt to present comparative data on absolute income poverty across both rich and poor countries, the United Nations and others have defined minimum levels of daily income requirements within countries of different wealth levels. In *Ending Poverty*, Marris provides a table comparing first, second, and third world income poverty using, respectively, the measures of less than $1, $5, and $15 a day. He concludes that, of those living in income poverty, 28% are in the third world; 20% in the second

Table 1.2
Income Poverty Profile of Select Countries:
Percent of Population Living Below $1 and $2 per Day

Country	Year of Survey	% Population Living on Less than $1/day	% Population Living on Less than $2/day
AFRICA			
Botswana	1986	33.3	61.4
Ghana	1999	44.8	78.5
Mozambique	1996	37.9	78.4
Nigeria	1997	70.2	90.8
Sierra Leone	1989	57.0	74.5
South Africa	1993	11.5	35.8
Uganda	1993		55a
ASIA			
Bangladesh	1996	29.1	77.8
Sri Lanka	1995	6.6	45.4
China	1999	18.8	52.6
India	1997	44.2	86.2
Indonesia	1999	12.9	65.5
Thailand	1998	2.0	28.2
FORMER SOVIET UNION			
Russia	1998	7.1	25.1
Ukraine	1999	2.9	31.0
Uzbekistan	1993	3.3	26.5
LATIN AMERICA			
Chile	1998		8.7
Colombia	1998	19.7	36.0
Mexico	1998	15.9	37.7
Peru	1996	15.5	41.4

Source: World Bank, World Development Report 2001 and World Development Report 2003
a. Data for Uganda using international measurement is not available. Data presented here is percent of the population living below the national poverty line.

world (the transition states of the former Soviet Union); and 10% in the first world (the industrial states) (Marris, 1999, p. 27).

In the OECD countries, patterns of poverty have changed. For example, in the 1960s, the elderly made up a large percentage of the poor. That is no longer true—now children constitute the largest percentage of the poor in rich countries. In the United States alone about 17% of the children under the age of six are growing up in poverty (Douglas-Hall and Koball, 2005). Among the nine richest industrial powers in the world, the United States has the greatest percentage of people living in poverty, with 32.3 million people or 12% of its population living below its own national poverty line (US Census, 2000). Several wealthy countries, for example, Germany, Spain, the United Kingdom, France, and Holland, have significant transfer payments and pro-poor tax strategies, which allows them to lower their incidence of poverty more than does the United States, demonstrating the importance of institutional differences (Haveman and Burtless, 2000).

A majority of the 1.2 billion people in the world living on less than $1 a day are children (UNICEF, 2000). Children and minorities are two defining characteristics that appear again and again in the poverty data across all countries. Demographic shifts account for part of this fact. Many wealthy countries (Europe, Japan, etc.) are experiencing an aging of their populations, while other, poorer countries are predominantly youthful. Many African countries have large percentages of their population under the age of 15: Uganda, 50%; Yemen, 47%; Angola, Zambia, 47% (UNICEF, 2000).

The period from 1990 to 2000 with its civil wars and AIDS pandemic has added extra dimensions of ill-being to children's lives in poverty. AIDS alone resulted in 13 million children being orphaned and seriously increased the infant and child mortality rates. Countries that had made progress in reducing, for example, infant mortality, such as Zimbabwe which had gotten its infant mortality rate down to 30 per thousand, saw that progress reversed inside 6 years as the rate doubled to 60 per thousand (UNAIDS, 2000). The rate of infection continues to increase and, as this is happening among young girls and women of childbearing age, the numbers are increasing exponentially. And AIDS is not the only health threat to children. While estimates vary, it is likely that at least a quarter of the world's children remain unprotected against polio, measles, tuberculosis, diphtheria, and tetanus (International Save the Children Alliance, 2001, p. 3).

The story of child poverty calls for a radical rethinking of policy choices to manage the multiple aspects of the problem. Adolescent-headed households are increasingly prevalent, especially in sub-Saharan Africa. That in turn leads to an increase in child labor and often means greatly truncated schooling, adding to the likelihood of deepening poverty for the next generation.

Minorities are also overrepresented among the poor within a great many countries—whether they are the Roma (gypsies) in Eastern Europe, Algerians in France, African-Americans in the United States, Dalits or scheduled castes in India, Burakumin in Japan, ethnic minorities in China, or indigenous people in Brazil's Amazonian states. There are also the newly poor—those Russians, Ukrainians, Georgians, Tajiks, Uzbeks, and other Central Asians for whom the transition away from communist rule came with job losses and dismantling of health and other social safety nets. Afghans and Iraqis, as a result of recent wars, have been added to those made poorer or newly poor by political events.

In short, these are the poor in our times: children, minorities, victims of war and economic turmoil. Poverty and insecurity are not only features of life in the poorer countries of Asia, Africa, and Latin America, but a problem found across the Balkans, the Caucasus, Central Asia, Tibet, and China, as well as Appalachia and Sioux Reservations in the United States, European slum neighborhoods, small, rural villages in Poland and Italy, immigrant neighborhoods and industrial slums in England, Algerian immigrant communities in France, and the Kurdish community divided among several countries—to name but a few.

WHY ARE THERE MORE POOR PEOPLE?

Our review of the scope of poverty does not fully answer the question of why people are poor and why in so many countries large numbers of people slip back into poverty even after once escaping it. Yet, since many countries have experienced significant economic growth and millions of people have moved out of poverty over the last decade, it is worth asking why others have not. What are the major factors driving this poverty problem?

A standard list would contain several drivers. Human disasters (caused by bad policies, genocide, wars, and lack of investment in people) outrank natural disasters as leading causes of poverty and of people falling back into poverty having once escaped it. And rural poverty still outranks urban poverty. Bad national policies that underinvest in agricultural development or misdirect agricultural investment are widespread serious issues for both rich and poor countries. Nevertheless, arguably, war heads the list as a driver of poverty today.

The World Refugee Survey, which is cautious in its data collection, resulting in conservative estimates, reports that there were 13 million refugees around the globe in 2003. Add to them the 21.8 million internally displaced people and you have 34.8 million uprooted people worldwide (World Refugee Survey 2003, Table One). There are six countries with more than two million uprooted people within their borders and an additional fifteen countries with more than 500,000 uprooted people within their borders. Natural disasters, epidemics, and environmental catastrophes—and, of course, miserable national policies—all play their parts in impoverishing people. Governance is often a central cause of poverty. Sometimes states collapse (Somalia) or turn violent (Afghanistan), or get locked into a war economy (Colombia). Or, governments turn upon their own citizens, paying more attention to extraction than to investment (Mobutu's Zaire; Mugabe's Zimbabwe). All these examples are poor countries; their own internal poverty played a role in the build up of tensions and issues that led to their dysfunctional and violent political choices.

The Center for Research on the Epidemiology of Disasters (CRED) collects data on natural disasters. It reports a clear increase in the number of natural disasters, probably due to changes in global climate. "In Latin America and the Caribbean region alone, from 1980 to 1999 there were 38 major droughts, floods, hurricanes, tropical storms, landslides, earthquakes, volcano eruptions, and El Nino episodes" (Skoufias, 2003, p. 1087). Jeffrey Sachs has data illustrating the striking decline in rainfall in Africa from the 1970s to the present in an already dry region dependent upon rain-fed agriculture (Sachs, 2004, p. 31, figure 8).

There are other causes of poverty, ones that are subtler and more pervasive, and often forgotten by the time they take their toll. Environmental degradation is just such a cause. Happening over decades, it slowly, but inexorably, eats away resources. Environmental degradation may also have adverse health consequences or lead to or exacerbate natural disasters. Jeffrey Sachs reminds us that geography also matters, as he points out that a large percentage of Africans live in landlocked remote rural areas too far from markets (Sachs, 2004). We all tend to look at proximate causes and forget the underlying ones. Patterns of underinvestment in human resources, especially in education, health, or human capital over time always take a toll. Or skewed tax systems that encourage aggrandizement rather than productivity—all of these factors contribute to the poverty story.

Poverty has roots in political, moral, social, economic, institutional, and environmental problems. Institutions that skew the rules so that credit is not accessible, contracts unenforceable, and ownership of assets impossible to document, cripple investment. These institutional problems deepen poverty. Economic choices, from the macroeconomic level all the way down through to the household, impact human well-being. Social causes range from embedded discrimination to practices that keep people away from assets. Legal frameworks that protect privilege at the expense of fairness are, for example, major problems. Another problem is that racism or discrimination is deeply embedded so that whole groups of people are denied access not only to income generating opportunities but also to opportunities for enhancing their own capabilities through improved education or health. This racism comes with heavy costs for the whole society and ransoms its chances for growth.

At a basic level, poverty is often caused by a socioeconomic and political system that does not provide all people with access to the opportunities and capabilities they need to secure their well-being.

Much more detailed work needs to be done in order to pry loose precise explanations of why poverty is increasing so that poverty reducing policies can be more carefully crafted.

Taking a step back from the more immediate explanations, then, are underlying structural issues at the root of the various causes of poverty. The International Convention on Economic, Social, and Cultural Rights expanded the concept of citizenship to include more than civil and political rights, to lay out the right to basic needs such as food, health care, and housing, and a voice in decisions affecting their well-being. States and societies rich and poor often fail to fulfill these rights. Progress will only be made on basic economic and social rights when more political will and administrative skill are mobilized to work on reducing poverty.

Much development work in the past did not focus on root causes, or consider that the poor had economic or social rights, in addition to civil rights. But NGOs are moving in that direction and more of them have adopted a rights-based approach to development. As pointed out by Oxfam America, which is reorienting its antipoverty programming work to a rights-based approach, past development efforts that focused on meeting specific needs have made some progress, but have failed to address deeper questions of social injustice. The problem has been that development work in the traditional sense does not change the status quo and "is not in any way transformative of the system that perpetuates the processes reproducing poverty, generation after generation" (Offenheiser and Holcombe, 2001, p. 5).

Looking at what does work can lead to some progress while more capacities are put in place to move toward a rights-based approach. Impressive results are to be found in the local level work being done every day by ordinary people committed to social justice who work in communities on their own problem solving. It is through learning from these smaller, but durable experiences, that one can build incrementally the essential political will for more attention to poverty reduction.

Dani Rodrik adds to the case for the importance of participatory problem solving. He has developed an equation that he has tested empirically: increased growth equals negative external shocks times latent social conflict divided by institutions capable of conflict management (Rodrik, 1999, p. 82). As he says, "I find that countries with more participatory political systems were generally better at handling the consequences of the shocks in the 1970s" (Rodrik, 1999, p. 84). We will explore this when we consider social exclusion in Chapter 2 and institutional development in Chapter 3.

POVERTY AS CAPABILITY DEPRIVATION

The broad and compelling definition of Amartya Sen—that poverty is capability deprivation—also directs us toward much more inclusive approaches to poverty reduction, especially those increasing access to assets and capabilities (Sen, 1981; 1984). Amartya Sen's definition of poverty as capability deprivation makes sense to us. In fact we developed in the early 1980s—without the benefit of knowing about Sen's work—a similar definition focusing on people's capacities and adding the concept of interdependent development (Bryant and White, 1982). By defining poverty as the poor's lack of access to capabilities needed in order to affect their own development in an interdependent world, we were (and still are) underscoring a focus on human development and people as agents of their own change as an end in itself rather than as an input to economic growth.

When Amartya Sen added the concept of capabilities to development theory, he turned away from the utilitarian approach, or the freedom from want approach, to ask about positive freedoms—what is possible for people. So the issue is not, for example, freedom from hunger, but rather the capability to be well nourished. And he expanded upon this to other freedoms. He writes, "...some capabilities (e.g., that of appearing in public without shame) may largely depend crucially on what clothing, etc., the person possesses relative to others and in relation to established standards in that community" (Sen, 1984, p. 28). Rather than thinking narrowly in terms of the instrumental aspects of income, the capabilities approach asks that we think in terms of the positive values that should be available for human beings: freedoms from more than hunger, freedom from ill health, freedom from racism, freedom from illiteracy, and many other freedoms.

The angry reaction of millions of people to the development agendas in the 1970s and 1980s led to a serious critique from the dependency school. People asked who got to decide on national development priorities. Why were so many of these priorities determined beyond their borders? Why was it that development was too often experienced as exploitative? (Goulet, 1971; Freire, 1973; Barnet and Muller, 1974; Evans, 1979). The impetus behind the development of a definition centered on capacities was that increasing people's capacities—their own problem solving skills, their access to wealth generating possibilities and to activities that would add value to their own productivity—was essential. But it also noted that there were, and are, constraints, as we are interdependent. My overuse of natural resources diminishes someone else's opportunities for those resources. There are also intergenerational problems: wealth extraction may enrich the current generation but contribute to the impoverishment of the next.

When we took a similar approach years ago by arguing that development, concerned as it is with poverty reduction at its core, should be defined as increasing people's capacities to affect their futures in an interdependent world, we were describing development as a larger systemic process. We wanted also to suggest the centrality of people in driving their own development agenda as a worthwhile goal in its own right. This approach also emphasizes the critical issue of agency in the development process—who decides what is, or is not, "development?" The critical literature on development is full of stories of failures. Many point repeatedly to the arrogance of development professionals presuming to know what is to be done in a locality or within a sector or even at the national level without much reference to the perspectives of people living there. Even today, after a great deal of writing and self-reflection within the development community, the problem remains. There is a strong and growing move toward bringing people into the decision-making process in order to hear their voices and incorporate their views. Participatory development is now widely acknowledged to be essential to the change process.

Principal-agent problems will always be an issue in poverty reduction work. In part because of the inevitable nesting of decisions (the accountability problems in moving from the international to the local level are serious) and in part because of competing interests and power inequalities. International events lead to internationally determined decisions; national political systems are widely variable in their accountability or participatory processes. Local governments are often locally captured by powerful elites.

A fundamental transformation is now emerging, building both on the concepts of capabilities and human development and on the work of development practitioners who consulted directly with the poor on the elements that define their poverty. Official definitions are beginning to move away from focusing on specific characteristics of poverty such as lack of income or education to focusing on the multidimensionality of poverty and a fuller understanding of the impact of choice and freedom on poverty. This includes an understanding of elements such as social exclusion, vulnerability, and powerlessness as key determinants of both poverty and the factors that limit the ability of people to move out of poverty.

The belief that human development is for rich countries and that poor countries need to focus on economic growth alone has by now largely been refuted. A comparison of UNDP's Human Development Index and a country's GNP reveals that income level and human development are not directly correlated. Costa Rica and Korea, for example, have very similar HDI ratings but Costa Rica has half the income of Korea (UNDP, HDR 2001, p. 13). As Sen points out, in East Asia, the focus on education, basic health care, and early land reform contributed to widespread economic participation, which in turn helped fuel economic growth in an environment of high employment. Brazil, which had an almost comparable growth of GDP per capita, did not achieve the same level of development in part because of severe social inequality, landlessness, unemployment, and neglect of public health care (Sen, 1999, p. 45). This illustrates the problems of focusing only on national economic growth without also working on enhancing other freedoms.

POVERTY, POWERLESSNESS, AND ILL-BEING

The conditions confronting the world's poor are of concern not only because of increasing absolute levels of poverty and inequality, but also because of disturbing trends that reveal increasing vulnerability of the world's poor. The poor bear the brunt of the growing number of violent civil conflicts, natural disasters, and financial crises. In East Asia, the financial crises of 1997 set back decades of progress in poverty reduction as more than 13 million people lost their jobs and real wages fell sharply (UNDP,

HDR 2001, p. 99). The volatility of financial markets and the global reach of its repercussions present new challenges for protecting the poor.

Even in stable areas, job and income security have diminished as a result of global competition, dismantling of social protection, loosening of labor restrictions, and mergers and restructuring that have led to widespread layoffs. Despite economic growth, Europe's unemployment rate averaged 11% throughout the 1990s (UNDP, HDR 2001, p. 99). With the global economy's increasing reliance on private sector markets, public expenditures have been declining.

In addition to income insecurity, the poor are facing increasing health insecurity. By the end of 2000, at least 36.1 million people had AIDS. These numbers undercount the total as data collection on AIDS in Africa is incomplete and the scope of the impact in China is not clear. AIDS has become the killing disease of the poor. In Botswana, 36% of the adults are HIV infected, as are 20% of South Africans. Three million people died of AIDS in 2000—2.4 million of them in sub-Saharan Africa. As one authority says, "[AIDS] is bringing a Holocaust every two years...it is the most lethal epidemic in recorded history" (Berwick, 2001, p. A17).

The health problems of the poor go beyond AIDS, however. Tuberculosis kills two million people each year. Malaria is as rampant today as it was in past centuries, killing one child every 30 seconds—and yet it receives far less attention and less research than AIDS. No one runs in "Find the Cure" marathons for malaria research.

Wars, and especially the inevitable refugee camps, are major public health catastrophes, as well as immediate human catastrophes for the refugees themselves. Diseases once thought to be conquered return (measles, polio). Inadequate sanitation systems in refugee camps spread diarrheal diseases. New viruses emerge—and spread with unmanageable contagion rates. Wars, in short, lead to epidemiological nightmares for public health workers, and researchers, across the globe.

The impacts of natural disasters on the poor are also devastating. As noted by Kofi Annan, "the vulnerability of those living in risk-prone areas is perhaps the single most important cause of disaster casualties and damage....Above all we must never forget that it is poverty, not choice, that drives people to live in risk-prone areas. Equitable and sustainable economic development is not only a good in its own right, but also one of the best forms of disaster insurance" (Annan, 1999).

RELATIONSHIPS BETWEEN POVERTY AND WAR

Poor people are more often victimized by violence than any other group in a society, whether in rich or poor countries. When asked about their problems, constant insecurity and violence are often cited by the poor as major, frequent problems (Narayan, Chambers, et al., 2000); from domestic violence to dangerous neighborhoods to simple conditions of daily life—huts without lockable doors or windows, beatings that come with robbery, domestic violence, unsafe working conditions, street crime. Worse, police—if summoned—can sometimes be abusive, rather than helpful. The risk of being defrauded is higher for the poor, whether by bureaucrats or by businesspeople when purchasing goods or services. (In poor countries without effective regulatory frameworks, medicines are all too often fraudulent; "aspirin" made of pressed chalk, fake malaria medications, high risk back alley abortions...the list is virtually endless.)

But what about the less observable relationships between poverty and violence? When and under what circumstances can it really be said that poverty, inequality, and social exclusion create the climate for wars? There is insufficient research to draw a direct casual link. And yet, mounting evidence suggests a deep interdependence. Of the eighty-two major armed conflicts that took place between 1989 and 1992, all but three occurred within rather than between states—and most of these states were poor (Economist, May 24, 2003). Paul Collier points out that when there are lootable resources that rebels can use to buy arms, wars in poor countries develop a war economy quickly, which makes it much harder to end, as has been the case in Colombia, Congo, and Angola. When there is a diaspora working abroad that harbors revenge against the current regime, wars get financed. When a poor country denudes its environment beyond the point of no return and loses its productivity, people migrate—illegally or legally into nearby poor countries—and friction develops over already limited resources in the receiving state.

Political theorists point out, rightly, that most of those who are chronically poor over generations do not rebel. (Marx; Nelson, 2001). Often those who are poor do not act out externally against their condition. They are far more likely to inflict pain upon themselves or one another, for example, with substance abuse, attacks on others within their community, child-battering, etc. Such self-destructive actions can reflect the sense of powerlessness to achieve a different kind of life and an eroding of the value of preserving life because it is so tenuous anyway (Bourgois, 1995). Poor people are not naturally rebels, but they are often deeply frustrated by impenetrable barriers to the good life for them and for their children. Through her participant observation and extensive interviews, Janice Perlman documented the extraordinary efforts of squatters in some Rio de Janeiro slums to conform to middle class behaviors—wishful that conformity might bring admittance (Perlman, 1970). Yet these same slum dwellers were often abused by those in authority with the presumption that they were likely to be criminals.

But do their aspirations mean they are never available for mobilization into violence? When and under what circumstances do poverty, social exclusion, and inequality create conditions for people to become terrorists, agitators, rioters, and rebels? That does happen. Often rebels or agitators, or revolutionaries, will react to circumstances of poverty and inequality and explain their actions as being on behalf of others—despite the fact that they themselves did not grow up in the conditions to which they object. Few of the leaders bringing about the French revolution grew up in poverty. But there can be no doubt that Danton and others were keenly aware of, and apparently offended by, extremes of inequality. They too acted on behalf of others in their quest for equality, liberty, and freedom, although it is interesting to recall that the French economy had experienced a series of bad harvests culminating in a nationwide economic disaster. By spring 1789 grain supplies were chronically low and bread prices in urban areas— where the revolutionary leaders lived—were rising, creating serious and widespread shortages (Andress, 2004). While revolutionary leaders tend to come from the middle or upper classes, they persuade those actually disenfranchised in society to join their fight for an improved livelihood. The worldwide terrorist organization Al Qaeda is a current case in point. The organization's leader Osama bin Laden comes from a wealthy Saudi family. Yet his support is strong among many poor who see him as working to fight the injustice they face in their lives.

While poverty and conflict are often found to be interwoven, research on the specific circumstances under which poverty breeds war is, however, contingent upon many factors—catalyzing events, networks, local collective action, agitators, available lootable resources (e.g., gems), remittances from vengeful diaspora groups. Some of the desperately poor become available for recruitment into more overt externally focused violence—gangs, cults, criminal activity, or rebellion.

If some of the poor come to be truly sure that they have no stake in their current situation and even less in the future, then criminal behavior, collective rebellion, or even war become more attractive. But it depends upon the specific mixture of catalysts, context, and cause. In the newer research being produced by the World Bank, at Oxford University, the United States Institute of Peace, and the International Peace Academy, there appear to be more underlying political economy causes for war than are popularly understood. One way of synthesizing some of this work is depicted in Figure 1.1.

The major point to be noted in this figure is that each of the drivers of poverty has rational (though tragic) connections to the drivers of war on the other side. For example, if one has no access to assets and limited capabilities, it is understandable, while outrageous, that one may well resort to looting natural resources (e.g., alluvial diamonds, gemstones, timber) for money. If an organizer has also "persuaded" the looters that fighting will

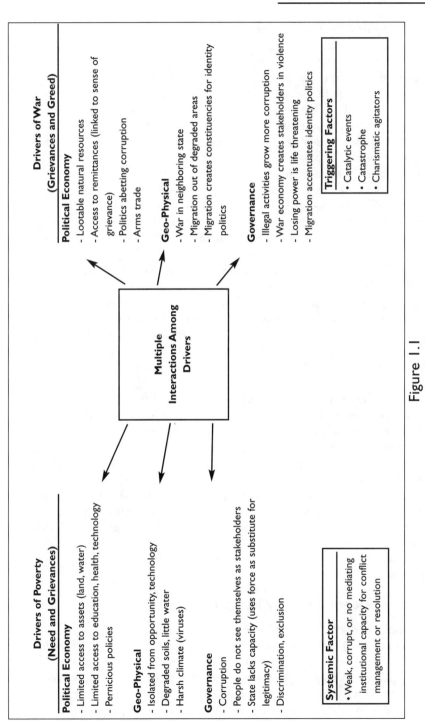

Figure 1.1

Interdependencies Between Drivers of Poverty and War

bring other gains, the battle is begun. The looting increases in scale—and a war economy is born.

Or war starts in a neighboring state and refugees pour over the border. Receiving populations can resent these intruders, especially if they were already poor before the refugees arrived. Ethnic differences become more salient both for the refugees and for the people who are receiving them. Pressure on resources worsens and so do tensions. If bloodshed breaks out, who is to say exactly which factor causes the war—the ethnic differences or the shortages of natural resources? Probably both. But the key point is that these factors interact with one another.

Governance is most often cited as a causal factor, and probably rightly so. But governance can be both cause as well as consequence of the political economy within which it functions. Looting and illegal activities bring bribery and corruption with them, especially as the scale of those activities grows.

Ted Gurr long ago described the concept of relative deprivation—a perception of injustice arising from a discrepancy between individuals' values and expectations and the lack of opportunities to realize these expectations (Gurr, 1968). People who have moved out of poverty during their lifetime and then are pushed back into poverty by crisis or disaster are more angry and frustrated than those who never escaped. This is why increasing inequality—or relative deprivation—is more volatile than long term poverty.

While we are still working on understanding the root causes, we know the consequences—countries that go through a war emerge poorer, with people killed, the environment damaged and infrastructure destroyed. The setback for human development and the environmental destruction and its economic implications means not only lower income levels, but reduced potential for future growth.

As noted, the widespread displacement of people and high concentrations of people in refugee camps bring with them serious health crises. Tuberculosis spreads. New viruses get introduced to populations with little or no immunities. And viruses now travel on jets, which alone should attract global public attention to the global poverty problem and its intersections with violent conflict.

A FRAMEWORK FOR POVERTY REDUCTION

Substantially reducing poverty is within our reach. We now know more about what works—and that opens up many more options for ways forward. We live in an era of new learning—and our social learning is changing too. Skills and techniques matter, however, in quickening the pace of social learning. Organizational capacity matters. Structural barriers can be torn down as the Berlin Wall was torn down. Precisely because we believe that substantial progress can be made, we will be elaborating on a framework for poverty reduction throughout this book.

A quick way to see the roadmap is depicted in Table 1.3. The major building blocks and the relationships among them are policy change, institutional development, community level collective action, and programs and projects as vehicles for change. These must be, of course, intermediated by agency and process—and achieving that intermediation requires skills. Thus, in the second half of the book we turn to many of the "how" questions—the operational questions for implementing change—of poverty reduction. Fortunately these skills are currently being acquired, and improved upon, through field work in several major development studies programs in universities around the world.

It matters that wide ranging networks in civil society keep poverty on the international agenda. As Strobe Talbott and Nancy Birdsall say in the foreword of a new book on the subject, "the plight of the poorest around the world has been pushed to the forefront of America's international agenda for the first time in many years" (Brainard, Graham, Purvis, Radelet, and Smith, 2004, p. iv). This is true.

Policy prescriptions for bilateral programs, however, are not enough. Too much focus on the narrow constraints of particular public bilateral assistance policies can mean eluding coming to grips with the global characteristics of the problem. We need to consider questions about access to assets, inequality, and social exclusion—drivers of poverty that also give rise to occasions for violence. And then we can turn to what has been learned about effectiveness by NGOs, as well as bilateral and international organizations. Poverty in all countries is now a global problem of

Table 1.3
Requisites and Their Drivers for Reducing Global Poverty
_____

Increased Institutional Capacities: Nationally and Internationally

$$\downarrow \qquad \downarrow$$

Pro-Poor and Pro-Growth Policies with Attention to Distribution

$$\downarrow \qquad \downarrow$$

DRIVERS:
- Community level collective action—learning through participatory projects
- National cooperation among non-state actors for national policy and institutional change
- Effective pro-poor projects and programs provide examples of success
- Transnational solidarity movements for conflict resolution and poverty reduction
- Advocacy at all levels of governance—winning support for pro-poor and pro-growth policies

the highest order. It is part of the security problem, linked as it is inexorably with people's needs for security. Global poverty is part of our shared global need for effective peace building.

NOTES

1. It should be noted that this figure was cited as marking an improvement in poverty in the United States as it represented a decrease from 17% in 1990. The short period of economic boom in the United States in the mid-1990s reduced the number of people below the poverty line, bringing it down to 12%. For a detailed account of poverty in the United States see Gary Burtless and Timothy Smeeding, "The Level, Trend, and Composition of Poverty" and Timothy Smeeding, Lee Rainwater, and Gary Burtless, "U.S. Poverty in a Cross-national Context" in Sheldon Danziger and Robert Haveman (eds.), *Understanding Poverty*, Russell Sage Foundation and Harvard University Press, New York and Cambridge, 2001.

2. These Central Asian countries are Kazakhstan, Kyrgyzstan, Uzbekistan, Tajikistan, and Turkmenistan. Neighboring Afghanistan is also seriously impoverished after decades of crisis including war with the Soviet Union, civil war, rule by the Taliban and the war in 2001. Shahrbanou Tadjbakhsh has documented this in "Development Aid Effectiveness in Central Asia: Progress or Regress? An Examination of Outcomes and Ownership of Reform Policies," unpublished mss, Columbia University, 2003.

3. The editions referred to here are: *Democracy in America*, the Henry Reeve text, revised by Francis Bowen and edited by Phillips Bradley, Vintage Books, New York, 1945; *The Protestant Ethic and the Spirit of Capitalism*, Talcott Parsons' translation, A. Knopf, New York, 1958; *Capitalism, Socialism and Democracy*, Harper Torchbook, New York, 1942; *Asian Drama, An Inquiry into the Poverty of Nations*, Pantheon, Random House, New York, 1968.

4. See the front page *New York Times* story by Amy Waldman, January 3, 2004. The "e-choupals" a word taken from the Hindi word for gathering place, have caught on in a substantial way. The company behind e-choupals, ITC LTD, has done much to bridge the digital divide. "There are now 1,700 in this state, Madhya Pradesh, and 3000 total in India. They are serving 18,000 villages, reaching up to 1.8 million farmers." When the soybean future market price sinks, it augurs ill for the soybean prices for millions of small Indian producers. Through the e-choupals, they can, and do, track the price at the Chicago Board of Trade.

5. A Poverty Reduction Strategy Paper (PRSP) is the document required by the World Bank and IMF of countries that are eligible and apply for debt relief. A Public Expenditure Review is a World Bank product analyzing the pattern and human development implications of current public expenditures in a country. These documents are used for policy dialogue with senior country leaders, including the President or Prime Minister and the Minister of Finance, in order to clarify what needs to be done in the future in regard to the use of public expenditures.

2
ACCESS TO ASSETS AND THE ROLE OF SOCIAL EXCLUSION

"The concept of social exclusion may be superior to that of poverty...it focuses on the multidimensional character of deprivation and thus provides insight into the cumulative factors that keep people deprived."
—A.S. Bhalla and Frederic Lapeyre, *Poverty and Exclusion in a Global World,* 1999

INTRODUCTION

Ensuring access to assets is centrally important for poor people as they seek to develop their own productivity. Accessing and utilizing assets is how they move out of poverty. As the vast majority of the world's poor live and work in rural areas, their access to assets (for example, land, water, agricultural research, technology, infrastructure, markets, and equipment) is clearly central to their efforts to escape poverty.[1] It is equally critical for the urban poor, whether they are subsisting in vast squatter settlements or in urban industrial slums. Ensuring access thus becomes a central underlying objective of any poverty alleviation strategy. But to do this means going beyond increasing the availability of services and opportunities to addressing the factors that block one's ability to get to them or make use of them. Access to assets may be impeded by geography, time, or by project or program requirements such as literacy, language, or targeting guidelines. In addition to these factors influencing access, a series of structural barriers embedded within a society such as discrimination, prejudice, racism, or tradition can exclude certain people from assets.

As noted in Chapter 1, there is a high correlation between minority status and poverty in countries around the world. The persistence of this poverty over decades (sometimes centuries) for many such groups points to processes and societal relations that are systemically excluding people, often minorities, from their full participation in society. The concept of social exclusion provides a framework for examining these processes and looking for the underlying multidimensional causes of poverty.

It is precisely the ubiquity of the presumption that some groups have always been, and therefore are likely to always be poor, that allows the majority to slip into believing that little can or should be done about their situation. A central contribution of the debates surrounding social exclusion is how social exclusion as a concept sheds light on this frequently encountered, yet infrequently addressed, situation. For marginalized people, this is experienced as silent violence. The marginalized, the minorities, groups excluded by virtue of their race, faith, or ethnicity—these are often people living in the midst of societies that have forgotten their problems and their basic human needs.

In this chapter we will examine the importance of access to assets in the poverty equation and explore the role of social exclusion in blocking that access and thus perpetuating poverty. We will review the debate over the definition of social exclusion and clarify the ways in which the term is useful for understanding poverty and for identifying approaches to solutions. We will also explore ways in which persistent poverty, when combined with social exclusion, can lead to an attack on one's well-being at many levels that constitutes a form of structural violence. Because the concept of inequality can serve as a lens for understanding persistent poverty within certain groups as compared to others, this chapter also includes a review of the current research and debates on inequality and the problems inherent in measuring it. In our conclusion we discuss how understanding these dimensions of poverty is an important step toward finding solutions.

INCREASING ACCESS TO ASSETS

Our definition of development emphasizes the rights of people to develop their capabilities to affect their own futures. This is consistent with Amartya Sen's concept of development as freedom for each person to realize his or her own potential. People's capabilities depend on the long term assets they possess. While access to jobs may provide short term alleviation of income poverty, sustainable access to assets such as transferable worker skills is key to ensuring long term solutions. It is assets that families turn to when crises occur—it is the viability of these assets that cushion shocks and families' vulnerability to those shocks.

Writing about the health crisis globally, Helen Bishop points out that "the physical suffering of the poor is not only abhorrent in its own right, but also serves as a barometer of the fairness of the underlying social order....the health inequities result from social injustices [such] as poor access to health care, inadequate food, impure water and air, unsafe working conditions, and extreme poverty" (Bishop, 2001, p. 33).

Critical assets range from health, nutrition, education, and shelter to technology, land, credit, and security. Assets also include the human and social capital of individuals and communities. The importance of an assets-based approach has gained acceptance in the development literature in recent years. The World Bank's World Development Report (WDR) 2000, which focused on poverty, laid out a framework for understanding poverty that is based on assets, returns to those assets, and the volatility of those returns. The WDR lists assets by type (natural, human, physical, financial, social, location and infrastructure, and political/institutional) and by level (household, community, and extra-community). The analysis by the World Bank acknowledged that a range of nonmarket factors, namely institutions, norms, and values, influences access to assets (World Bank, 2001).

Poverty alleviation programs can aim to build assets explicitly or provide incentives for the accumulation of assets. When assets are not taken into account, programs are less likely to help people move out of poverty sustainably. Experience in the United States, for example, has shown that families can get caught in poverty dependent on public assistance if the right incentives are not provided to build assets that can move a family out of poverty. The criteria for receipt of public assistance in the United States have traditionally created *disincentives* for acquiring assets, by setting relatively low limits on the level of assets a family can own and still receive assistance. Thus, the very policies designed to assist low-income families can contribute to the perpetuation of poverty by penalizing those who accumulate assets. Following reforms in 1996 that transferred greater responsibility for public assistance to the states, many states began to modify the asset requirements, with some states eliminating the asset test altogether for certain types of assistance. However, these changes have not been consistent across the country and in some states, small levels of savings or a single car can make families ineligible for cash assistance, food stamps, and public health insurance (Dinan, 2003, p. 1). Overall, the policy continues to be one of discouraging asset accumulation among families who need to receive public assistance to meet their basic needs.

Experience has shown that strategic, even if modest, interventions can produce significant results when they focus on increasing access to essential assets. For example, primary education for girls led to incremental increase in control over household income for women, as they gained an increasingly higher investment rate in household welfare. Similarly, access to secure land registration in China allowed smallholders to increase their productivity between 1977 and 1985 (Lipton, 1993). Increased access to education has been noted by many researchers as a key element to ensuring not only more rapid economic growth, but also better distribution of wealth when growth occurs.

As the importance of technology grows, and with it the debilitating impact of the technology gap, there are very large gains to be had from increasing access of the poor to technology, especially appropriate technology. The impact of appropriate technology when it meets specific local needs is illustrated by the instance of a group of women in Mali who managed through their collective action in a women's association, and with help from UNDP, to acquire a mechanical grinding machine (Thurow, 2002). While prior to having this machine, the women needed 3 days to grind by hand 100 pounds of corn, the machine ground the same quantity in 15 minutes. Similarly, grinding peanuts, a traditional foodstuff, took hours for small quantities, while the machine did it quickly and with better results. The process of acquiring, installing, and maintaining the machine involved training and that in turn led to more demand for education; the women made much of these opportunities. The compelling facts around this case illustrate the complex social benefits, as well as economic gains created by one relatively modest increase in access to technology. A key to the success in this case was that the women themselves defined their need and the technology they wanted.

Assessing the level of access to assets is often a key step in determining development objectives, especially at a local level. For example, CARE uses a tool it developed, the Household Livelihood Security Index, as a means of measuring assets and identifying when households are depleting assets and thus reaching potential emergency situations. This tool also helps define what type of assistance households and communities need in order to determine appropriate intervention strategies.

As part of the focus on the role of assets in fighting poverty, many development practitioners are making an important shift from a needs-based perspective to one that builds upon existing assets within a community as the core way to identify approaches for moving out of poverty. This approach differs from the traditional needs-based approaches as it starts from the assumption that all communities—even the poorest ones—have some assets that can contribute to the development process. Given the long-standing development paradigm of seeking solutions through the application of external assets and the dependency mentality that such an approach generated, practitioners must often work with communities to change attitudes and begin to identify and appreciate the assets the community itself has.

In the United States, this approach, spearheaded by Jody Kretzman and John McKnight, was developed into a model known as Asset Based Community Development (ABCD). While the concepts and language of ABCD have been finding their way into international development, limited experience exists to date with its implementation. The role that large sums of external financial resources traditionally play in international development run counter to the ABCD model, as the essence of the model is to prioritize change within a community by using the community's own resources. When done successfully, the ABCD approach uses broad-based community participation, empowers the community to be more self-reliant, and increases access to assets by building on the community's own assets (Kretzmann and Knight, 1993). It also links a community's internal assets with those provided externally.

The distinction between the ABCD approach and traditional approaches to international development is highlighted in two projects with similar objectives of revitalizing local communities in post-conflict Serbia. One project funded by USAID overwhelms local communities with large sums of external assets in the form of financing and technical assistance that is disbursed in a very short time frame: approximately $200 million to be disbursed at the community level over 5 years. A project financed by the Swedish Government's aid agency (SIDA) also presents an inherent challenge to ABCD because it injects substantial financial resources into communities. However, the sums are smaller and the project team executing the project has chosen a deliberate strategy of pursuing an ABCD approach. SIDA designated $600,000 over an 18-month period for one municipality comprised of twenty-seven communities. While the basic project structure is similar to a conventional Social Investment Fund, the differences include using participatory planning and supporting communities in developing proposals for projects in which local community assets are combined with international assistance. Local facilitators are trained to conduct the planning in the communities. The project provides full support for the development of community project proposals, but will fund only $5,000 for implementation per project, thus ensuring relatively small projects that the community can manage (Bergdall, 2002).

There are several challenges to the ABCD approach. First among these is the traditional development mentality—of beneficiary populations, as well as of donors—that external funding provides the core solution to community problems. Accustomed to development agencies pouring substantial resources into projects, community members may question why they should be expected to take on greater responsibility. In the case of Serbia, the population has had limited experience with development and even less with participatory processes. Furthermore, in post-conflict situations, the identification of existing assets can be more difficult and projects must help communities in many instances to regain assets that were depleted during the war.

While the assets within one's own community are important, another essential piece of the puzzle is the ability to access external assets; that is, those assets that must be obtained from outside an individual's or community's sphere of influence. The key is optimizing and strengthening local assets while leveraging needed complimentary external assets.

STRUCTURAL BARRIERS TO ACCESSING ASSETS

Lack of access to assets entrenches poverty within certain groups and persists over time—often irrespective of economic gains enjoyed by the country as a whole. Across countries there is a consistently high correlation between poverty and minority status. Not all minorities are poor, and not all of the members of any minority group in any country are poor, but in aggregate terms they are more likely to be poor than nonminorities in any given country. Minority refers not only to ethnicity or race, but to minority status based on any factor that distinguishes a group from the majority culture such as, for example, disabilities.

Native Americans, African-Americans, and Hispanics in the United States, West Indians in England, Algerians in France, North Africans in Italy, Dalits in India, Roma in Eastern Europe, Bushmen in Botswana, Burakumin in Japan—these are just the beginning of a list of groups recognized within their societies as minorities. People in these groups experience discrimination when they try to access assets critical for their productivity and wealth generating possibilities.

Often, members of a minority group have been among the poor for so many generations that their poverty comes to be accepted—both by the mainstream majority and by the members of the minority group as well. Consider, for example, how accepted it is that Roma—colloquially known as gypsies—are assumed to be beggars in European urban centers. In these cases, often structural barriers exist that inhibit members of certain groups from accessing the assets needed to improve their livelihoods and the opportunities to apply those assets. Barriers faced by minorities may be the result of customs, widely practiced behaviors, or, in the worst cases, laws that either tolerate or enforce discrimination. For example, not allowing Roma to go to school, own property, or hold certain kinds of jobs is legalized discrimination.

This problem of widespread and regularly practiced discrimination that impedes people from improving their own life chances is sometimes termed social exclusion. The ways in which dominant social groups will quietly coalesce in order to exclude different groups from potentially productive income generation, asset accumulation, or specific access to education, training, and health services essential to productivity is at the center of the social exclusion process. The term social exclusion gained in popularity during the 1990s. Although debate is ongoing over its precise meaning and use, we believe it is a useful concept for understanding the processes and relationships at work in a society that can lead to structural barriers impeding access to assets for certain minority groups.

DEFINING SOCIAL EXCLUSION

While sociologists have talked about social exclusion for some time, the concept was given broader recognition in Europe by Rene Lenoir, Secretary for Social Action (Secrétaire d'État à l'Action Sociale) in the Chirac government in France, when he published his 1974 book, *Les Exclus.* (In English, *The Excluded.*) Lenoir was discussing those excluded from the employment-based social security systems. Interestingly, he was citing not cultural or social minorities, but those excluded on the basis of characteristics for which they were discriminated against—for example, alcoholics, the disabled, the aged, or abused children. Their numbers, Lenoir said, accounted for 10% of the French population and he therefore called for attention to be paid to them in the social security programs at that time as part of a plan of national inclusiveness.

Today social exclusion is getting attention in many arenas. The European Union (EU) has a specific focus on solidarity programs to prevent social exclusion in member states and has developed protocols on social inclusion of the Roma that member countries are expected to uphold. Moreover, the EU, using some of its funds, works with countries in the queue for accession so that they can begin to address the problems of social exclusion in their midst. The British Government established a Social Exclusion Unit in 1997. NGOs, especially Médecins Sans Frontières, picked up on this issue in France, while other NGOs—Oxfam, Save the Children, CARE—have also incorporated it into their work and outreach (Lindenberg and Bryant, 2001, pp. 109–115). The Inter-American Development Bank (IDB) has included addressing social inclusion as an integral part of its development agenda. At the IDB, the issue is linked directly with race and the exclusion of minorities in Latin America—particularly Afro-Latinos and indigenous peoples. As stated by the Executive Vice President of the IDB in June 2001, "social and economic exclusion is on the agenda of the IDB....We cannot address poverty unless we address race" (Burke, 2001).

Although the term is now widespread in industrialized countries, many have noted that it is similar to the conceptualizations of poverty that have been prevalent for some time in developing countries, where social analysis has focused on issues of marginality, invisibility, and vulnerability (Oakley, 2001). The concept has allowed for a convergence of the dialogue on poverty across rich and poor countries. The framework of analysis is similar even though the focus on factors of exclusion varies—with more emphasis in rich countries on access to labor markets and decent housing and in poor countries on access to basic public goods, sources of livelihood, political participation, and security.

While the range of specific factors varies, dimensions of exclusion can include the following: economic exclusion, including exclusion from the labor market, agricultural land, credit, or land title; exclusion from public goods such as education, health care, or social protection; and political exclusion, including exclusion from civil and political rights, social and political participation, organizational representation, government transparency, and the judicial system.

Precise definitions of social exclusion vary among practitioners and analysts, but the core concept focuses on the exclusion of people from participating in the life and benefits of the larger community within which they reside. In broad terms, it refers to the societal and institutional processes that exclude certain groups from full participation in the social, economic, cultural, and political life of societies (Narayan, 1999, p. 4). There are groups of people excluded from full economic, political, and social participation for a variety of reasons—disabilities, drug use, different cultural practices, or immigrant status, for example. If a group is actively denied access to social welfare programs otherwise available to those in the majority, then their barriers to assets grow.

Social exclusion is not interchangeable with the term discrimination or the term poverty. Discrimination is but one of the processes that can lead to exclusion. The concept of social exclusion provides a lens for examining the implications of acts of discrimination when that discrimination leads to the exclusion of people from participation in mainstream society. The distinction between social exclusion and poverty is an important one. Not all poor people are socially excluded and not all members of groups who are excluded are also poor. For example, gender studies have demonstrated many ways in which women are excluded even within industrialized countries where they continue to face exclusion from certain levels of politics, powerful institutions within society, etc. Yet these women are not necessarily income poor, though they may experience other dimensions of poverty from a capabilities perspective.

An example that highlights the distinction between poverty that is embedded in long histories of exclusion and other forms of poverty is provided by a comparison between a poor community in Northern Uganda and the Roma in Serbia—illustrated through pictures of their respective homes (Photographs 2.1 and 2.2). In the picture at the top (Photograph 2.1), of Northern Ugandan homes near Teso, one can see that these traditional thatch homes and storage facilities reveal much that is positive about their residents. These people appear to have a sense of style, of culture, of being in a valued place. In short, there appear to be social, as well as economic incentives for them to build and maintain their facilities. The picture

Photograph 2.1
Ugandan home

Photograph 2.2
Roma Home

of a Roma home reveals a different story. Roma are denied many basic rights in Serbia, so that for example they cannot claim rights to tenancy or ownership of their land. While it is likely that the Roma have more than $3 a day to live on—and the Ugandans less than that—the social exclusion encountered by the Roma present a set of barriers to their working their way out of poverty that are different than those faced by their Ugandan counterparts. As we have said before, income is an incomplete measure of poverty. Social exclusion can, and often has, impoverished people for generations.

OUR USE OF THE CONCEPT OF SOCIAL EXCLUSION

While debate is ongoing on the use of term social exclusion, many researchers and policy analysts have come to the same conclusion as we have that the term provides a useful framework and analytical lens. In a conference that debated the topic at the Institute of Development Studies, one conclusion in the conference paper was that "on the value of social exclusion, there was general agreement that it was useful to direct attention to the multidimensional nature of poverty, to the problem of multiple disadvantage, to the psychosocial elements of poverty, and to the importance of agency and participation in the widest sense" (O'Brien et al., 1997, p. 16).

Some argue that the term is too imprecise and too all encompassing. Its broad scope poses problems for measurement and detailed analysis. With that in mind, we believe it is important that social exclusion not be seen as a new definition of poverty, but instead as a means of understanding the dynamics at play within society that lead to and perpetuate poverty. In this respect, we agree with Arjan de Haan, who argues that "social exclusion is primarily a framework for analysis and not...a new term for specific marginalized groups" (de Haan, 1998, p. 1). We contend that the concept provides a meaningful lens when defined somewhat more narrowly. For our purposes we are defining social exclusion as the process through which systemic barriers are imposed upon a minority group that impede members of that group from access to assets widely available to the majority.

As noted by de Haan, "the concept's advantage is that it focuses attention on central aspects of deprivation, equally relevant to analysis and policies: deprivation is a multidimensional phenomenon, and deprivation is part and parcel of social relations" (de Haan, 1998, p. 2). The notion of social exclusion is also closely related to the notions of relative deprivation and vulnerability. Social exclusion helps to focus the poverty debate on causes rather than outcomes. Income level, health status, level of education, etc., describe symptoms of poverty, but not the reasons for these outcomes.

Another advantage is that it encourages analysts to look at the trajectory of disadvantage over time (Oakley, 2001).

Because participation in the life of a community is linked to capabilities, social exclusion is also useful when examining poverty from a capabilities perspective (Sen, 1999, p. 89). Because capability deprivation looks at the ability of people to lead the life they value, relative poverty can lead to absolute capability deprivation—in other words being relatively poor in a rich country can significantly limit people's capabilities, even if in absolute terms they have a much higher standard of living than the poor in other countries.

The lens of social exclusion is also helpful in comparing and contrasting poverty within rich and poor countries and encouraging dialogue about approaches traditionally used in one or the other. As noted above, the concept has helped to bridge the gap in discussions about poverty in rich and poor countries. We used to say there is a third world inside the first, and a first world inside the third. But even that aphorism does not capture the complexity of poverty and social exclusion in the new millennium.

One last point bears mentioning with respect to the definition of social exclusion before we move on. Exclusion refers to a process in which people are systematically denied access to assets that they need and desire if they are to overcome their poverty. So, for example, if an indigenous population purposefully and willfully chooses to live separately from mainstream society and not to access the society's education or health care but rely on their own practices, that group is not being structurally excluded from accessing those assets (e.g., the Amish in the United States or an indigenous group striving to rely solely on its traditional lifestyle). However, if mainstream society encroaches on the indigenous group's own assets by denying their right to land ownership and granting logging rights to another group on the same land, then the lens of social exclusion may come into play. As it would, of course, if members of the group wanted to access mainstream education but were denied access.

CONTINUUM OF SOCIAL EXCLUSION

While the concept of social exclusion provides a useful framework, a more nuanced examination of the ways in which people are excluded and how the exclusion is played out is needed in order for us to understand its complex dynamics more clearly and articulate the tools that can be used to effectively address various facets of the problem.

Social exclusion occurs along a continuum—with distinctions from one extreme to the other related to the degree of exclusion and institutionalization of the processes that lead to exclusion. The way in which exclusionary practices are implemented play a role in determining where practices fall along the continuum. Exclusionary practices can be legalized, embedded within laws and formal institutions, or informally practiced, embedded within cultural attitudes and behavior. State efforts to end legalized exclusion may be ineffective if attitudes and behaviors do not also change; the interplay between the two provides an important dynamic. When the state is a participant in exclusionary practice, it can be so through a role of acquiescence in which it chooses to "overlook" the exclusion or through a role of state sanctioning of exclusion. More specific aspects of each of these are discussed below and represented in Figure 2.1.

Social exclusion in worst cases can be institutionalized through laws that dictate who can and cannot access certain assets. The apartheid regime in South Africa and segregation laws in the United States prior to the 1960s are examples of state sanctioning of exclusion leading to the enactment and enforcement of laws that excluded certain ethnic and racial groups from access to mainstream society on many levels. The genocide in Rwanda, of course, represents an extreme case of state sanctioning of not only exclusion but also the actual murder of people from a particular ethnic group. In other less extreme instances of state sanctioned exclusion, such as the lack of voting rights for women or other groups, laws deny access to certain institutions, but the groups are not excluded from all facets of society.

The selection and enforcement of languages for public services that are not inclusive of minority group languages are also a common means of legalized exclusion. While, on the one hand, such policies can aim to augment commonality and inclusiveness across groups with diverse languages, on the other hand such practices often deny language-minority groups from accessing a variety of services and can even serve to wipe out a native language. In Guatemala, for example, all official business is conducted in Spanish, despite the fact that the great majority of the population is indigenous and speaks languages other than Spanish as native tongues. In India, the policy of providing primary education in native languages, but all higher education and official business in English, creates barriers to pursuing advanced education and positions within government for those from rural areas. Despite efforts to promote language integrity in India through the Three Languages Formula, inequities persist, in part because languages other than the mother tongue are not introduced until upper school and then the second and third languages are taught, but are not the medium of instruction, thus lessening acquired competency in those languages (Mallikarjum, 2001).

In the United States, recent policies toward immigrants have increasingly articulated explicit policies of exclusion that differentiate the rights of different categories of legal immigrants. With welfare reform and the passage of the Personal Responsibility and Work Opportunity Reconciliation Act of 1996, the federal government of the United States limited the access of noncitizens to public benefits (such as Medicaid, food stamps,

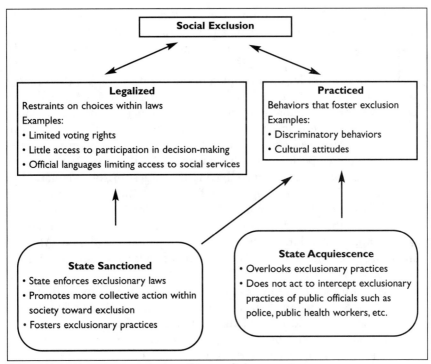

Figure 2.1
Continuum of Social Exclusion

and temporary assistance payments), thereby excluding many immigrants residing legally in the country from accessing services (Kappaz and Siegel, 2001). Several analysts are exploring the implications of these policies not only in terms of institutionalized exclusion of certain minority groups, but also in terms of segregation and exclusion of citizens. As the majority of children of immigrants are native US citizens, although their parents are often not citizens,[2] the differentiation of rights to access has had the consequence of denying services to many children who are themselves eligible if born in the United States but whose parents are not (Fix and Zimmerman, 1999).

Organizations can often be structured in such a way as to create barriers to access and in some instances exclude specific groups of people. Several key government institutions in the United States are structured so that entire industries have evolved around them to help people navigate the system. This is true, for example, in the case of the public benefits (welfare) system, as well as the Internal Revenue Service (IRS) and the Citizenship and Immigration Services (USCIS; known prior to 2003 as the

Immigration and Naturalization Service or INS). In the case of the USCIS, the barriers are not only linguistic and cultural, but also administrative— procedures are so complex as to require lawyers to assist applicants to do what, in essence, is completing an application form.

Without outright legal sanctioning of exclusion, states can also support exclusionary practices through acquiescence. This occurs when laws are not enforced or discriminatory practices get by under another guise. Police profiling is an example of state acquiescence to an exclusionary practice. The apparent prevalence of discrimination in the court system is another example. While working within the law, the judicial process in the United States has resulted in the country having the largest prison population in the world (at a record high of 6.6 million in 2002). A disproportionate share of those prisoners are minorities. While African-Americans represent only 11% of the total US population, they represent 46% of those in prison. And, while a larger percentage of the prison population, African-Americans represent a smaller proportion of those on parole—31% as compared to 55% white.

The institutionalization of exclusion can take place at many levels. As we will discuss in Chapter 3, institutions comprise not only organizations, but also the norms and rules of the game that govern various aspects of societal behavior. Exclusion can be prevalent within a society even when not legalized or sanctioned by the state. What we term practiced social exclusion refers to the dominance of cultural attitudes and accepted behaviors that serve to systematically exclude certain groups. The interplay between legal and practiced exclusion is not linear. In some ways, you need cultural attitudes to change in order to push legal change; but legal change can sometimes come ahead of change in practice in mainstream society. For example, in the United States and other countries, antidiscrimination laws moved forward by those opposed to discrimination preceded changes in the dominant culture; over time, the legal protections led to increasing changes in practice and norms. The existence of the laws does not mean people are no longer discriminatory, but it has made it unacceptable behavior and opens up the possibility for more improvement over time.

The degree of social exclusion within a society varies and often involves a complex interplay among different factors. In the case of Native Americans in the United States, for example, several instances of exclusion with state acquiescence or even state sanctioning have been documented. However, at the same time, there are members of the country's majority who support Native Americans and have helped use the legal institutions of the country to uphold the rights of the minority group against those exclusionary practices. One case in point is the misuse of the Indian Trust Monies funds by the US Department of Interior's Bureau of Indian Affairs. While the federal government agency misused funds for decades, civil society groups working together with Native Americans were able to win cases in the federal courts that denounced the practices of the Bureau and mandated changes. While this was an important step forward, the story of Native American exclusion and violence is ongoing and we turn to it again later in this chapter.

INEQUALITY

While social exclusion and inequality often go hand in hand, analytically they are different phenomena. Income inequality can be measured and therefore is the focus of a great deal of research. Yet, when income inequalities become extreme, they, like social exclusion, reflect the fact that the existing system is working well for some and failing others. There is some seminal research indicating that extreme inequality negatively impacts economic growth.[3] Analysts now increasingly talk of "pro-poor" policies by which they mean policies that encourage growth with positive distributive impacts. In order to understand the policy implications of inequality for growth and poverty reduction, at least a quick review of some of the measurement issues and cross national comparisons is needed to reveal a little of the complex debates concerning inequality.

When people compare themselves to others, they are most likely to make those comparisons with proximate counterparts—their neighbors or peers. Some of the strongest feelings about one's poverty are evoked in light of such comparisons. Thus it can be that inequality, especially as it increases, poses serious social and political problems more than does chronic poverty, especially chronic poverty that is geographically isolated or remote. Sadly, "out of sight, out of mind" is most true for the chronically poor living in remote places. They live with their isolation, and it compounds their discomfort. We need to remember that the social welfare of a society depends not only on *average* incomes, but on the *distribution* of income (Marris, 1999, p. 7).

Regional differences in income poverty (noted previously in Table 1.1) are a sign of the large inequalities that exist between countries, as well as regions. The inequality of the global political economy is one issue in the active current debates over poverty, its implications, and what might be effective in reducing it. Debate exists on trends in inequality, with researchers using different data sets and methodologies. While some contend that inequality is declining (Wolf, 2003), most studies conclude that the gap is indeed widening globally between nations, and in several instances widening within nations as well (Schultz, 1998; Firebaugh, 1999; Milanovic, 1999; Ravallion, 2001). According to the UNDP, using World Bank data, the ratio between the average income of the world's richest 5% and the poorest 5% increased from 78 to 1 in 1993 to 123 to 1 in 1998. The income gap between the richest 20% of countries and poorest 20% of countries went from 30 to

1 in 1960 to 60 to 1 in 1990 to 74 to 1 in 1997 (UNDP, HDR, 1999). In 1997, the richest countries (representing 20% of the world's population) had 86% of world GNP as compared to the poorest 20% of the world with 1% of world GNP (UNDP, HDR, 1999).

Precise measurement of inequality is affected in part by the use of income divided into deciles in order to measure distribution within a country. But there can be wide differences within the top decile of income distribution, especially in countries with large populations. Often, as a result of the growth in incomes achieved in the past decade, for example, the top 10% of income distribution now contains a subgroup of billionaires with concentrated wealth on a level and scale never seen before.

Painstakingly careful work in this area has been carried out by Branko Milanovic, who distinguishes among three kinds of inequality: first, unweighted countries' GDPs per capita; second, population-weighted GDPs per capita; and third, inter-national and internal income distribution to derive "true world income distribution." He finds, in his clearly written work, *Worlds Apart: Inter-National and World Inequality 1950–2000*, that

> over the period 1988–1993 [the third concept, inter-national income distribution], shows an important increase in inequality caused by slower growth of rural incomes in populous Asian countries compared to the rich OECD countries, as well as by rising urban-rural income differences in China, and by declining income in transition countries (Branko Milanovic, 2002, p. 1).

With that increased inequality has come increased tension between rich and poor nations, such as that voiced by NGOs in their protests at international trade meetings. While the past decade has been compared by some to the Gilded Age of the end of the nineteenth century in terms of the wealth aggregated by elites in major northern industrializing countries, levels of inequality are much larger now than they were then. The poverty we have been discussing exists alongside extreme wealth. The combined assets of the world's top three billionaires are more than the combined GNP of all the least developed countries—home to 600 million people (UNDP, HDR, 1999, p. 3). The richest 200 people in the world more than doubled their net worth between 1994 and 1998, bringing the total to more than $1 trillion. The difference in income per capita between richest countries and poorest countries 250 years ago was about 5 to 1. The difference between Europe and South Asia was about 2 to 1. The difference now in income per capita between Switzerland and Mozambique is estimated at 400 to 1 (Landes, 1998).

Some countries are not only failing to gain, but are actually growing poorer. Russia is poorer than it was two decades ago. The Republic of Congo is poorer. Rwanda, Burundi, Sierra Leone, Myanmar, Iraq, Zimbabwe, Tajikistan, Afghanistan...people who, by accident of birth, live in these places have seriously poorer health, nutrition, education, access to land, capital, and personal fulfillment. They may well also be working harder than did their grandparents, with more of the household committed to working for wages or self-employed and unable to work their way out of their constrained circumstances. Some are not working at all—they have been mutilated by fellow citizens during civil wars, or turned into refugees, or rendered homeless.

A central issue in the inequality debate is the extent to which current economic policies, particularly globalization and market liberalization, are benefiting the poor, as well as the rich. One study, by Lundberg and Squire, finds evidence that trade openness increases inequality. They point out that openness to trade is correlated negatively with income growth among the poorest 40% of the population but strongly and positively with income growth among remaining groups (Lundberg and Squire, 2003).

Part of the problem in the inequality debate is that researchers use different data sets and define and therefore measure factors differently. In short, there is no consensus among research economists on exactly what the trends are in income inequality. In a major Brookings Institution Conference on the subject in 2004, Martin Ravallion presented a thorough paper summarizing that debate (Ravallion, 2004).

Despite the ongoing debate, the World Bank's PovertyNet points to inequality as rising within several countries. Sharp increases in inequality resulted in the years following the transition from communism in Eastern Europe and Central Asia. Inequality within OECD countries increased in the 1990s, especially in the United States, Sweden, and the United Kingdom. Some countries experienced decreases in inequality from early 1980s to early 1990s, most notably Korea, Indonesia, and Malaysia. But Malaysia's progress was reversed in the 1990s. In the same time period, China, Russia, and Thailand had the largest increases in Gini coefficients, the standard measure for inequality (World Bank PovertyNet).

These levels of inequality reflect a serious divide between rich and poor that cuts across national boundaries. There are pockets of extreme poverty within wealthy countries and pockets of wealth even within the poorest countries. In the United States, 10 million households (9.7% of all households) were food insecure between 1996–1998. These households did not have enough food to meet their basic needs (Nord, Jemison, Bickel, 1999).

In 1998, for the fourth consecutive year, average household incomes rose in the United States, but the persistence of inequality resulted in only a statistically insignificant change in the poverty rate—from 13.4% in 1997 to 12.7% in 1998 (Dalaker, 1999). Despite a record economic boom in the United States, both the poverty rate and level of inequality remained statistically unchanged from 1993 through 2000. The long term trend in the United States has been toward increased income

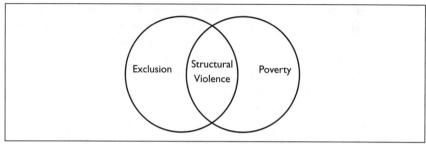

Figure 2.2
Structural Violence: The Intersection of Exclusion and Poverty

inequality. In 1996, the share of household income received by the highest income quintile was 49.0%, an increase from a share of 43.8% in 1996. While the rich's share of the country's income has been increasing, the share of the lowest quintile has been declining—from 4% in 1967 to 3.7% in 1996. This also implies that the middle 60% of the income distribution has received a declining share. The Gini index for the United States in 1998 was 14% above its 1967 level (Weinberg, 1999).

IMPLICATIONS OF SOCIAL EXCLUSION AND INEQUALITY FOR VIOLENCE

Inequality and social exclusion have implications for conflict and violence. When we talk of social exclusion, we are talking about the systemic denial of access to the same freedoms and rights that others in a society enjoy. In circumstances where social exclusion is pervasive and combined with chronic poverty and inequality, it creates an ever-present denial of a group's acceptance by society that results in a silent, structural violence felt in the day-to-day life of a people. This can lead to entrenched resentment, frustration, and anger, which have the potential to erupt into physical violence. Understanding exclusion thus has important implications for peace building. In this section we will examine two forms of violence that can be fueled by, and associated with, social exclusion: structural violence and physical violence. As discussed in Chapter 1, our concern here is to explore key associations and linkages between violence and elements of poverty such as exclusion, but not to provide evidence that there is a direct causal link between the two.

There are, more likely, intervening variables that drive whether or not social exclusion leads to structural violence. As noted in Figure 2.2 below, not all circumstances of poverty or exclusion also entail structural violence, but particularly where poverty and exclusion intersect, structural violence tends to occur.

Structural Violence

Just as peace was defined in Chapter 1 more broadly than simply the absence of war, violence must also be understood to encompass many forms. As Martin Luther King, Jr., noted, "Violence is anything that denies dignity and leads to a sense of hopelessness and helplessness" (Cited in Uvin, 1998). John Galtung, a leading peace and conflict theorist since the 1960s, defines structural violence as a condition "in which the poor are denied decent and dignified lives because their basic physical and mental capacities are constrained by hunger, poverty, inequality, and exclusion" (cited in Uvin, 1998, p. 103).

In an analysis of the role of the development complex in the Rwandan genocide, Peter Uvin expanded on the concept of structural violence, defining it as "a structural process characterized by long-standing dynamics of exclusion, marginalization, inequality, frustration, and racism" (Uvin, 1998, p. 7). Elements of structural violence include "ethnic inequality; institutionalized, state-organized racism; regional politics; lack of dignity and self-respect; the generalized presence of impunity and the absence of justice; human rights violations; [and] the oppressive presence of the state" (Uvin, 1998, p. 45).

Researchers of poor inner city populations in the United States, especially those looking at African-Americans and Hispanics, have also described the life experience of the poor in these circumstances as one of structural violence (Bourgois, 1995; Kaljee, 1995). Structural violence is the combination of poverty with the persistent life experiences of rejection and exclusion, fueled by racism and prejudice, that diminish a sense of self-worth and reinforce the perception of oneself as an outsider unable to join mainstream society and improve one's living condition.

The concept of structural violence thus allows us to identify and acknowledge the type of nonphysical violence that is inflicted upon people who are daily confronted with injustices embedded within their society. The violence is in the form of deprivation and denial of an adequate livelihood and in the form of emotional violence against a person's sense of self-worth and hope for his or her future:

> In short, it seems that the same elements appear over and over again: for poor people, meaningful development is not simply about increases in income but also about increased access to the means of production; reduction in insecurity and vulnerability, and the creation of a sustainable and hopeful future; empowerment through participation, justice, freedom, and access to information and education; overcoming physical weakness through access to health and nutrition; and social relations characterized by human

dignity, cooperation, and a sense of equity....The systematic absence [of these various processes] for certain groups, especially under conditions of macroeconomic growth, can be called structural violence (Uvin, 1998, p. 107).

Impunity is an important factor in creating structural violence since the inability of the judicial system to punish criminals and acts of injustice hampers the ability to fight for change and perpetuates the image of helplessness. For example, in India, caste Hindus annually rape, murder, and maim hundreds of Dalits, usually with impunity (Meerman, 2001, p. 1465). Even after a 1989 law was passed to protect Dalits (the Prevention of Atrocities Act), violence continued, with 8,540 crimes against Dalits reported in 1997, including 261 murders and 302 rapes (Meerman, 2001, p. 1465).

The development industry can help perpetuate the processes of exclusion if it does not challenge and indeed change the patterns of who benefits from development assistance. It can also perpetuate structural violence if development work enhances the presence of inequality within a society. Particularly in societies where structural violence already exists, development aid can often end up working within those same systems of exclusion. Studies have found that most of the development aid ends up in the hands of the richest 1% of society (Voyame, 1996, and Godding, 1993, cited in Uvin, 1998).

One way in which these processes are perpetuated is when some people continue to live in abject poverty, while development workers live in privileged conditions in poor countries. A job announcement for a position in Haiti with a large international NGO exemplifies this problem. Despite the extreme poverty that permeates Haitian society, the ad describes working conditions for expatriate staff in Haiti as follows:

> The living and working conditions in Haiti are generally quite good. The office and compound are among the nicest in the [NGO name] world. Housing is of good quality, most houses having pleasant gardens. Public services such as electric and telephone service are not dependable, but the office and residences have back-up systems such as water cisterns, radios and generators. Good schools are available in French and English medium through high school level. Medical facilities locally are basic, with serious illness being treated in Miami.

No doubt it is difficult to recruit professional development staff with families to live in poor countries, yet it is also important not to replicate the very problem one is striving to overcome. If development workers are to overcome social exclusion, they need to consider carefully their lifestyle choices. This does not mean they need to deny family members quality health care or education, but they do need to look for opportunities in social interactions to signal support for inclusive and affirming ways to include and listen to minorities in their social lives. In reaching out in those ways, they will also keep themselves informed about the patterns of inequality and social exclusion under way in the places where they are working.

The historic treatment of Native Americans in the United States is another example of structural violence. The Hollywood version of the American West obscures a harsh reality of social exclusion, given real form in reservations for Native Americans following a trail of broken treaties. Today, Native Americans and Alaskan Natives have the highest poverty rate of any ethnic group in the country and are the only group for whom poverty increased rather than decreased from 1998 to 2000 (US Census Bureau, 2002). On average from 1998 to 2000, 25.9% of the Native American and Alaskan Native population were living below the poverty line (US Census Bureau, 2002).

Writing about Native American affairs in the Western United States in the 1980s, Paula Limerick points out that in the ongoing battles between Indian and non-Indians over land disputes, fisheries, grazing rights, leases of reservation natural resources, majority culture far from reservations professed a "generalizable fondness for the Indian as a symbol of ecological restraint and primal wisdom...closer to the epicenters of the claims disputes, however, the sense of injury turned in the opposite direction" (Limerick, 1987, p. 338). In every instance in the American West, Native Americans lost access to land and their way of life, as well as their traditional foods. The bloodshed was the overt physical violence; the malnutrition, shortened life expectancy, stunted children, and lost heritage constitute the structural violence that remains with us today.

The persistent structural violence against people within the Sioux nation illustrates the point. Dee Brown told the earlier story of the Sioux in *Bury My Heart at Wounded Knee* (Brown, 1988). More recently the *Wall Street Journal* carried the story of the Sioux today—a people whose life expectancy—at 48 years—is the second shortest in the Western Hemisphere. (Only the Haitian life expectancy rate of 46 years is shorter.) This tragic Sioux life expectancy rate in 2002 is in large part the legacy of hundreds of years of structural violence, including, most recently, the budget cuts of the 1980s under President Ronald Reagan. As Limerick points out, President Reagan cut back substantially the payments made to a range of programs to Indians on reservations, including the Indian Health Service.[4]

Many of the federal payments originated in agreements on compensation for land taken by the government. Reservation land is owned in trust by the federal government. Indians residing on reservation land cannot use it as collateral for loans, which adds to their problems in securing credit. In the mid-1980s, when the programs were cut, reservation unemployment was 50% on average and in the worst cases—Pine Ridge and Rosebud Sioux—it was as high as 70%. This is structural violence at work.

The history of Native Americans in the United States is a long story of other Americans trying by means fair or foul to change the culture of the various Indian tribes. Frightened by these different cultures—Sioux, Apache, Ute, Chippewa, or Iroquois—every effort was made to change Indian traditional life. If not the religious fervor of Reverend Meeker in Colorado trying to get young Indians to forego hunting and pony racing in favor of farming, it was the efforts in the 1960s to take children away from Indian parents to school them in wholly different contexts in order to erase their culture. What has happened, of course, is a deepened sense of Indianness as a political statement, as well as a cultural heritage.[5]

Physical Violence

When several of the elements of structural violence exist in combination and persist over extended periods of time, they create an environment of frustration and hopelessness. Structural violence, which is fostered in an environment of exclusion, can erupt into physical violence. We cannot, obviously, claim empirical proof that structural violence and exclusion directly cause physical violence or war, but we do contend that the two are correlated. At the very least, it can be argued that environments where structural violence exists not only do not promote peace, but provide a breeding ground for physical conflicts. As Uvin points out, "a society characterized by structural violence produces profound popular anger, frustration, cynicism, ignorance, and desire for scapegoating" (Uvin, 1998, p. 8).

In an examination of the linkages between exclusion and conflict and a review of the literature it was found that "there is no evidence that exclusion per se leads to violent conflict" (Martin, 1999, p. 6). When it does is contingent upon catalytic events, and political leaders who choose to capitalize upon it for their own political ends. Such critical intervening events can be found in accounts of, for example, the bloodshed in the Balkans, in Kosovo, in Rwanda, or in the history of the partition of India into India and Pakistan. Recently, the discovery of oil in the context of unresolved violence in the Sudan has been among the events leading to the disastrous violence in Darfur in western Sudan.

Exclusion without such events, or catalysts in other political and economic contexts, is likely to induce different survival strategies, some negative and personally violent such as battering children or wives, alcoholism, or other substance abuse. Far less violent, and more common, responses are retreat from society, heavy reliance on core-family, and distrust of outsiders.

More positive approaches are the strengthening of traditional forms of solidarity and social capital within the excluded group, building up of the informal economy, and strategies of integration or collective action.

The strategy chosen depends "on contextual factors such as the historical patterns of conflict resolution, political regime characteristics, the degree of civilian control over the military and the police, the degree of fairness and independence of the judiciary, the presence of armed groups" among others (Martin, 1999, p.11). These conclusions mirror our hypothesis that exclusion can be thought of as a permissive condition of conflict, even if not a direct cause. While direct causation cannot be empirically proven, the conditions of social exclusion and structural violence do lend themselves to violence. And it is likely that the more extreme the levels of structural violence and the more excluded people feel from other means of expressing discontent, the fewer the options there are for nonviolent responses and peaceful change.

CONCLUSION—IMPLICATIONS FOR POSITIVE WAYS FORWARD

An understanding of poverty based on access to assets and the framework provided by the concepts of social exclusion and structural violence as processes that limit access suggests several implications for designing ways to move forward on these complex, nested problems. As we noted at the beginning, social exclusion always brings us back to actors and institutions. The search for ways to move forward means looking and listening to the actors. These are, among others, social groups, the state, businesses, local authorities, local elites, military leaders, religious bodies, and community organizations (Oakley, 2001). Each of these has a role to play in shifting norms, practices, and values in local communities, civil society, and the state.

While there are no quick fixes to historic problems, there are steps, policy changes (legal reforms, punishment of discrimination, funds for inclusion), and project interventions (microcredit, education support, social funds for small local projects) that can, over time, with good will, help to undermine and thus erode bad practices. Institutions are created by people, thus they are also open to be changed by people. Bringing about institutional change is often thought of as entailing both political and economic change. Fair enough, but it is also cultural change. Cultures are inherently dynamic and cumulative, shifting incrementally, and sometimes relatively rapidly, with each new generation. Basically, they change as people change their minds and behaviors in light of events (new information, new desires, or different incentives).

In severe cases of social exclusion, legal and regulatory sanctions are needed to create incentives for change. The European Union with its focus on social inclusion and solidarity requires that member governments and governments of candidate countries for accession prepare national strategies for social inclusion for groups that have experienced social exclusion. Thus, for example, several of the countries that were admitted to the EU in May 2004 were required to develop national strategies for overcoming the problems experienced by the Roma, a group traditionally deeply marginalized in many EU member states and socially excluded in Poland and Slovakia. The Aquis Communitaire of the EU serves as the major legal foundation, which each country must enact. In one of its chapters, the *Aquis Communitaire* details the legal requirements for social protection and overcoming social exclusion.[6] The European Union's sanctioning of social exclusion and provision of funds for promoting social inclusion are working to change historic patterns of social exclusion in local communities across Europe, much as did the Civil Rights legislation of the 1960s in the United States.

Institutional change that facilitates access of formerly excluded groups to key services such as education moves sweeping change along. The introduction of free primary education in the United States grew into an institution—now taken for granted—and constituted a major building block for change and invention in the nineteenth century. Integrating gender concerns in the latter years of the twentieth century into all levels of public services is another example of institutional change. In short, changing legal frameworks and opening up access to the judicial system is fundamental in the process for overcoming exclusion, especially those factors that impact directly upon property rights and access to jobs such as equal opportunity. Laws, however, do have to be enforced and people must have access to legal recourse for their grievances.

Thus frameworks for social inclusion are multidimensional in their policy choices. Jacob Meerman's analysis of the relationship between minorities and poverty points to the three-way relationship among poverty, minority status, and options for reducing tensions (Meerman, 2002). Although Meerman purposely does not use the term social exclusion, the treatment and conditions of the minority groups he describes fit well within the framework as we have defined social exclusion. He looks at four minority groups in country contexts where policies have made efforts to reduce the poverty of a specific minority: Dalits in India, blacks in Cuba and the United States, and Burakumin in Japan. What he finds is some empirical confirmation of Gunnar Myrdal's older assertion—that stateways can change folkways (Myrdal, 1968). He also finds that Cuba stands ahead of the others in finding ways to enhance the inclusion of blacks so that their quality of life is the same as that of the majority.

Meerman positions his research firmly within human capital theory and therefore provides useful reminders of the relationship between human capital and longer term economic growth. Moreover his research focuses on governments that made an effort to improve the mobility of minorities out of poverty. And even where there was some commitment and, importantly, policies supporting that goal, progress was very slow. Nonetheless there was progress—improvement in the mobility out of poverty—and thus much can be learned from looking at what works, which is the major theme we stress throughout this book.

Cuba's success, he tells us, was due to a combination of state policies that were effective at providing Afro-Cubans with assets that allowed them to achieve parity with the majority. Parity was measured in terms of income, occupational distribution, educational attainment, and health status. Cuba's policies included increased access to quality education, provision of employment, and support from the highest levels of government for a philosophy and behaviors that promote equality of all people. The success was due in part to the particular political circumstances following the revolution that facilitated a fundamental paradigm shift in society and to the policy of the government of taking control of the means of production and thus of employment. It should be noted that the Cuban experience was also accompanied by a mass exodus of professionals that opened up more room for rapid ascension of minority members in society.

The social exclusion and structural violence frameworks for understanding poverty also have implications for program and project design. On one level, programming should aim to be inclusionary—for each program and project, an analysis of the ways in which different groups will be impacted and will have access is needed, with community input to ensure long-standing exclusionary practices are broken and that barriers to access are not unintentionally included in the program or project design.

Furthermore, programs and projects should be developed that specifically aim to change long-standing patterns of exclusion. In the case of Rwanda, after the genocide, development aid was directed at peace building, justice support, strengthening civil society, monitoring human rights, conflict resolution, etc.—all of which aimed at breaking down practices of exclusion. Before the genocide occurred, such programs did not exist, as development aid was focused on more traditional poverty-alleviation strategies (Uvin, 1998 p. 100). As stated by de Haan, "increasing social cohesion can be a precondition for poverty alleviation rather than a second priority" (de Haan, 1998, p. 14).

Other types of projects that can specifically address problems of exclusion include those that aim to increase multicultural aspects of programs. Incorporating multiculturalism into education is one important step—in terms of teaching children about valuing different cultural identities and also using teaching techniques and curricula that are respectful of different cultures and minority groups (including programs for and about people living with disabilities, for example). Both microcredit projects and small projects under the aegis of social action funds are especially well suited for providing previously excluded groups access to assets where the market has previously failed to do so. Projects can also work specifically at strengthening the ability of service providers to provide services in ways that are accessible to people of different cultures. In the United States, there is a growing focus on the need for what is known as cultural competence among providers, particularly in the health arena. Cultural competency has been defined as a set of congruent behaviors, attitudes, and policies that come together in a system, agency, or among professionals and enable the system, agency, or professionals to work effectively in cross-cultural situations (Cross, 1989).

Another area that has come into focus through the social exclusion lens is the need to reassess research agendas and data collection. As the IDB pointed out in its 2001 strategy for addressing social exclusion, providing accurate statistics on the status of minority groups will help "make the invisible visible" (IDB, 2001). For example, in Latin America, the rights of Afro-Latinos have traditionally received very little attention compared to the rights of indigenous populations. However, recent studies have shown that the Afro-Latino population, which has also been systemically excluded in most Latin American countries, actually significantly outnumbers indigenous populations. Estimates of the population of Latin Americans with African lineage range from 80 to 150 million (Oakley, 2001). The areas where Afro-Latino populations are concentrated tend to have high concentrations of poverty—the Pacific coast of Colombia and Ecuador, the northern fringes of South America, the Central American Coast, and Brazil's Northeastern region.

Research agendas change with the social exclusion lens because it calls for a focus on processes and relationships that lead to deprivation. Research on employment should look not only at outcomes of job status but also at the labor market practices that determine those outcomes (de Haan, 1998, p. 12). Research needs to focus on actors and processes—what Sen calls the relational roots of deprivation. Ultimately, social exclusion calls for a closer look at issues of human rights, particularly the long-neglected economic and social rights, as well as civil and political rights.

All of this brings us back to the importance of participation. Listening to, and getting input from, the poor and the excluded themselves is essential not only to building our understanding of the problems they face but in moving forward toward more fair and equitable solutions.

NOTES

1.   One of the most thoughtful and complete accounts of the issues confronting the rural poor is to be found in the *Rural Poverty Report 2001* published by Oxford University Press for the International Fund for Agricultural Development. See its account of the need for access to assets throughout, but especially on pp. 3–12.

2.   For example, in Chicago, 78% of the children of foreign-born mothers are native-born children and therefore, under US law, citizens (Cherlin et al., 2001).

3. See the World Bank's PovertyNet website, which updates its reporting on the ongoing research on inequality regularly. On February 2, 2003, that website carried the following account, among others, "Empirically the proposition that initial inequality seemed to be associated with lower growth rates was put forward by Persson and Tabellini (1994) and Aleksina and Rodrik (1994). Using data sets available to them, both studies found that inequality variables had significantly negative coefficients in growth regressions, when controlling for a number of the usual right hand side variables, such as initial income, schooling, and physical capital investment. A survey by Benabou (10996a) listed a number of other cross country empirical investigations of this relationship, and reported that the vast majority of them reached the same conclusion." Later they discuss contrary studies, but most of those come from the use of a different database, the Deninger and Squire database. See this and more in "The Effect of Distribution on Growth." Accessed on-line at www.worldbank.org/poverty/inequal/econ/growth.htm.

4. When American Indians were forced onto reservations in the United States, they were given salted meat and flour, which constituted major components of their diet, as they had been moved to land where they could not produce their own food. In their previous life, their diet was fish, berries, fruit, venison, squash, nuts—a nutrient-rich diet. Major health problems resulted within a decade of reservation life with its deadly combination of inactivity and poor diet.

5. In 2004, the Smithsonian Institution added the first national Museum of Native American Art.

6. We are grateful to Ivana Aleksic, Joanna Brzeska, Christophe Merdes, Renata Nowak-Garmer, Gullaume Roty, Marta Schaaf, and Gelu Sulugiuc who researched and wrote, for the World Bank Social Development Unit, the Columbia University Workshop report, *Great Expectations: The EU and Social Development in Poland and Serbia,* for their account of the social protection work of the EU in accession countries (May 2004).

3

POLICIES, INSTITUTIONS, AND COLLECTIVE ACTION

"How can we explain the radically different performance of economies over time?...Institutions, together with the standard constraints of economic theory, determine the opportunities in a society."
—Douglass North, *Institutions, Institutional Change and Economic Performance*, 1990

INTRODUCTION

The framework we have defined thus far for understanding and addressing poverty and violence places an emphasis on participation and on structural change to tackle the root causes. The systemic factors affecting poor people's access to assets and hence their ability to move themselves out of poverty lies at the core of the poverty problem. This framework for reducing poverty implies a critical role for institutions. Institutions influence people's behavior, define the parameters within which participation takes place, and directly affect access to assets and inclusion in society. Institutional development is thus our final foundational concept before we move on to discuss practical policies, projects, and techniques for effective poverty reduction work.

We argue that a different conceptualization of development is needed—one that makes fewer distinctions between "developing" and "developed" countries and simply focuses on reducing poverty. That is not to say that there are not major institutional differences between—and among—largely wealthy countries and countries with widespread poverty. But, while the differences are recognized, there are more institutional similarities than is commonly acknowledged. Many of the same dysfunctional institutions exist globally, not just in first or third world countries; for example, regressive tax systems, corruption, absence of transparency in public expenditures, human rights violations, etc.

Moreover, the same general types, or categories, of institutions play important roles across societies, even while vast differences exist in the details of each institution in different contexts. Understanding the importance of institutions, recognizing various types, and knowing how to look for them when engaged in development work is central to effectiveness. Failure to do so can lead to myriad problems and poor results. Institutional differences are a major factor affecting the application of successful antipoverty problems from one region to another.

This chapter will examine the role of institutions in fighting poverty. We will look in some detail at the institutional issues inherent in improving the access of poor people to assets and the importance of institutional legal frameworks, in particular as they relate to common property. And we will also talk about institutional change, in particular the pivotal role of collective action in bringing about change and the way in which social capital interacts with institutional change.

INSTITUTIONS AND POVERTY REDUCTION

To get a good sense of how institutions enable or impede poverty reduction, one needs a clear understanding of what is meant by *institutions* and all the roles they play. We follow the definition of Douglass North and other institutional economists who agree that institutions are the "rules of the game"— policies, norms, and widely repeated behaviors are all included in their use of this concept (Williamson, 1985; Eggertsson, 1990; North, 1990; World Bank, *Governance Policy Paper*, 1991). Institutional economists mean by institutions far more than simply those policies passed by legislatures— though those are indeed part of the rules of the game. They also mean by institutions those highly valued behaviors demonstrated through sturdy, lasting combinations of "rules" and "roles." Thus, for example, the rule of law is not found in any one piece of legislation but is embedded in widespread practice and ethos over a large number of entities. Institutions as values, rules, and roles are much larger than policies or organizations.

Indeed, some of the ways in which people use the term institution interchangeably with organization muddies the singular importance that institutions have in our lives. Not all organizations are institutions, although many are. For example, it can be argued that football is an institution in the United States—but it takes many different organizational forms. There are the local kids playing in the school playground, and there are the professional clubs, and the National Football League (NFL) itself. Some of these organizations come and go, but the institution of football carries on. On the other hand, sometimes there are organizations that are place specific and can be said to be institutions—the New York City Public Library,

Table 3.1
Institutions versus Organizations

Institutions

Institutions are the rules of the game of a society, or, more formally, are the humanly devised constraints that structure human interaction. They are composed of formal rules (statute law, common law, regulations), informal constraints (conventions, norms of behavior, and self-imposed modes of conduct), and enforcement characteristics of both.

Organizations

Organizations are the players: groups of individuals bound by a common purpose to achieve objectives. They include political bodies (political parties, the senate, a city council, a regulatory agency); economic bodies (firms, trade unions, family firms, cooperatives); social bodies (churches, clubs, athletic associations); and educational bodies (schools, colleges, vocational training centers).

Source: Douglass North, 1995, p 23.

for example. So institutions can take organizational forms. This point is important since below we will talk about the need for greatly strengthened and reformed international institutions, many of which take precise organizational form, such as United Nations agencies or the World Bank.

Thus, institutions take many forms, both formal and informal. Some are embedded in culture, and others codified in laws. While institutions can encourage positive collective action and provide order to systems of behavior, they can also lead to patterns of exclusion and violence. When understood as the rules governing behavior, it is clear that institutions play a vital role in determining livelihood strategies of the poor. The shift in development practice to participatory approaches, which build upon communities' own adaptive strategies and capabilities instead of relying on externally defined and imposed solutions, requires a more in-depth understanding of the institutions at work in a community and the dynamics that can lead to institutional change. As others have also argued, "participatory development is impossible without understanding the underlying institutions or rules of the game between different stakeholders" (Davies and Hossain, 2000). To illustrate some of the key institutional factors and complexities that come into play in any effort aimed at addressing the structural causes of poverty, let us turn to a brief discussion of indigenous institutions, as well as the concept of dysfunctional institutions.

The nature of indigenous institutions—by which we mean the norms and rules embedded in a culture—affect the ways in which people in that culture take up change, or innovate by incorporating what they have learned from outside their culture. Many aspects of indigenous institutions are also referred to as social institutions, defined as "the rules that individuals share and use to regulate collective behavior" (Johnson, 1997). Anthropologists and behavioral psychologists have had much to contribute to our understanding of those processes. But the need for more research is particularly acute with respect to this issue. Think about how the intersection between deeply held values and human motivation drives daily choices for every one of us. Our cultures are institutionalized within us, shaping us in ways we do not always recognize. And we, in turn, shape our institutions. Cultures—and their institutions—are inherently dynamic, always changing and adapting, yet often in such incremental steps that the changes are not readily identified even as they take place. In times of increased multicultural interaction, the rates of change increase, and, with them, tensions or conflict. Among other things, indigenous institutions affect how people adapt or learn when engaged with those who are very different.

The differences among ethnic communities in the countries of sub-Saharan Africa and the roles that indigenous institutions have played in the social, economic, and political lives of those countries is not one story, but volumes. Indeed, the African novelists have given us more compelling insights (Achebe, Soyinka, Ngugi) into these dynamics than have many political scientists. One interesting recent nonfiction work on indigenous institutions that moves forward our understanding is Mamadou Dia's *Africa's Management in the 1990s*, which directly addresses the disconnect—and its devastating costs—between Western cultural values and those inherent to these African communities (Dia, 1997).

Powerful leaders—from Mahatma Gandhi to Genghis Khan or Ataturk—invoke indigenous institutions precisely because of their strength as core values and their relationship to how trust is embedded in those values within a place. They know that institutions matter...and that change only happens when people sense that the change needed is in fact inherently valuable in light of deeply held norms. Unfortunately, some deeply held values can also be problematic. Superstitions and prejudices can be deeply held values—and they can be foundations for dysfunctional institutions.

A vivid example of complex indigenous institutions combining functional and dysfunctional characteristics is provided by Heike Behrend, who writes from extensive research on the origins of the Lord's Resistance Army in Uganda and, in particular, on the powerful role of the founder, Alice Lakwena (Behrend, 2000). Lakwena was a young woman who claimed she had been possessed by a spirit—a spirit that was asking her to lead the north in resistance to the government located in the south, and often dominated by southerners, in light of the serious poverty and environmental problems experienced by northerners. She did lead such a resistance—some 7,000 marched toward Kampala and terrible deaths resulted when they were overwhelmingly defeated. While Alice Lakwena eventually fled, there remain to this day bands of militants and groups of thugs loosely grouped under the banners of the current Lord's Resistance Army who continue to inflict violence on people, mostly civilians, and often children, in northern Uganda.

Lakwena's behavior, beliefs, and demeanor seem bizarre to us, unaccustomed as we are to spirit possession. Yet she could be likened to Joan of Arc, who also had a vision of armed resistance. The analogy illustrates the point that Westerners tend to relate to Joan of Arc from within their Western tradition and yet feel estranged by the concept of spirit possession in what is to us a distinctly foreign setting. Both are embedded in indigenous institutions. Both had institutional consequences and led to bloodshed. Lakwena's origins in poverty, illiteracy, and environmental devastation have social and psychological counterparts that in turn have further consequences for future choices. There were a number of institutions at play in northern Uganda leading to a situation of poverty and disenfranchisement, which made the people open to the practices proposed by Lakwena. And at the same time, violence and conflict took on a life of its own as the war economy, as well documented by Paul Collier, became institutionalized (Collier, 2000).

Let us look more carefully at dysfunctional institutions, because they often need to be acknowledged and addressed in the development process. By dysfunctional institutions, we mean ones that lead to destructive acts or choices that undermine human well-being. Institutions can be functional or dysfunctional. Corruption, racism, violence—all can be institutionalized. Dysfunctional institutions account for large parts of the poverty problem. Social exclusion, prejudices and practices about "acceptable" behavior often grow out of different accounts of history. But histories vary with faith, ethnicity, and gender. Repeated patterns of behavior can result in people being excluded from the opportunities available to the residents of a place. Encountering discrimination, either overtly or covertly, against those who are different—ethnically, physically, religiously, culturally—results in people being denied the opportunities they need to meet their human needs. This is dysfunctional institutional behavior. Writing about dysfunctional institutions, Alain De Janvry and coauthors say:

> In particular to be explained are why dysfunctional institutions tend to persist for such long periods of time and why new social norms have such difficulty in imposing themselves? This is usually explained by either path dependency, the Prisoner's Dilemma, or imperfect information about future gains. In the first explanation, high sunken costs induced by past institutions make transition to what could be superior institutions socially unprofitable. In the second explanation, without cooperation, the cost of breaking an existing rule may be too high on individuals, and it is thus individually rational for suboptimal institutions such as castes to remain in existence. Finally, in the third explanation, a bias for the status quo emerges from uncertainty

in the distribution of benefits from change (De Janvry, Sadoulet, Thorbecke, 1993, pp. 567–568).

Dysfunctional institutions may be widely privately practiced. They may also be publicly accepted in law, regulations, and bureaucratic behavior. When public policies and their implementation exclude people from their legal rights to access public services, the problem becomes a public problem. Local bureaucrats as public officials have responsibilities for the rule of law. Yet some officials—especially in criminal justice and policing systems—are notorious for their abuse of power. When this happens, dysfunctional institutions can lead to structural violence.

INSTITUTIONS AS POLICIES

Policies are important forms of institutions. Certain actions or behaviors get institutionalized as policies, and in turn policies play an important role in forming and maintaining other institutions. Policy shortfalls can result in some people gaining more than others—thus deepening existing inequalities. Policies do not always create level playing fields. Regressive taxes, weak or no law enforcement in poor neighborhoods, underinvestment in health and education facilities, and weak or missing environmental protection in poor communities are but a few examples. And, it should be noted, regressive tax policies are among the hardest for poor people to correct. Doing so requires considerable organizational time and documentation—yet the very people who need this change are least likely to mobilize for this goal given the transaction costs of doing so and the low probability of wining.

Getting an environmentally cleaner and healthier neighborhood in poor communities is almost as difficult as getting tax reform. Environmental issues for the poor are often at a scale of abuse not seen in middle class neighborhoods. Theirs are the environmental problems of raw sewage in rutted dirt paths in squatter settlements, soot-filled air, crippling fumes and dust in work spaces, and peeling lead paint in filthy hovels. Damaged lungs, stunted babies, diarrheal diseases—all result from environmental neglect. The illnesses alone strip away the energy for collective action.

Policies do matter and policy reform that can foster institutional change can be the central engine in reducing poverty. But winning support for policies that have positive gains for the poor is singularly difficult. Getting them implemented once they are enacted matters too—and often proves to be even more challenging than getting them enacted.

A well-crafted policy means nothing if it is not appropriately implemented. This point was brought home in Gunnar Myrdal's Asian Drama in the 1960s, which emphasized the legacy of "the soft state"—the government that passes laws defining policies that say more than the government ever intends to do (Myrdal, 1968). Politics may dictate that the legislature or executive be seen to expound certain views as "policies," but not implement them. The grinding, slow, iterative process of making policy come to life—implementation—is the area most neglected.

One of the reasons that we talk about programs and projects as much as about policies in this book is because many of us who work on poverty problems have most frequently had to work within policy frameworks that are not pro-poor. Working in the social and political space available, and with whatever opportunities are at hand, grassroots projects can often still make a difference. Moreover, over time, they help to build awareness of what might be done and influence policy change.

ROLE OF INSTITUTIONS IN ACCESS TO ASSETS

As we have already discussed, people's access to assets and their ability to fully realize their potential by putting their assets and capabilities to use are affected by their degree of inclusion in various areas of society. Social exclusion can be institutionalized on a variety of levels—from formal laws and regulations to informal rules and societal norms. Institutional change, often of deeply rooted indigenous institutions, as well as of policies, is needed in the fight against social exclusion. A look at institutional factors affecting exclusion in health care illustrates the point.

Health care provision, financing, and research is determined by institutions. Which health crises and diseases will gain public attention and financial support depends largely on norms, on what are seen as pressing concerns, and on the rules determining whose influence and power tend to prevail in defining policies. AIDS is devastating in its impact. A leading demographer points to its deadly impact, especially in Africa:

> The increases in life expectancy that happened in Africa in the late 1980s were seriously undermined by the HIV/AIDS epidemic. In the past 20 years, more than 60 million people have been infected by HIV/AIDS worldwide, of whom 10 million are still alive. Of these cases, only 6% are in more developed countries while in Africa HIV/AIDS has become the leading cause of death. The United Nations projects that in some African countries, more than two-thirds of children aged 15 years in 2000 will be infected with HIV/AIDS before they reach 50 years of age (United Nations 2002). For the thirty-five countries in Africa most affected, life expectancy at birth has been reduced by 6.5 years in the late 1990s, an effect that is projected to rise to 9.0 years in 2000–2005 (Lee, 2003, p. 172).

Other diseases get less attention but are often brutal killers. Malaria, tuberculosis, and measles attract less public attention and get far less financial support for research on curative or symptomatic treatment, despite the fact that they are incapacitating hundreds of millions of people, especially children, in poor countries every day. These are known as "orphan" diseases—diseases for which there is no major investment in finding good drug treatment because pharmaceutical corporations argue there is not enough profit in developing the drug. Too few of the sufferers of these illnesses could afford to pay much for the medicine.

Malaria is one of the most insidious of diseases. Independent malariologists believe it kills two million people a year, mainly children under 5, and mainly in Africa. Until overtaken by AIDS in 1999, it was Africa's leading killer (Rosenberg, 2004, NYT Final Edition, pp. 38). Once one has had malaria, and, if fortunate, recovered from that episode, one lives with the fact that many varieties go into remission and resurface at unpredictable intervals for the rest of one's life. There is no cure for malaria, only treatments that vary in their impact on symptoms. New drug-resistant strains of malaria keep evolving. First-time visitors to Africa are struck by the impact malaria has on day-to-day life. Integrated into life patterns, it is accepted as part of the landscape—it is an institutionalized illness. The acceptance of its ubiquity suppresses public outcry at the underinvestment in research for a cure. In Africa, people just cope, while it continues to drain strength and energy. In richer countries, it is a distant problem difficult for many to place among their urgent concerns. AIDS, on the other hand, is affecting people across the globe, rich and poor alike.

The institutional issues in access to health include market failures; public sector performance shortfalls; failure of delivery systems to be responsive to the needs of the poor; and underinvestment in training, facilities, research, and development. Underlying the way in which these issues are addressed are political and social norms affecting what level of health care is considered a right and hence a public responsibility. For example, in the United States, the political assumption is that health care is a private responsibility. Yet market failures exist within the insurance systems of rich, as well as poor countries. More than 40 million people lack health insurance in the United States for regular health coverage or catastrophic health care. The health problems of Native Americans in the United States are as serious as those in many poor countries. As the cross-national research of Timothy Smeeding and Katherin Ross Phillips points out, transfer payments and social insurance or social assistance programs in the United States are much less developed than in many other countries; their impact on reducing poverty is much less than in Europe or Scandinavia (Lustig, 2001, pp. 272, 273).

Norms about private responsibility for health care in the United States are primarily rooted in political culture. There is not a sufficiently strong counterbalancing social norm in the United States regarding access to health care so as to create a public outcry about the fact that millions have no health insurance and that the public health system meant to meet the needs of the uninsured is woefully under funded. And as countries around the world strive to find effective solutions for providing health care in light of limited public budgets, they are increasingly moving away from old norms about health care as a public good available at low or no cost to all citizens. Rather, they are adopting new norms in which the burden of costs are shared between the private and public sectors.

The scale of the public health problems afflicting the two billion poor people on the globe is overwhelming and poses fundamental questions about how these needs might be met. What combinations of social insurance schemes or social assistance policies could be afforded and put in place? Before turning to the collective action needed to mobilize the political will to address these choices, let us look briefly at some of the most important developments in changing formal and informal institutions related to health care, particularly in the areas of insurance schemes and cost-sharing mechanisms.

The best of the research on alternative insurance or assistance policies has focused on Latin America and Asia, unfortunately not on Africa. Nora Lustig, in *Shielding the Poor*, discussed the varieties of social protection policies in both rich and poor countries (Lustig, 2001). The problem for households is how to manage when severe or catastrophic illness strikes. What economists call consumption smoothing, or relying on savings in order to maintain household standard of living during crises, is not possible for the very poor. When work becomes impossible for primary breadwinners, the combination of caring for them and devising alternative income possibilities is the challenge for the household. Asset depletion is the result—households in those circumstances call on interhousehold transfers; take children out of school, and send them to work or beg; sell homes, tools, or draft animals; and eat the seed corn. These strategies have long term negative consequences for the poor (Moser, 1998; Lindenberg, 1999).

Many countries try combinations of private and public insurance schemes. Despite demand, families have difficulty purchasing insurance from private sources because of inadequate information or because those who most need it are screened out and disallowed in the private market. Governments must assume a central role—either through universal, publicly financed and delivered health care (e.g., the United Kingdom's National Health Service), or a public/private mix in which the government funds health care for those below a certain income. Financing options often include employer-mandated health care or mandatory payroll taxes. But these latter approaches only reach a small fraction of the very poor—and even fewer of the rural poor. Given the weak financial base of public systems, especially in the very countries with the greatest public needs, this effectively means that health delivery institutions meet only a tiny fraction of the public need.

It was in this context that donors began demanding cost recovery through user fees for medical care in the 1980s and early 1990s. The public policy debates over user fees and their impact continues to rage. In an empirical study of panel data from Indonesia and China, Paul Gertler concludes that user fees are not always appropriate, especially not in the case of catastrophic illness (Gertler, 2001, p. 109). There may be a case for user fees to deter overuse of publicly provided service for relatively inconsequential illnesses, but user fees in the case of catastrophic illnesses impact the weakest when they are least able to provide. Moreover, while many poor countries do have both public and private sector insurance schemes of one sort or another, most often households are unable to purchase insurance for major catastrophic illnesses. There are real market failures in that part of the private social insurance market; hence, there is a role for governments to address income loss due to disability and medical care expenditures.

Access to education and its institutional features is comparable, yet different in important respects from the public health story. While the scale of the need is as great, the likelihood of progress is more encouraging, and, in general, there is more acceptance of a public role. There are a number of formal international institutions supporting education for all. Most countries have signed the United Nations Human Rights Covenant on Economic and Social Rights in which education is defined as a right; world leaders meeting at the 1995 United Nations Social Summit signed a declaration promising to provide primary education for all by the year 2015; and the Convention on the Rights of the Child, ratified by all of the world's countries except for two (the United States and Somalia), reaffirms the right of all children to a *quality* education. However, written policies are but the first step and must be accompanied by a range of other institutional commitments to ensure implementation. Advocates and policy analysts have determined that the 2015 goals will not be met at current levels of action. Global advocacy campaigns, such as the Global Campaign for Education spearheaded by Oxfam, are pushing world leaders to implement strategies to meet their commitments.

As in the case of health care, a number of social norms must also be addressed in order to ensure access to quality education. Traditional behaviors and norms must be taken into account including such things as attitudes toward education in general and for girls in particular, and survival strategies that require parents to focus on short term benefits of children as income-providers rather than longer term benefits of having educated children. Customs and norms regarding free access to education have been challenged by governments who have imposed user fees in light of insufficient public resources. This has been done despite the Convention on the

Rights of the Child specifying the right to "free, compulsory education for all children" (Pegozzi, 2001). Recent research examining the impact of user fees on education reveals their negative impact on access and hence exclusion of the poor. According to Oxfam International, it costs the poorest 40% of the population in developing countries over 10% of their annual income to send two children to primary school (Oxfam, 2001). In Zambia, between one-half and three-quarters of total education spending at primary level is met directly by parents (Oxfam, 2001). Case studies have revealed that fees are keeping parents from sending children to school and, when Malawi actually removed fees in 1994, school enrollment almost doubled within 1 year (Oxfam, 2001).

Government-financed education for all, however, requires significant increases in financial resources dedicated to improving both access to and the quality of public education. This requires work at several levels to set budgeting priorities and find means to increase overall public funds available in the budget. Debt relief has therefore become a key arena for this battle, as advocates argue that funds used for debt repayment should be redirected at social spending including education. While these debates go on and government funding remains inadequate, institutional innovation is occurring in communities around the world as they confront the demand for improved access to education—or demand for access to improved education. For example, in sub-Saharan Africa, communities have begun to organize community schools—ones that they build and control.

INSTITUTIONAL LEGAL FRAMEWORKS

Another critical set of institutions affecting the poor are those related to legal frameworks, both formal legal institutions and the rule of law. The poor's access to physical assets, such as housing, land, draft animals, tools, and technology, depends not just on having capital, but also, importantly, on access to credit and to such institutional features as contract enforcement, legal rights, and a judicial system for the enforcement of those rights. Much has been written about the importance of the rule of law—usually, however without much discussion of what needs to be done to institute it. Yet with the rule of law, as with many other large issues, the devil is in the details. Legal systems and the quality of their enforcement vary within any country. Poor people are most likely to be deprived of their rights either because few rights are legally secured, or because the enforcement processes are inadequate. They often are at risk when endeavoring to protect whatever small claims they may have to property.

One important example of the fragility of legal rights to assets can be seen in the problems of land or home ownership. One of the key steps is registering the title to property. As the home or shelter is most often a family's major asset and is crucial for access to credit, the absence of clear title is a major constraint for improving income. A system for recording property transactions and providing clear titles is a critical institution in a functioning real estate market (Bryant, 1996, 1998; de Soto, 2001). The fact of the matter is that getting a clear title to their land or home is often impossible for poor people. Sometimes it is an issue of the vagaries of land law, sometimes of the history of land records. Brazil, for example, has land registries that date back to the sixteenth century arrival of Portuguese and Dutch settlers. Disputes over legal rights to land coupled with high rates of landlessness have led to raging disagreements and even violent conflict as the poor have begun to mobilize to assert the right to land ownership.

Land registries and title companies are susceptible to corruption. One of the major causes of landlessness in many poor countries is that large landowners are able to control rural land registration processes to their advantage (Lipton, 1993; Bryant, 1996, 1998; de Soto, 2000). Poor farmers and the urban poor are highly vulnerable to the vagaries of inept, inadequate, opaque land registries. Smallholders may believe that they have registered their land claims, only to discover that this is not the case when they endeavor to borrow against that land for credit for crop inputs. The poor occupants of a shelter in a squatter community may think that the "receipt" they purchased entitles them to ownership, only to find later that the "receipt" means nothing more than that they paid money for it uselessly.

The issue is compounded by problems of contract enforcement and bureaucratic processes. When poor people run small enterprises, they are often at the mercy of the high interest rates charged by the local moneylender. In part, the moneylender is rightly worried about risk. But it becomes a vicious circle—getting credit for small enterprise is critical to reaching the output needed to earn from it. Running the gauntlet to get the various required business permits is another blockage. Moreover, if the small producer sells to others on credit, enforcement of the agreement is likely to be wholly dependent upon social pressures. Contract enforcement and ready access to, for example, a small claims court, are not widely available in regions with high densities of poor people or in inner cities in largely poor neighborhoods.

Legal environments matter. They matter for human rights. They also matter for income generation and property rights. Hernando de Soto's researchers illustrated this problem when they "set up a one man clothing workshop on the outskirts of Lima, and tried to register it. The team worked for six hours a day, filling in forms, traveling by bus into central Lima and queuing before the relevant official desks. It took them 289 days to make their microenterprise legal, and cost $1,231—31 times the monthly minimum wage in Peru" (The Economist, 2001, p. 21).

Establishing legal environments that enable rather than disable poor people from earning their living is a major kind of institutional change needed for reducing poverty. Institutional work needs to be done upstream, such as developing law schools, supporting public record keeping and the right to public information from public records, developing court systems, improving accountability of local bureaucratic systems, and enhancing public education about property rights.

An area where there has been considerable institutional innovation is in the communal management of common property. Assets that are "owned" by a community and jointly managed by them are an important feature of life, especially for the rural poor, in many countries. These "common property resources" range from village forests in Mexico to communal land in Malawi. Social institutions play a central role in common property because they dictate the accepted behaviors governing their use. The management of common property resources has recently been emphasized because of its role in the generation of social capital. The skills and energies generated by people acquiring capabilities to manage common resources have important consequences for their resolution of other problems. In that sense the term "capital" is accurate as it shares the characteristic of fungibility inherent to capital (Ostrom, 1990).

Developing explicit common property regimes requires an understanding of the complex institutional arrangements affecting any particular resource. As is the case with control over any type of property, the successful application of rules governing common property depends on the legitimacy of norms governing entitlement and use of the resource. While there are many successful cases of local communities managing sustainable resources under common property regimes, some researchers have found that the success depends on the availability of resources, as well as the number of conflicting demands on the resources. For example, C. Johnson argues that socially shared rules can encourage sustainable livelihoods provided the rate at which benefits are extracted from the resource base is low and the distribution of benefits is wide; when rules reinforce narrow distribution of benefits, livelihood can be unsustainable (C. Johnson, 1997).

By taking into account an analysis of existing institutions and creating systems that support and reinforce local institutions, sustainable management under common property regimes can be established. In addition, much can be learned from existing examples of sustainable common property management within poor communities where traditions support collective efforts to maximize the livelihood of all members of the community sharing a common resource. As more is learned about common property management in poor communities around the world, the potential for ways in which collective action can be mobilized to make a difference emerges.

COLLECTIVE ACTION, CIVIL SOCIETY, AND POLICY CHANGE

The most salient aspect of institutions, noted by every commentator no matter the differences among them, is that institutions are socially constructed. That is also the most encouraging point. Evolving social constructs make institutions dynamic and open the possibility for institutional change. Dysfunctional institutions, for example, can be impacted by other institutions. That process happens most often through collective action—groups of people working together.

Starting at the grass roots, people in communities the world over are working together on their own poverty problems. The numbers of local organizations and community-based organizations is not well documented, but it is known that, fueled by urbanization and improved levels of literacy, millions of local groups, associations, clubs, and NGOs have flourished in most developing countries in the past three decades (Uphoff, 1998; Bebbington, 1999; Lindberg and Bryant 2001). In 1995, the OECD estimated that the number of formal local NGOs in developing countries was approximately 250,000. By 2000, the estimate was that worldwide the number was likely close to one million local NGOs.

In the mid-1980s, Albert Hirschman was asked by the Inter-American Foundation to visit several grassroots projects while he was on sabbatical leave from Princeton's Institute for Advanced Study. After observations and interviews conducted over 14 weeks in six different Latin American countries, he cited several results that surprised him because they ran counter to what one might hypothesize would happen under such circumstances. Chief among these was the amount of cooperative behavior and collective action, which provided the title to his book, *Getting Ahead Collectively*.

Hirschman became curious about why the cooperative action he saw in the Inter-American Foundation projects had occurred. Among the many points made in the book, he included the "principle of conservation and the mutation of social energy." In his words:

> A large number of these [complex situations of collective action] shared one striking characteristic. When we looked into the life histories of the people principally involved, we found that most of them had previously participated in other, generally more radical experiences of collective action, that had generally not achieved their objective, often because of official repression. It is as though the protagonists' earlier aspirations for social change, their bent for collective action, had not really left them even though the movements in which they had participated may have aborted or petered out. Later on, this social energy becomes active again but it is likely to take some very different form...a renewal of energy rather than

a wholly new outbreak. I shall refer to this as the Principle of Conservation and Mutation of Social Energy (Hirschman, 1984, p. 43).

This theme of "surprises" is a favorite point made also by another development scholar, Norman Uphoff. He too has pointed out that among the great things about field work is that so many positive things you would think could not happen are in practice possible—and surprising. Uphoff's prime example was the success of ethnically mixed water user associations in the Gal Oya project in Sri Lanka. Even at times of rising violence between Tamil and Sinhalese, these water user associations included both Tamils and Sinhalese in the same water user groups, without major incidence of unfair behavior. Water rights can be very conflictual, especially between those upstream and those at the tail end. But the Gal Oya story is a major demonstration of how a system of small, well organized water user associations can defeat the usual problems of free riders or hijacking. Uphoff often points out how the Gal Oya experience was counter to the predictions of standard social science theory that collective action in these circumstances would not work.

How different this is from the nineteenth century view that the rural peasantry was largely passive while the urban poor provided the impetus for change. Recall, for example, Marx's fury at the peasantry in The Eighteenth Brumaire of Louis Napoleon in which he railed against the rural peasantry for behaving as passively "as a sack of potatoes." Peasants' anomie was their enemy. It is not clear that Marx was accurate then, but it is surely true that peasants and smallholders and the poor are more organized, literate, vocal, and collectively active in their struggles for improved well-being in the twenty-first century than in any previous period.

Sometimes the local groups are protest groups, in other cases they are groups formed in response to opportunities for attracting resources, for example, from social investment funds. But from barrios to shanty towns, from squatters to farmers' groups and workers' groups, from mosques to temples, there has been an upsurge in local collective efforts—for protests, projects, advocacy, for fun (sports, performances), or for shared conversation and mutual support. Local collective action in much of Africa, Asia, and Latin America is increasing. It has played a central role in some of the historic bloodless revolutions—toppling the Marcos regime in the Philippines in the mid-1980s, dismantling the Berlin Wall in 1989, and, more recently, leading to the change of leadership in Indonesia.[1] In short, collective action can be depicted as a continuum from the occasional collective effort in building a local group to the more systematic organizing of larger community-based organizations to the longer term advocacy work of coalitions of organizations for systemic change.

SOCIAL CAPITAL AND INSTITUTIONAL CHANGE

We have been discussing both the new management strategies of the poor and the emerging civil society. These factors are related to institutional change on several levels (Ostrom, 1988, 1990, 1992; Putnam, 1993; Fischer, 1998; Helliwell, 2001). Simultaneously, at a macrolevel of aggregation and intervention, there is more thinking about the work of the multilateral development banks and international financial "architecture." Authors working at this macrolevel are also addressing institutional development—by which they mean major systemic changes in legal frameworks and structural change (Bryant, 2001; Eichengreen, 2001; Kennen, 2001). Institutional change at the macrolevel can work in synergistic ways with broad-based grassroots collective action to have positive effects or they can work in opposite directions. Either way, they have implications for one another because what happens at one level affects the other. A positive instance, for example, is the clear linkages when local community-based organizations are pushing for more protection of tenurial rights and land title registration and simultaneously there is leveraging by a multilateral development bank for judicial and legal reform in order, among other things, to make contract enforceability available to all citizens.

Yet macrolevel–microlevel actors can also pull against one another. For example, when IMF conditionality pulls decision-making back into formalized and centralized structures, it counters local community groups struggling for local level autonomy. Getting microlevel change and comparable and synergistic changes at the macrolevel moving together toward pro-poor development is the challenge. It is not the old debate about centralization versus decentralization or about balanced and unbalanced growth—although these debates remain relevant—but a new discussion about which combinations in which sectors and in what sequence are most conducive to improving people's capacities to affect their futures in this interdependent world (Bryant, 2001). Moreover, these struggles about IMF conditionality point yet again to the need for international institutional change, especially in those international institutions such as the IMF that have an impact upon a country's poverty reducing policies.

NEXT STEPS: WHAT CAN BE DONE

Within this framework, we can now look at what needs to be done from an institutional perspective to bring about the structural changes needed to get at the root causes of poverty. Policy changes, especially in those policies that directly impact people's access to assets, are vital. And there is a need to increase our ability to take local institutions into account in formulating and implementing programs and projects, as well as policies. Attention should also be paid to fostering an enabling environment for institutional growth and change. Many development practitioners talk about the need for institutional strengthening; in many cases this refers more specifically to organizational strengthening, but there are a number of ways in which development work can help to strengthen institutions, as well as organizations. Policy dialogue, attention to legal frameworks, and strengthening judicial systems are but a few ways to build institutional capacity.

In terms of policy change, there are already NGOs hard at work advocating access to certain assets. As mentioned earlier, Oxfam International has a major role in the Global Campaign for Education in which it is leading a coalition of NGOs in calling attention to the need for access to quality education. Médecins Sans Frontières and others are hard at work on the problems surrounding drug pricing and access to medicines for the poor. Coalitions of NGOs are working together more effectively today than ever before—in part thanks to the changes in global communications technology that have accompanied the rise of the Internet. The communication that can now occur across vast distances enables policy change to be both locally driven and monitored, while also informative to those who are friends of the poor but who live at a distance. These technological changes, together with growing concern for addressing underlying policy issues affecting programs and projects, have led traditionally operations-focused organizations to turn increasingly to advocacy work.

These coordinated advocacy efforts are all instances of effective collective action. Some of the most interesting breakthroughs are coming about because of the connections between larger NGOs and their partners in poor countries. The adoption of the debt relief programs for Heavily Indebted Poor Countries (HIPC) is an excellent example of complementary roles of NGOs in rich and poor countries, as well as of effective NGO advocacy on a highly technical and politically charged issue. Local NGOs in developing countries, especially those associated with political and social movements, had been voicing concern about the debt in their countries since the debt crisis first hit in the early 1980s. Protests grew as the structural adjustment programs of the 1980s and 1990s exacerbated conditions for the poorer segments of society without relieving the debt burden. While NGOs in the indebted countries played an active role and organized themselves into networks around this issue, it was the large NGOs based in wealthy countries who eventually took leadership of the advocacy effort and helped push the issue onto the agenda of donor governments and international financial institutions (Lindenberg and Bryant, 2001). This collaboration has continued into policy implementation, as local partners help monitor governments' promises on social investments following debt relief. Among the critically important roles for those local organizations is monitoring how resources freed up by debt relief are used by their country's government.

In addition to effective collective action, successful advocacy work also requires sound policy analysis. One of the essential technical tools—institutional assessment—can help with policy analysis, as well as with the development of more effective programs and projects. An institutional assessment involves mapping out the rules of the game, norms, roles, and issues that are at work in an organization, a community, a geographic region, or a sector. This kind of work began to be applied in mainstream development practice during the 1990s, including substantial work by the World Bank. The tools continue to be developed by research institutions and universities. Mapping out the configuration of institutions at work in a particular setting helps ground future prescriptions.

Institutional assessments are helpful for working in communities. They are also useful when beginning capacity building work. Or when working on policy reform in a sector—such as education—to allow key decision-makers to discern how that sector as a whole functions. Or, alternatively, when a donor is working with NGOs or community organizations, an institutional assessment is useful in order to identify the capacities, or shortfalls in capacity, that will affect the projects being implemented.

So how does one do an institutional assessment? Ideally one should do an institutional assessment through a series of participatory workshops. If that is not possible, using interviews and focus groups also works. As a last resort—and often that is all that is available given limited resources—a rudimentary institutional assessment can be done through a document search coupled with telephone interviews to clarify one's reading of documents and relevant literature.

A functional approach to institutional assessment is most useful. There are several core functions that are most likely to be undertaken within any institution. These are Decision-Making, Financing, Staffing and Motivating, Communicating, Monitoring, and External Demand-Making. These functions happen with different degrees of specificity, conscious effort, levels of sophistication, and detail. For example, these functions are played out in clubs, groups, and families, as well as in large complex organizations and in whole sectors. In short, somehow these functions have to happen and looking systematically at who are the stakeholders in the functions and how they happen helps us to identify possible aspects that need strengthening, as well as existing strengths to be built upon. They also help to identify the various stakeholders who need to be involved in the development process. The organizing device for presenting the information gathered through an institutional assessment is a matrix that looks at these core functions that happen in all institutions, preferably at various levels, such as at the national, district, and community levels. A sample structure for such a matrix is presented in Figure 3.1.

An institutional assessment is a diagnostic tool, a kind of x-ray. It has some of the advantages and disadvantages of a single set of x-rays. First, it

AREA / LEVEL	Policy and Decision Making	Financing	Staffing and Motivating	Communicating	Monitoring and Evaluating	External Demand-Making
National						
Rules						
Roles						
Issues						
District						
Rules						
Roles						
Issues						
Community						
Rules						
Roles						
Issues						

Figure 3.1
Institutional Assessment Matrix

is a photograph at one point in time. Second, it can be used to inform prescriptions, but the matrix itself is not prescriptive. The assessment is to illuminate what works and how.

The overwhelming advantage to doing a participatory institutional assessment with a community or community-based organization is in how much more can be done with the matrix. For example, in a workshop process, community members or organizations can both do the mapping and then discern which factors are within their control or amenable to their collective influence and which ones are not so amenable. Having done their own sorting, armed with their own collectively devised assessment, they can work to improve their own condition.

Let us look at an example in order to clarify how an institutional assessment matrix might look. For example, the World Bank's Northern Uganda Reconstruction Project of 1992 contains a small grant facility—a community action fund—aimed at helping people identify projects that they really need and that will enable them to rebuild their lives. (The community action fund component—now a social fund—of this project has been expanded; the most recent follow-on project went to the Board of the World Bank in 2002.) If we looked at an institutional assessment, or map, of the institutions that may affect, or be affected by, this fund, we can identify where there are critical issues likely to affect the performance of the small grants.

For example, across the rules row at the national level, one would find entries such as: financial disparities between the North and the South; too few branch banks to facilitate small accounts; positioning the implementation unit in the office of the prime minister exerts too much centralizing authority; too little auditing and hence limited financial accountability. At the district level, one would find entries under the financing column that detail the potential bottlenecks in the local systems and banks for managing flows of funds to small community groups. Those charged with monitoring this project did encounter just these problems after implementation started. As one might predict, they were harder to fix after the fact than they might have been if identified at the outset.

One can also use the institutional assessment tool to look at the potential for policy change within a sector by mapping the array of rules, roles, and norms in that sector by different agents or groups clustered under the functions on the matrix. Or, the institutional assessment can use an abbreviated matrix focusing only on those functions of immediate concern to the user of the assessment. For example, if planning how coffee growers in a large cooperative might get their produce labeled and certified as organic, one could adapt the institutional assessment tool in order to focus on the policy making process of the certification authority, while a second institutional assessment might focus on the decision-making, financing, and staffing functions for the cooperative as it applied for and received certification.

The institutional assessment matrix can also be used when a donor is working with a relatively modest community-based organization and wants to strengthen that organization. Often a donor starts off with the intention of strengthening, but the donor's own procedural requirements are already beyond the capacities of the smaller community group. Thus, rather than strengthening, the donor strains that community group. Had the donor done an institutional assessment early on, it might have been better able to strengthen the local group. For example, it might have identified which functions needed clearer lines of communication or could be done in a different sequence or required more staffing in order to increase the capacity of the community-based organization. Efforts at institutional strengthening often include the development of mechanisms such as cost recovery aimed at improving financial sustainability of local groups. In such instances, institutional assessments can help determine the feasibility of various cost recovery schemes by analyzing characteristics of the group's clients and the nature of the demand for its services, among other factors. By delving into the rules and behavioral norms of an organization's stakeholders, institutional assessments can help define appropriate and realistic institutional strengthening projects.

Institutional strengthening does involve much more than organizational capacity building. At the policy, program, and project level, an enabling environment needs to be in place to ensure that institutions can develop and change. At the policy level, factors such as tax codes and the use of deductions for philanthropic donations can affect institutional development, as can registration requirements for the formalization of institutions through organizational structures. The legal environment and in particular property rights, contract enforcement, and freedom of expression and organization have important consequences for the degree of institutional development and institutional change that takes place within a country. All of these are specific areas that need to be examined and addressed. At the program level, institutional strengthening can involve judicial reform, the development of professional associations, exchange programs, and independent research institutes. At the project level, the key for an enabling institutional environment is the extent to which collective action is fostered through participatory projects.

CONCLUSION

Institutions play an integral role throughout all levels of society and as such play critical roles in any poverty reduction strategy. It is key to understand institutions in a broad sense, as rules of the game, norms, and behaviors, rather than mistaking them narrowly as simply organizations. Institutions both define the parameters in which antipoverty work takes place and provide the mechanism to fight poverty, as progress at removing obstacles to moving people out of poverty will involve institutional change at one level or another. Although institutions can be very slow to change, they are dynamic. But change must eventually be driven by those within an institution, which thus requires participatory approaches. A clear understanding of the institutions involved in any community provides insights for creating more effective policies, programs, and projects.

NOTES

1.   Although there was violence associated in varying ways with each of these revolutions, the ultimate change occurred thanks to peaceful action of large portions of the population.

4

POLICIES, PROGRAMS, OR PROJECTS?

"'Would you tell me, please, which way I ought to go from here?'
'That depends a good deal on where you want to get to,' said the Cat."
—Lewis Carroll, *Alice's Adventures in Wonderland*

INTRODUCTION

At the beginning we promised readers that in the second half of this book
we would turn to what can be done. Much has been learned in the search
for effective poverty reduction. What works, and what else could work?
This is risky, of course. Most books on poverty stop after their analytical
work is presented—the reader then is to infer how to move forward. Some
books detail failures from past efforts. Yet another group demonstrates the
success of particular approaches. We, however, are heading down a different path—one less traveled.

This different path will delve in more depth into the "how" questions.
We will talk about the relationships among policies, programs, and projects—with a focus upon what has worked, rather than dwelling on what
has not. We also want to keep in mind how the three different levels of
development work and their interrelationships. Some learning occurs up
and down the chain from policy to project and back again. But those feedback loops are imperfect. The communication flows are noisy and incomplete. Our key point is that successful projects are not rare—but they rarely
make it onto the radar screen of powerfully positioned decision-makers.
But successful projects in villages and communities provide insight into
what is needed.

Three levels are at work—policies, programs, and projects. In addition,
there are not only national governmental decisions about the policy rules

of the game, but intermediate levels (provinces, districts), local level governance, NGOs, and civil society actors. Private sector-public sector–interactions matter all the way through these processes, affecting every decision one can imagine—from taxes to health investments, from energy policy to local water availability.

We will start with policies, keeping in mind that policies are often implemented through programs and projects. Policies are part of the essential rules of the game—the overarching embedded norms, behaviors, and formal rules governing the allocation of resources and the patterns of their distribution. Policies are most often large aggregated rules (for example, to increase school attendance and quality of education throughout a country) and programs are the approach to be used (for example, improve quality by improving teacher training, or increase attendance by providing school lunches). Projects, then, are the sturdy vehicles through which policies and programs most directly reach and engage people (for example, starting school lunches in specific disadvantaged parts of the country). Projects provide opportunities to learn about what works—and what contextual factors affect outcomes. Feeding that information back up the chain can help in the next round of policy change or reform.

WHAT HAVE WE LEARNED ABOUT POVERTY POLICIES?

There is much debate about what combination of policies are most effective in reducing poverty. This debate has moved in recent years beyond the confines of development agencies, political institutions, and academia and out into the streets. Ever since they first made international headlines at the WTO meeting in Seattle in 1999, heated protests now accompany practically every international economic or trade meeting. Protestors come from rich and poor countries alike and often cut across a range of ideological positions. The protests are fueled by the assertion that current policies must clearly be at fault since poverty persists (along with environmental degradation and other social ills) and, worse still, current policies must be inherently unjust since inequality also persists and some people are clearly benefiting from the current prescriptions while others are losing out. The debate has become very polarized with two opposing camps—"globophiles" and "globophobes" as coined by Oxfam—taking extreme views that make dialogue difficult.

Although the debate rages on, solid research is emerging that we believe begins to build a strong case for policies that do work for reducing poverty. Let us first briefly explore the core ideas fueling the debate, and then turn to what has been learned about what works.

At the center of much of the debate is the set of policy prescriptions often referred to as the "Washington Consensus" because it is promoted by the Washington-based IMF and World Bank, with support from major

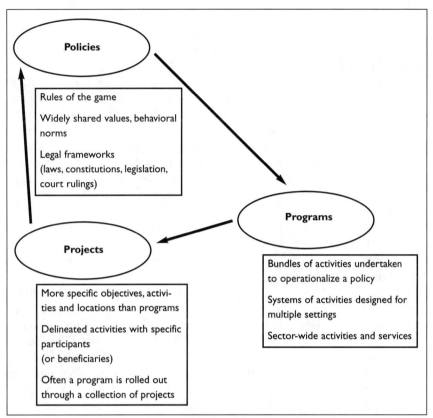

Figure 4.1
Characteristics of Policies, Programs, and Projects

donors of the industrialized world. "Washington Consensus" came to be popularly used to connote policies promoting free markets, open trade regimes, and a reduced role for the state. (The term is often attributed to John Williamson, although he was more careful in his use of the term.) In reality there was never quite so much true consensus around these issues and debates were common even within (and between) the World Bank and IMF. It is important to remember that the IMF is focused on short term stabilization lending, often in order to leverage improvements in a country's macroeconomic policies, exchange rates, money supply, and inflation. The World Bank, on the other hand, is focused on long term development. Given these different mandates, it is the case that they will, and do, disagree upon occasion about what is to be done in any given country.

The applicability of the model also varied from country to country. Small countries are more dependent upon donors for a variety of reasons (some having to do with limited internal financial capacity), while large countries (China and India, for example) are far less reliant upon them. Hence the actual history of what happens is very dense and more complex than some current popular literature reflects. Nevertheless, there has been a relatively standard set of macroeconomic policies that dominated international development policy since the mid-1980s. The basic policies that comprise what has come to be known as the Washington Consensus began to emerge during the 1970s, when it was called the neoorthodox macroeconomic approach. According to Joan Nelson, this approach "called not only for corrective macroeconomic policies but also for medium-term structural reforms, including shifts towards outward-oriented trade policies, reductions in the role of the state, and public sector reforms" (Nelson, 1990, p. 11). At the height of the Washington Consensus in the late 1980s and early 1990s, policy prescriptions included an emphasis on economic growth fueled by increased openness and free markets with a push for very rapid trade liberalization, privatization of state owned enterprises, and elimination of domestic subsidies.

As the record in terms of poverty reduction, as well as economic growth and stability, has come under scrutiny, the validity of the Washington Consensus has come increasingly into question, even by those who initially supported it. One of the most ardent critics of the Washington Consensus is a former "insider": Joseph Stiglitz, Chief Economist of the World Bank from 1997 to 2000, who began his critique, particularly of the IMF approach, while still at the Bank. In an article written in 2000, Nancy Birdsall, who served as the Executive Vice President of the Inter-American Development Bank during the heyday of the Washington Consensus, points out that the optimism about the impact that economic growth and free markets would have worldwide is now "tempered by the more checkered record of the reforming countries in improving income distribution and protecting their citizens from external shocks and volatile international capital flows" (Birdsall et al., 2002, p.1). Indeed, she notes, the very architects of the Consensus are now seeking a new paradigm.

A great deal went wrong during the 1980s and 1990s as a result of the advice and conditionality that the IMF and the World Bank insisted upon in many countries. The first and most obvious problem is that the prescriptions were imposed upon countries without attention to their institutional context, financial institutions, or social or political systems, and hence their capacity to adapt or reform (Wade, 1990; Nelson, 1998). In many cases, the drafting of conditions and the way in which they were monitored left everything to be desired; this was especially true in small, landlocked African countries. When the East Asia financial crisis came— starting with Thailand, then moving quickly through several East Asian countries that only a few years earlier had been lionized as great examples of success—people slid back into poverty, the kind of poverty that they had only recently thought they had escaped, creating added political tensions.

Of course, these were times consumed by a wave of conservative ideology, starting with President Reagan and Prime Minister Thatcher. Many countries, especially those in transition in the former Soviet Union, needed real help with both reforming the public sector and developing the private sector. And it was not just that their financial institutions and banking sector needed institutional development—their decision-making processes, legal frameworks, implementation capacity, and conflict resolution institutions needed serious strengthening as well. The leadership of the Group of Seven industrial powers was afraid of the disintegration of the Soviet Union—hence every pressure was on to stave off chaos by moving as much money into the Russian economy as fast as possible. Little attention was paid to those who cautioned that more in-depth preparation and institutional development were needed.[1]

The imposition of rapid liberalization, austerity, privatization of state-owned enterprises, and removal of subsidies often resulted in worsening the poverty problems within those countries. The increase in poverty in Russia and Eurasia is a prime example (Nolan, 1999; Stiglitz, 2002). The Russian economy went through the equivalent of several great depressions, with GDP shrinking by more than a third in the first few years—only to contract further in the following years. Life expectancy dropped. In Africa, adjustment programs with strong conditionality often could not be implemented—and parts of those programs also generated serious social tensions. In the worst cases, they reignited ethnic tensions that lay beneath the surface as, for example, Hutus in Rwanda feared that the adjustment process would strengthen Tutsi economic power and access to land at their expense. These tensions might have been managed had there been more arenas for public expression and discussion of alternatives; in short, more channels for articulating and managing real fears and opposition. While there were several other unresolved issues underlying the outbreak of violence in Rwanda, it remains true that designers of adjustment programs in ethnically tense contexts did not take that ethnic situation into account. We have a long way to go in learning more about how to facilitate institutional development that enables the management of real conflict before it erupts and leads to major losses of human life.

GENERAL LESSONS ON SETTING PRO-POOR POLICY

Several general lessons regarding the development of appropriate pro-poor policies have emerged out of the experience with the Washington Consensus. One is that effective poverty reduction requires policies appropriate to each country's particular context and not a uniform prescription applied equally to all countries. At the core of Stiglitz's criticism of the Washington

Consensus is that it represents "cookie-cutter" economics, meaning that a standard set of prescriptions is recommended for countries regardless of their particular social, historical, or institutional contexts, and without regard to information asymmetries (Press, 2002).

A second overall lesson about policies is that they must be phased in gradually as appropriate to the particular country context. Again turning to Stiglitz, who summarized this point well,

> Perhaps of all the IMF's blunders, it is the mistakes in sequencing and pacing, and the failure to be sensitive to the broader social context, that have received the most attention—forcing liberalization before safety nets were in place, before there was an adequate regulatory framework, before the countries could withstand the adverse consequences of the sudden changes in market sentiment that are part and parcel of modern capitalism; forcing policies that led to job destruction before the essentials for job creation were in place; forcing privatization before there were adequate competition and regulatory frameworks (Stiglitz, 2002, p. 73).

The failure to pay attention to the existence of appropriate institutions and to the needs for strengthening institutions was particularly problematic in the poor sequencing of policies. There was far too little attention paid to, or investment in, the real needs for institutional development in many poor countries. Related to institutional structures is the issue of transparency and accountability. Imposed policies further undermined the development of accountability in many countries—it meant that donors could be blamed (often deservedly) and that that which needed to be done could be disregarded while powerful leaders enriched themselves.

A third lesson is that policies need to be coordinated with projects— a topic we will explore further in the latter half of this chapter. The policy debates about the Washington Consensus were complicated by the use by the IMF of stabilization lending and by the World Bank of structural adjustment lending (quick disbursing loans that were contingent upon countries' meeting prespecified conditions and were not disbursed through projects but generally were disbursed directly to the state treasury). The heavy use of conditionality was true of each modality. The use of quick disbursing money directly to government budgets meant bypassing participatory efforts.

There were many task managers at the World Bank, nonetheless, that labored on doing what they knew to matter—participatory projects. But they were a relatively disregarded group. People actually working in the field on projects were among the least listened to, or even invited to participate in, this essentially macroeconomic debate. Conditionality, and quick disbursing loans, by definition meant less interest in project work and limited attention to capacity building and implementation. In many instances, donors mistakenly presumed that capacity could be built by dictating the need for increased capacity in the loans' conditionality. One example of this was including civil service reform as a condition of lending, without supporting the reform itself.

This was not a time in which much learning happened across projects, programs, and policies. As Judith Tendler reminds us, in general, mainstream economists do not read much sectoral literature, or focus upon social systems as they interact with political economy, or follow the breakthrough work in industrial organization or management theory (Tendler, 2000). As a result, it was very hard for project people who worked with these subjects in mind to communicate to mainstream economists the potential problems that would result from too harsh and rapid an imposition of policies that were—in fact—not experientially based but most often only theoretically presumed.[2] Again this highlights the need for engaging, consulting, and working with people—a people-centered approach—rather than imposing top down edicts without local ownership.

CLUSTERS OF EFFECTIVE POLICY AREAS

While a definitive list of policy options is beyond the scope of this book, we do believe that experience has shown that the following four policy clusters are critical for poverty reduction: (a) policies that provide sufficient security that people within a country can conduct their daily lives; (b) policies that facilitate pro-poor economic growth *and* the distribution of the benefits of growth; (c) policies that improve the accountability and openness of governance; and (d) policies on a global level that promote fair participation in global trade. Each of these is explored briefly below.

Policies that Provide Sufficient Security

Poor people live with high degrees of personal insecurity in terms of physical, economic, and health security, whether from crop failures, domestic violence, crime, police brutality, gangs, bandits, and, in the worst cases, state acquiescence in ethnic or religious attacks. Their housing, if they have homes, is often not secure (squatter housing often lacks title, appropriate infrastructure, or even ways to lock doors). Public transportation, if available in their neighborhoods, is unsafe, as well as unreliable. Water is often unsafe and, in many places, unavailable.

Policy changes to address each of these situations range from strengthened regulatory policies and their enforcement (housing codes, inspections, water management, working conditions, rights to access publicly provided safety nets), police reform, legislated and enforced human rights, judicial reform, law enforcement with attention to organized crime, interdiction of drug markets, recognition of property rights for the poor (land titling and registries, banking regulations), and disclosure rules to counter corruption (public disclosure of contracts, financial reporting, and auditing standards). These are all difficult to achieve. Indeed, they cannot be achieved without extensive consultation with communities and people impacted by these policies.

Policies That Facilitate Pro-Poor Economic Growth and Distribution of the Benefits of Growth

Poverty reduction does require macroeconomic stability and economic growth, but growth is only important for poverty reduction if it is in sectors that affect the poor and if the benefits of growth are indeed realized by the poor. The requisites for growth in a nation's economy are rooted in its productivity and capacity to engage in trade with other countries and within the country among its own citizens. Macroeconomic policies— export capacity, liberalized trade policies, avoiding an overvalued exchange rate, and reasonable incentives for foreign direct investment—constitute a part of successful growth stories. But these kinds of policies are not sufficient if there are severe inequalities within the nation's income distribution.

Although economists continue to debate the relative importance of growth, even those that see it as one of the most essential elements for poverty reduction acknowledge that particular types of growth are needed to have an impact on poverty. As stated by Nicolas Stern, chief economist of the World Bank in 2001, the "twin tracks of a pro-poor growth policy are getting the investment climate right to boost productivity, investment, jobs and growth...and the empowerment of poor people to participate in the growth process" (IMF, 2001, p. 7). Cross-country studies have found that the more equal the distribution of income in a country, the greater the impact of growth on reducing the number of people in poverty (Ravallion, 1999). Adopting much of the research findings of Ravallion and others (Datt and Ravallion, 1992; Kakwani, 1993; Ravallion, 1999), the World Bank and IMF's guidelines for developing poverty reduction strategies now highlight the fact that the impact of growth is dependent on the "distributional patterns and sectoral composition of growth" (Ames et al., 2001, p. 5).

In terms of sectoral composition, research has shown that growth will have a greater impact on poverty reduction if the growth occurs in sectors of the economy where the poor are concentrated. In countries where most of the poor live in rural areas, agricultural growth reduces poverty because it increases income for poor farmers and increases demand for goods and services that can be provided by the poor. Studies have found that, in such countries, growth in agricultural and tertiary sectors have an impact on poverty reduction, but growth in manufacturing does not (Ames et al., 2001, p. 6).

Policies that improve the distribution of assets within a society, such as land tenure reform, pro-poor public expenditure, and measures to increase the poor's access to financial markets, are recommended components of policy reduction strategies (Ames et al., 2001, p. 3). We contend that a progressive tax policy also matters (with distributional equity, earned income tax credits, etc.). Access to assets and the marketplace directly influences the extent to which the poor will benefit from economic growth and trade. For example, land holdings impact who will benefit from increased agricultural trade. Smallholder agriculture has been shown to be highly effective in poverty reduction, but in many countries agriculture is dominated by large landowners; in Latin America, for example, more than half the rural poor lack access to land (Oxfam, 2002, p. 86).

In terms of policies that foster economic growth, we agree with research that shows that the level of openness is not as key to growth as the level of public investment and macroeconomic stability. As Rodrik demonstrates, "the countries that have grown the most rapidly since the mid-1970s are those that have invested a high share of GDP and maintained macroeconomic stability" (Rodrik, 1999, p. 1). East Asian success cases such as South Korea complemented gradual import liberalization policies with a cohesive strategy of domestic investments. As discussed further in the next section on global trade policies, the pace of liberalization is also key to its impact on growth. The Oxfam 2002 report on trade notes that the countries that are "integrating most successfully into world markets—such as China, Thailand and Vietnam—are not rapid import liberalizers," while those countries that did follow the Washington Consensus prescription of rapid liberalization, such as Peru, have not fared as well and have experienced negative impacts on poverty, particularly in certain sectors of the economy (Oxfam, 2002).

Public investments (especially in primary health, health insurance, and education) are critically important. These investments directly affect people's productivity and ability to take part in the benefits of growth. Investments in infrastructure are needed to attract investment (transport, electricity, and telecommunications) and facilitate farmers' reaching markets.

The importance of investment in institutions underlines the importance of an adequate state role in achieving pro-poor growth and equitable distribution. Markets need governments to provide access to information, stability, predictability, and the rule of law if they are to flourish. People need to know that contracts can be readily enforced (otherwise they can only lend or borrow within families or cliques—clearly suboptimal if growth is to occur). They also need to have access to assets with clear records (imagine buying a home when unable to do a title search or know if your payments are in fact securing ownership). These are a few of the things governments, not markets, do. Governments in turn need markets that are decentralized (for example, accessible by the rural poor) and transparent and accountable enough to avoid fraud and corruption.

Policies That Improve the Accountability and Openness of Governance

Especially because the role of government is so important, governments must be accountable and transparent. This requires policies that ensure open and contestable elections, strong legislative oversight for greater accountability, and rules for government financial management and reporting standards. Accountability and openness are interrelated. Public access to information, freedom to question, and rights to opposition affects the climate within which poor people can bring their demands into the debates over who gets what. Poor people are most often, as noted in Chapter 2, among the least powerful actors within any political system. While the information revolution has made something of a difference with regard to their access to information, the digital divide limits their use of this revolution in order to get more responsiveness to their very real needs.

Policies on a Global Level That Promote Fair Participation in Global Trade

Global trade is important for economic growth and poverty reduction—but the potential benefits of trade can only be realized when trade is practiced on a level playing field. Few countries can grow and help people within their borders prosper without being engaged in international trade. (Even very large countries, such as China—that could afford to pay the cost of being more insular—have not chosen that route. Insularity is not then an option, for example, for landlocked, small countries in Africa.) But the fact is that currently there is nothing close to a level playing field. There are many aspects of trade regimes in northern industrial countries that adversely affect the chances for poor countries to sell their products in first world markets.

The issue of trade and globalization is at the heart of the fierce debate on policy. We side with those in this debate who seek common ground for moving forward—not rejecting globalization but rather finding a way to make it beneficial to all parties and not unfairly advantageous to some, as it is now. As Amartya Sen stated, "the basic objective is to combine the great benefits of trade to which many defenders of globalization point, with the overarching need for fairness and equity which motivates a major part of the antiglobalization protests" (Oxfam, 2002, p. 17).

Improving the terms of trade has the potential to have a significant impact on poverty reduction by directly increasing the income of developing countries. Oxfam International estimates that a 1% increase in Africa's share of world exports would result in $70 billion in increased revenue, five times the amount Africa receives in aid and debt relief (Oxfam, 2002, p. 6). For all developing countries, it estimates that a 5% increase in their share of the world export market would result in $350 billion in revenue, seven times as much as they receive in aid (Oxfam, 2002, p. 6). While acknowledging that these numbers are only estimates, as trade is dynamic, these figures nevertheless provide a useful glimpse of the type of impact increased trade can have for developing countries. The World Bank has also noted the cost of trade barriers to developing countries, estimating that tariffs and subsidies in industrialized countries cause annual welfare losses of $20 billion for developing countries (World Bank, WDR, 2001).

In order to realize the benefits of trade, poor countries must have access to markets in rich countries and must compete in the global marketplace on equal terms. Currently, poor countries face uneven tariffs, subsidized production and oversupply from wealthy countries that result in dumping and reduce world prices, and international trade rules that do not work in their favor.

Uneven trade practices, and the double standard between what rich countries preach through development policies and practice at home are acknowledged facts by those on all sides of the debate. As noted in the *Wall Street Journal*, the World Bank and industrialized governments are pushing free trade in Africa "even though the United States, for one, is expanding the subsidies it pays to its own farmers....Industrialized countries continue to pay their own farmers the subsidies that [donors claim] stymie development in poor nations—a total of $311 billion last year alone. The subsidies not only protect American and European growers from low world-market prices; they also depress global prices by encouraging overproduction" (*Wall Street Journal*, 2002, pp. A1, A14). Overall developing countries exporting to rich countries face tariff barriers four times higher than those encountered by rich countries (Oxfam, 2002).

The impact of tariff barriers on the poor is heightened by the fact that the sectors most affected are those where the poor are usually employed— agriculture and labor-intensive manufacturing such as textiles. Subsidies in agriculture in wealthy countries result in export dumping, meaning that agricultural products are exported at prices below the actual cost of production. Oxfam estimates that the United States and EU export at prices more than one-third lower than the costs of production.

Structural oversupply also leads to falling commodity prices. Low prices for commodities prevent trade from working for the poor. The price of coffee, for example, has fallen 70% since 1997 (Oxfam, 2002, p. 11). While commodity prices are low for products like coffee and cocoa, the market for processed products from these raw commodities is strong. For example, while the export of cocoa generates $2 billion, chocolate sales by confectionary manufacturers produce in excess of $60 billion (Oxfam, 2002, p. 161). Trade barriers contribute to the difficulty that poor countries have in taking advantage of the more lucrative value-added markets, since tariffs escalate based on the amount of value added to a product.

Policies that promote a fair playing field in international trade are thus essential for poverty reduction. These include tariff and subsidy reductions, elimination of export dumping practices, and global commodities agreements.

UNIVERSALITY OF THE POLICY LIST

Even this abbreviated policy list illustrates the enormous amount of work to be done on the policy change front in order to redress poverty. Moreover, as poverty, inequality, and social exclusion in powerful countries also need more attention, this list could be reconfigured to address the policy changes that any large, powerful, post industrial country should do to redress poverty.

Consider for a moment the applicability of that list to a specific rich industrial country. When we began, we defined poverty as a global problem. It is a global, not merely a national, problem. But what then does that mean for the policies in powerful countries toward the poor of their own country? Where is the global pressure to redress that situation? What national policies would be most helpful in that case?

Look back at our list—how many of the issues are equally applicable to, for example, the United States? Our list started with security. If the United States were to have a more focused and coherent national strategy to reduce domestic poverty, would it need to address its own poor people's need for more security? As shootings are the major cause of death for African-American young men, one can hardly argue that security is not an issue. City governments in the United States that have made the effort to consult with community groups about their experiences with police brutality, crime, and drug-trafficking in their neighborhoods have developed more effective security policies working in tandem with the poor.

Distribution of income and access to assets affect the impact of growth on poverty reduction across the globe. Trade policies at the global and national level affect rich and poor countries, obviously requiring some reexamination of public support to domestic sectors in rich countries in order to achieve greater trade parity globally. Reducing state support to large agricultural producers may also free up public money to fund additional pro-poor programs in the wealthy countries.

We contend that the policy list is equally applicable within the United States (as well as in other industrial powers). Given the institutional capacities in the United States, more direct focus upon these questions— and the others that each in turn evokes—could be useful in making progress on the poverty problems in the country. Redressing the internal poverty problem is not impossible. We recognize that many will say that it is, however, rather improbable—due to a lack of political will, not because of a lack of capacity. Nonetheless, political will is generated by people across a country changing their minds about what is to be done. That in turn puts wind into the sails of change. That has happened in the United State before—most recently during the civil rights movement of the 1950s and the antiwar movement of the 1960s—and it could happen again. One of our hopes is that this book might contribute toward that shift in public perception and political activism.

GETTING TO REFORMED POLICIES

So in order to achieve poverty reduction, policies will often need to be developed and/or reformed. Policy reform, however, is extremely difficult. Nonetheless, let us consider how—in circumstances more felicitous than those of externally imposed conditionality—policy reform can, and does, happen. Policies need to be well researched and articulated, but one of the most crucial aspects of policy reform is building the political will and public support to get certain policies on the agenda and adopted. A wide range of stakeholders come into play in this process.

One of the more encouraging changes in our times is the growth of civil society. Literally hundreds of thousands of groups have organized themselves in order to promote particular aims. These groups might be community-based NGOs, or local units of a national organization, or partners with an international NGO such as Oxfam, CARE, Save the Children, or Catholic Relief Services. Recall that estimates suggest there are close to a million local NGOs worldwide today.

While often community-based organizations focus on specific issues of service delivery in their communities, these organizations are increasingly becoming engaged in advocacy for particular policy changes (see Lindenberg and Bryant, 2001). In fact one of the major changes of our times is the amount of advocacy work being done by groups, often through coalitions, within and among countries in ways that were not happening a decade ago. The information revolution has accelerated this process—and has made it far easier for international coalitions to develop. The process, in short, for pressuring the state for policy reform has opened up—and simultaneously made policy reform both more possible and yet more complicated. The complications come in that larger numbers of people need to be brought on board, and it is far more challenging to reach agreement with a large number of people so that decisions can be made.

But the clock will not be turned back. The increase in advocacy and the focus on policy reform are here to stay. In many ways the increased role of advocacy in development organizations reflects a new level of sophistication in the development community, which is now focusing on the policy environment that is at the root of the poverty problems it seeks to address.

In getting at policy reform, advocacy can encompass a wide spectrum of activities that includes not only direct lobbying of legislatures, but education and development and dissemination of tools that inform policy choices. Products include analysis and papers, speeches, newspaper articles, media products, books, and mobilization efforts like demonstrations.

Advocacy can be directed to change or introduce specific legislation, to influence special groups or the general public's attitudes and behavior. These activities fall along a continuum from passive to direct engagement—from having consultative status with international organizations to broadly defined education and public awareness campaigns to very focused lobbying on specific legislation at international, national, or even local levels.

Coalition building and engaging the right stakeholders are essential in effective advocacy work. Given the scope and complexity of most issues of concern related to poverty reduction, coordination of advocacy efforts has emerged as an effective—and in most cases, necessary—means of affecting global policies. Globalization is making such coordination efforts easier and opening the possibility for inclusive coordination with partners from around the globe. Coordinated global efforts utilizing technology for mass communication are allowing civil society to push specific policy reforms onto the agendas of national governments and international organizations. Advocacy is thus one tool that can be used effectively to fight poverty by bringing about effective pro-poor policies. Some of the other techniques required for building support for policy reform among diverse stakeholders are discussed in Chapter 5.

PROGRAMS AND PROJECTS: WORKING IN HOSTILE POLICY ENVIRONMENTS

We now move the next level down—from policies to programs and projects. One important issue as we begin this discussion is whether or not programs and projects can only be effective in an optimal policy environment. People doing fieldwork in the past three decades have often had to work in countries that lacked democratic governance. While recently there has been much discussion about the real need for open, democratic, and accountable governments, there were few such governments in Africa, Asia, and Latin America in the 1960s, 1970s, and 1980s. Often due to Cold War geopolitics, donor organizations were not willing to enter into dialogue with national leaders about the need for more openness and democracy. Bilateral donors sought clients, rather than good governance, and multilateral donors were stalemated.

Only with the end of the Cold War could attention to governance be put on the table. The first breakthrough came when the World Bank's Board accepted the Governance Policy Paper in July 1991 (World Bank, 1991).[3] Governance policy papers from the Asia Development Bank, the Inter-American Development Bank, and the UNDP followed rapidly.

Yet, by 2002, a new view had emerged: lending to poor countries should be contingent upon their having more open and democratic regimes. Conditionality had been used to bring about reform in economic policies;

why not use it to bring about greater openness in governance? As official development assistance is in short supply, the argument goes, and as governments matter (a sea change from the 1980s belief in the miracle of the market!), good government should be the entry ticket for assistance.

The debates about how to do this, and under what circumstances conditionality of this kind can be effectively used, are endless. As one of us was a major participant in writing and negotiating the World Bank's *Governance Policy Paper*, we readily acknowledge the importance of good governance. Yet we do not believe that poor people who happen to have the misfortune of being born into repressive or irresponsible political systems should be excluded from any developmental help. Our perspective is that people who are poor should have help to reduce their poverty wherever they are. People matter more than governments. Of course, one of the differentiating issues is whether official development assistance is channeled through a government, rather than directly through NGOs, bypassing government.

The main point is that projects can be successful in even the most politically unfriendly contexts. Thus we can see a reason for continuing to work in hostile environments. Just as doctors do not refuse sick people medical attention on political grounds, neither should development professionals. Moreover, over time participatory projects may help in their own small way to shift the winds of change in their favor—and to contribute to changing political will in a country. But even if we cannot be sure that will happen, we can work with people in hostile environments and still facilitate their improving their own well-being. Moreover, heavily conditioning aid upon good governance is rather like "cherry picking"—working only on the easy cases where success is already on the way.

But we also acknowledge that the answer is not always a simple one. In fact, in some circumstances, such as in conflict countries, it is often morally laudable when, for example, NGOs withdraw as they do not want to be complicit with the adverse and inhumane acts of a government. There is a difference—though it is a difficult line to draw—between working in a hostile environment when you are making a difference and working in a situation in which your work is being used in order to worsen the problems of the people with whom you are working. Building a Tibetan Business Center in Tibet when the governance problems of a minority population within China remain unresolved can be, and has been, for example, positive.[4] But withdrawing a humanitarian feeding program is also the right thing to do if one discovers that terrorists are using it to feed their cadres.

In short, circumstances dictate when it is wise, useful, or humane to work in hostile environments. These are tough decisions. Often among the questions to ask is when, or whether, the activities of the program or project are only taking pressure off a government to do that which it should be doing. Or when is it better to use advocacy pressures on the government to get it to deliver, rather than doing its job for it? It is no surprise that these questions are often raised when NGO leaders talk with one another. NGO leaders struggle for sure footing through this tortuous territory, in their domestic programming, as well as abroad.

Let us try to establish a few guidelines. First, participatory projects can, and have, made significant changes in hostile environments when local ownership was deeply enough rooted that governments stayed out of the way and allowed the projects to go forward. One example is David and Fran Korten's almost legendary work with water user associations in Marcos's repressive Philippines in the 1970s and early 1980s. We all learned a great deal more about how to organize water user associations from the Philippines water user associations' experience. But most importantly, water short, poor rural people gained reliable and sustainable access to water, learned to manage their own irrigation systems, and improved their own well-being as a result of these projects. Was it a mistake to work there when President Marcos's human rights record was appalling and the government was sorely in need of reform? Or, perhaps, having mastered collective action vis-à-vis water management, some of these rural people later participated in the nonviolent change of government that rocked the world with its force in 1986.

Consider the even more impressive achievement of the Gal Oya project in war-torn Sri Lanka (Uphoff, 1997). Should this project not have taken place because of the political climate in the country? If so, all that extraordinary learning by Tamils and Sinhalese about how to share management of their irrigation system while elsewhere their counterparts were killing one another would not have happened. Nor would those of us in project management have learned how amazingly things that our theory tells us cannot work, do work. Somehow people in the Gal Oya project were doing what social scientists said they could not do—work together. Fortunately, those Tamils and Sinhalese did not know that body of theory. In short, projects are sturdy vehicles, able to go to places that other kinds of development endeavors cannot. People working together can manage more than one can predict. Projects that work have a demonstration effect, and people learn from that success.

On the ground, those working directly on poverty reduction programs often manage to devise ways forward. Below, for example, we will discuss how Bolivia's leaders tried a wholly different kind of program—providing grants to local groups that came up with projects meeting real needs. Tendler also describes successful projects at work in Northeast Brazil—an area with generally weak institutional capacity for good government (Tendler, 1998). That kind of local risk-taking and innovation led to breakthroughs—but these breakthroughs were at a level well below the radar screens of economists whether in London, Brussels, or Washington at the IMF or the World Bank. As stated in the introduction to this chapter, the problem is not that successful projects are rare—but that powerfully positioned decision-makers rarely learn about them.

And yet when political leaders do get to rural places and see projects that work, they express great surprise at their discovery as if no one knew about these things. We remember, for example, US Treasury Secretary Robert Rubin speaking at a large development conference in Washington— and talking about how fascinated he was with a project he had visited. Development practitioners in the audience with decades of experience were bemused, and frustrated, at his "discovery" of what worked. A subsequent Treasury Secretary, Paul O'Neill, seemed equally pleased with his discoveries during his visit to Africa in 2002 with the musician Bono. People who work on programs and projects rolled their eyes and said, "Hello?" Experienced project people know about all kinds of projects that have worked, and multiple others that could work, if there were more political will for reducing poverty.

INTERACTIONS BETWEEN POLICY CHANGE AND PROJECT PERFORMANCE

There are multiple interactions between policy change and program and project performance and learning. Projects are not passive vehicles carrying out aspects of policies. They often need to be adjusted to work in different contexts. Thus adapting projects to work in widely different contexts means comparisons can be made—leading to learning more about replicability and effectiveness. Because projects are central to policy and program implementation, they are on the front lines of learning about what works, or fails. The feedback loops between project learning and policy choices need to be strengthened, as they are rich opportunities for experimentation and learning.

Strengthening those learning feedback loops is an area that needs more attention. Few studies look in depth at these feedback loops between policies–programs–projects. That said, the Operations Evaluation Department (OED) of the World Bank does undertake this kind of research. But few other donors are both funded and organized to do so. And, as OED is independent of operations—reporting directly to the President and Board—its recommendations do not necessarily always get much ownership from those working on projects. But in all development agencies and organizations, bilateral or multilateral, the channels for communication between evaluation and operations are noisy and congested; information gets lost along the way. We will turn in Chapter 6 to a more detailed discussion of learning processes and how effective monitoring and evaluation can help facilitate these feedback loops.

WHAT HAS BEEN LEARNED ABOUT EFFECTIVE PRO-POOR PROGRAM AND POLICY DESIGN?

While programs and projects help inform effective policies, the programs and projects themselves also benefit from continual feedback loops to improve their effectiveness. What happens during implementation is of course key to effectiveness and is discussed in detail in Chapter 5; but getting the design right is also critical. Ironically, many of the donors driving development, including bilateral agencies and multilateral development banks, have traditionally dedicated most of their attention to design. Sometimes a kind of organizational culture dynamic is at work—frequently those staff who do design work become an elite corps. Sadly their work can become increasingly esoteric and even more divorced from implementation realities. Ideal types of projects come to be preferred over components that work.

Elements of effective design for programs and projects that work are (1) participatory projects, made appropriate to the local context and needs by the people within the reach of the project, (2) achieving local ownership from those affected and those who will ultimately implement the project, (3) incorporating lessons from similar projects and integrating learning processes into design, (4) constructing appropriate budgets that take into account local assets and absorption capacity, and (5) remembering that appropriate does not always mean big.

There are two key pieces: getting the design right and integrating design and implementation teams. Projects should be designed through participatory processes. This is central to gaining support from various stakeholders on their needs and ways to address those needs through the program. When designed in a consultative fashion, programs and projects are more likely to meet local needs, be appropriate to the local context, and have support from those that will be affected and involved in implementation.

Such participatory design is still not commonplace despite significant strides at incorporating it into standard practices of many development agencies. (For example, the World Bank has a toolkit in their Participation Sourcebook.) Participation takes time and is costly. But, if used appropriately, participation can lead to increases in effectiveness, thus lowering the costs of implementation. Participation has been used more in the development of general program approaches, with some consultative process involved in developing a country strategy or poverty reduction strategy. Often, however, a donor will design projects that the donor views as being in line with the overall policy or program strategy (which was developed through a consultative process), without more consultation with the people most involved in the country.

In some instances, design teams incorporate the latest innovations and international best practices, but, if these are not integrated into the local context and capacity, the project will not be effective. As noted in evaluations of IDB-managed grants, projects that were designed primarily by the IDB teams with external consultants rather than being generated by local organizations tended to be less effective in meeting project goals (Kappaz, 2003).

Input needs to come from those who will be responsible for implementation, as well as the stakeholders affected by the project. Bceause so often in development, the teams involved in managing implementation of a project are external to the community itself, the managing teams should have input in design as well. Current dominant practice is for development agencies to design a project and issue a "Request for Proposals" to select and hire consultants to manage implementation. Although the consultants will be responsible for ensuring project outcomes, they have very little to say about the design. There are thus several disconnects between design and implementation within development agencies. It has been said that bureaucratic politics and misbehavior within the church becomes, for some, an argument against Christianity. To a far greater extent, development agency bureaucratic politics and misbehavior greatly undermines support for poverty reduction work.

What Programs and Projects Work Effectively?

So what works in reducing poverty? Lots of programs and projects work. As proof, remember, for example, that real progress has been made in increasing life expectancy, reducing infant mortality, improving literacy, and building local community-based organizations, in many different countries. There is more of a technical core today than ever before in program and project effectiveness. *Much has been learned in the course of the past 40 years of program and project work in both relief and development and in a variety of sectors.* For example, more is known not just about why participatory development is centrally important—but also about how to start participatory processes, how to listen, correct, and record what is learned through participatory consultative processes with people in urban, rural, or post-conflict communities than ever before. Participatory rural appraisal now has an ample toolkit.

The past two decades have also seen significant innovations in programming in a variety of sectors—microcredit and microenterprise programs and projects have grown and spread to every continent. The use of social action funds—grants to local communities for their own programming—has led to a blossoming of locally owned innovation in meeting needs. Very different kinds of groups and organizations are doing this work: governments, donors, private individuals who built NGOs, or private–public partnerships. Below is just an indicative, not a comprehensive, list, yet it is one that provides a wide range of options for effective action in reducing poverty in either rich or poor countries. Consider, for example, the following kinds of programs:

Microenterprise development

Microcredit and savings

Social action funds

Locally appropriate farm technology and agricultural research

Community schools

Preventive health programs

Self-help housing

Land trusts to increase low cost housing

We will discuss each of these very briefly in order to provide readers with a sense of the range of program possibilities. We also want to note that often we have used the terms "program" and "project" linked together. Operationally they are linked—though it can be that a major policy initiative is first rolled out through several different programs, and projects then follow within each of the various programs. In short, program is a larger category than project. And our list above is a case in point—we have listed programs within which one would find literally hundreds of different projects in many different parts of the world. We turn now to say a few words about our program list above and the ways in which it exemplifies some of the innovation and learning of the past twenty years.

Microenterprise Development

We started the list with microenterprise development as this is the sector that has grown most dramatically in the past two decades. Starting with the reality that many poor people are keen to increase their own earning capacities, microenterprise projects begin with people who want to produce a good or service and need small combinations of technical and investment support to assist them in their endeavors. The first of these projects were started by local NGOs, most notably in Asia. (See discussion of Grameen Bank, below, a microcredit and microenterprise support NGO established in 1976 in Bangladesh.) Donors had been aware of the size of the informal sector, but had not focused on the implications. Then, in the late 1970s, USAID supported the Program for Investment in the Small Capital Enterprise Sector (PISCES), which helped very small producers market their goods. The impetus for the project came in part from USAID research in squatter settlements in Haiti that found higher than expected economic activity rates among poor residents, primarily in very small enterprises. That research also found that "many of the activities reported upon remained small and precarious, not so much because of lack of entrepreneurial capabilities or of market opportunities, as because of lack of working capital, storage space or access to only slightly higher levels of technology" (USAID, 1981, p. vi).

Jeffrey Ashe, the task manager for the PISCES project, later founded Working Assets, a US-based group that assisted a wide range of microenterprise and microcredit projects both in the United States and abroad. TechnoServe and FINCA are two of the larger NGOs working today with a variety of small producers in myriad ways to increase their profitability whether they are small cooperatives trying to find new markets for pigeon peas, or alpaca producers marketing wool. The Eurasia Foundation supports microenterprise development projects all over Russia and Eurasia. One of those projects, for example, works with the Union of Small Entrepreneurs of Saratov—business owners in the Russian city of Saratov who have organized in order to further the prospects for small businesses. Among their major endeavors currently is working on gaining support for a better legal environment for small enterprises. These different groups and agencies and NGOs are but a tiny selection in the large and vibrant sector of microenterprise development.

Microcredit and Savings Associations

Some of the greatest work in starting and sustaining microsavings and credit groups was undertaken in Asia by local organizations that subsequently, in some cases, grew to set the standards for excellence in this sector. The work of the Grameen Bank and of the Bangladesh Rural Advancement Committee (BRAC) is now well-known. In both cases, they began simply by organizing small numbers of people—often of women—to form savings groups. The women would each contribute an agreed amount every month to a joint pool that would then be lent by the group to one member for her investment, to be repaid over time as agreed with the group. The group would then rotate the loan to other members—and hence over time—members would be able to increase their small savings by investing them in income producing activities. This is a much-abbreviated version of the process, but the key points are that (1) local small groups needed to be organized, and (2) mutual savings secured through local and direct face-to-face groups led to substantial increases in members' well-being.

Both BRAC and Grameen Bank grew as a result of their successes. Of course in both cases their leaderships had also to learn daunting lessons about scaling up, achieving sustainability, and managing what became complex organizations. Those stories have been documented. What is less well known is that the Grameen Bank is now working to organize local level saving groups in poor neighborhoods in the United States—a striking instance of our premise that lessons learned in developing countries have implications for working on poverty in wealthy countries too.

Social Action Funds

A type of project that has been used by the large development agencies as a means of supporting local level initiatives is the Social Action Fund (SAF), also known as a Social Investment Fund (SIF). These SAFs or SIFs were first launched in Bolivia in 1980 in what was called in that instance the Bolivia Emergency Social Fund. The idea of the social investment funds was to have a fast disbursing facility that could reach large numbers of the poor through projects of their own making. Thus greater flexibility was built into several dimensions of the project process. Social action funds are one of the modalities helpful in very different contexts—in long term development, or in short term post conflict reconstruction, or in multicultural countries where encouragement of horizontal trust among otherwise potentially competing groups is a step toward building peace.

The basic mechanism of the SAF is that a pool of funds is made available, through competitive application processes, for local activities to fund programs within specified parameters. The SAF facilitates the approval, disbursement, and oversight of many small projects within one larger project. A key element of the SAFs is that they aim to support community-initiated activities and strengthen local capacity to design and implement those initiatives. The scale, execution mechanisms, and results have varied greatly among SAFs. Over time, experience has shown that SAFs are most effective when they respect and support local institutions and decision-making processes. While institutional strengthening is sometimes needed, it is important to avoid external NGOs or rent-seekers from dominating the process.

An IDB evaluation of its poverty reduction programs found that SIFs "have benefited communities and mitigated the adverse effects of structural adjustment. Though not a long-term solution to poverty, SIF activities have generated short-term employment and the social infrastructure has improved health, education, and transportation" (IDB, 2000).

Locally Appropriate Farm Technology and Agricultural Research

When poor rural farmers—who account for 70% of the poorest globally—are active partners in identifying their own capacities, assets, and needs, as well as participants in the management of their critical resources (e.g., technology, pest management, or critical inputs), improvements in their well-being occur and spread. For example, working with their own seeds to breed more disease resistance into their stocks is more sustainable than heavy reliance on pesticides. Ugandan farmers have bred cassava resistant to a new strain of mosaic virus by combining frontier plant genetics, national research, and local extension—thereby reversing huge economic and nutritional losses that had resulted from the new virus. Norman Uphoff has also identified farmers who have devised a system for growing rice that achieves yields far above other methods (Uphoff, 2004).

Linking formal research to farmers' traditional methods also has a high pay-off. For example millions of pigeon peas—grown by small farmers—are lost to pod-borer. In India in 1993, costly chemical controls predominated. At a farmers' meeting organized by the NGO Research in Environment, Education, and Development Society, an elderly farmer showed other farmers his traditional method. This involved shaking larvae gently onto a plastic sheet and feeding them to chickens. IFAD subsequently followed up with tests in a large watershed, found it to be effective, and by 1999 the traditional method was back in widespread use for thousands of farmers. Similarly, the Research Foundation on Science, Technology and Ecology headed by Vandana Shiva in India is spearheading a grassroots movement to preserve—and reintroduce—traditional agricultural techniques that have been leading to improved incomes for farmers previously strapped by debt incurred by trying to keep up with technologies and pesticides needed with "modern" farming techniques and genetically modified seeds promoted by agribusiness and local governments (Lappé and Lappé, 2002).

Community Schools

In rural areas in, for example, Zambia and Malawi, people decided that the distances to schools, as well as these schools' serious limitations, meant that it was better for them to build and organize their own schools. Over time this process came to be called the community school movement. These community schools are now sometimes recognized by the formal Ministry of Education in several countries as playing a most useful role. Yes, they raise complex policy problems about national standards and teacher quality, but the fact is that the movement in this direction was so deeply locally grounded that governments and donors such as UNICEF have found they have more to gain by working with, rather than against, this change.

There is an interesting counterpart in the United States, in the widespread push in many communities to improve the access to quality education and range of school choices through either home schooling or charter schools. As education is under the authority of state and local government, with some federal support, the charter school movement in the United States has also succeeded in several states to develop a process for such schools being formally recognized. These charter schools now operate within the public school system, although they are initiated, designed, and supported by residents of the community. Each school aims to test new educational methodologies and meet specific needs of community members. The Boards of Education support these schools by allowing them to apply for recognition as charter schools.

Community Preventive Health

Judith Tendler provides us with detailed accounts of several successful community preventative health programs in Northeast Brazil. Her accounts of these are especially helpful as she describes the inner workings that made for success in implementation (Tendler, 2000). One of these cases covers the statewide Ceara Health Agent Program. Ceara, prior to the initiation of this program in 1987, had some of the worst health indicators not just in Brazil, but in Latin America as a whole, with an infant death rate of 102 per 1000. After only 5 years of operation, infant deaths had declined 36% and vaccination coverage for measles and polio had tripled—reaching 90% of the population. Small towns had nurses where previously there had been none.

How was all this brought about? The program began as part of an emergency employment program following a drought and was financed out of temporary disaster relief funds from both the central and state governments. The state decided in 1989—given the success of the program—to fund it permanently. The program hired people, mainly women, through a rigorous selection process and trained them to be health agents. They worked for minimum wages (nurse supervisors were paid more) on a contract basis to work intensively with families, often through household visits. It was embedded in a decentralization strategy that was underway, but it is noteworthy in the ways in which it called upon and created new relationships between all three levels of governance—local, state, and central. It also illustrates the importance of preventative measures and the impact of utilizing local community members to lead project implementation. The model of local community outreach workers has been used successfully for community preventive health in the United States as well—through the use of "promotoras" that work in their own immigrant communities.

Self-Help Housing

Self-help housing programs were one of the most interesting innovations in approaches to housing in the 1970s and 1980s. Self-help housing projects were used to address the serious shelter shortages in the squatter settlements in many African, Latin American, and Asian urban areas. In the projects undertaken in these programs, squatters were offered secure tenure on small lots that had access to water. Important elements of the projects were engaging the residents through community meetings, covering a range of issues and subjects, and providing credits for access to basic materials essential for building housing.

Families could then either build their own shelters or contract with others locally to build shelter. They could buy, sell, or rent the resulting homes. But at the core, they had to build their homes or get someone to help build them. It was essentially sweat equity that provided them with shelter. Since their inception, these initial self-help housing communities have essentially stabilized and even led to the embryonic development of a middle class (Bryant, 1980, 1996).

Inclusive Zoning and Land Trusts

Access to shelter is a key concern among the poor. Real estate markets contribute to concentrations of poverty, as the poor can only afford to live in certain areas, or in the case of most developing countries, in illegal squatter settlements that often ring major cities. In the United States, innovative housing policies and projects have worked to provide affordable housing, while also increasing integration across classes and minimizing the creation of pockets of poverty. They have done this through inclusionary zoning laws that require new residential developments of more than a specific number of units (ranging from four to 50) to set aside a fixed percentage (often 15%) of the apartments or homes for moderate- to low-income people. Moreover, the apartments are required to be largely equivalent to the others in the development. Such programs exist in Maryland, California, Massachusetts, Colorado, and a growing number of other states.

First conceived of as a way to maintain affordable housing for people whose services are essential in a community but whose salaries are not commensurate—store clerks, police, teachers, postal workers, etc.—this kind of zoning also preserves diversity and enlivens a community, averting the deadly homogeneity that comes with rapid, ill-conceived suburbanization (Jacobs, 1963).

Such policies are often supported by land trusts that serve as a means of redistributing resources, land, and homes, for low-income housing. Burlington, Vermont, for example, has a land trust that buys land with, or without housing on it, and sells the housing—but not the land—to new buyers. Buyers have full use of the house as long as wanted or needed and can sell it, but not the land, back to the Land Trust. The drawback is in part that families are not acquiring the same asset as other home buyers—but they are getting housing in locations generally closer to work and schools than they could otherwise afford. Land trusts are usually financed through taxes that may include a tax on taking down buildings, which is especially relevant in areas undergoing rapid gentrification.

CONCLUSION

Throughout this chapter we have focused on what works in reducing poverty and thereby builds opportunities for peace. But to get there we also needed to consider the relationships among policies, programs, and projects. And because the policy debates of the past decade have been especially contentious, the nature of those differences of view warranted attention. Getting to reformed policies and strengthening the learning among programs, projects, and policies are the major points in this chapter. Then too, we turned to the issue of whether it makes more sense to work only with those countries already making some progress. In short, should those concerned with poverty reduction give up on working in hostile environments? Cherry picking is always seductive; it is also worth resisting as the vast majority of poor people should not be blamed for having had the misfortune of being born in the wrong place.

We looked also at seven specific areas where there have been notable successes in reducing poverty. A characteristic of the projects within these sectoral areas was that often the projects were locally owned via participatory processes. Participatory projects are sturdy vehicles for reducing poverty. Locally owned and valued projects contribute to a sustainable process of poverty reduction, and can, over time, deepen and enrich social capital. Those changes in turn can help to build an atmosphere providing space for more peaceful problem solving skills to be practiced and levels of violence reduced.

NOTES

1.   A senior division chief at the World Bank tasked to work on public sector development in the emerging Commonwealth of Independent States (CIS) countries once said with disdain in this period, "We might as well drive a truck into Russia and dump the money—that's how little attention we can get to the usual quality controls for lending."

2.   The core disciplines in development studies can be said to be economics, political science, sociology, international relations, and development management (public administration and the management sciences). Within each sector, for example, health, education, agriculture, environment, energy, transport, etc., there are obviously large bodies of specialized literature on theory and practice as well. Within economics alone, there is the division between agricultural economics and other specializations, as well as the mainstream macro and microeconomics split. But worse, there are real tensions between more abstract theoretical work (exemplified by the Economics Department at Stanford University) and field-oriented empirical work (exemplified by Cambridge University in England). Versions of that tension reappear within political science, especially as it has become increasingly theoretical. In general, there has been less work in political science on development theory and practice than is needed. It is hard, given the core critical focus within political science, for political scientists to focus on the "what can be done" questions. Political scientists are especially ill-equipped by their discipline and its culture to explain why, when things work that their theory says should not work, how that came to happen. We saw this, for example, in the Sri Lanka water users association described in the previous chapter. It was equally true of their inability to predict or explain the release of Nelson Mandela from prison, or the "velvet" [non violent] revolutions in Eastern Europe after the fall of the Berlin Wall.

3.   The document, *Governance and Development*, published in July, 1991, grew out of a World Bank Task Force that worked to get acceptance from the operational staff of this major change in World Bank policy. All other multilateral development banks and the United Nations Development Program subsequently issued their own versions of a governance policy. The World Bank followed up the policy change with regional governance progress reports, and commenced lending on technical assistance to provide strengthened capacity—for example, judicial reform, strengthening of research capacity for legislatures, and more generally institutional development to put institutions in place to enable more open engagement with civil society.

4.   This work, financed by the Trace Foundation, was facilitated by its staff member, Ashok Gurung in the late 1990s.

5

ACHIEVING RESULTS: STRENGTHENING IMPLEMENTATION

"Implementation...is the ability to forge subsequent links in the causal chain so as to obtain the desired results....The longer the chain of causality, the more numerous the reciprocal relationships among the links and the more complex implementation becomes."
—J.L. Pressman and A. Wildavsky, *Implementation*, 1973

INTRODUCTION

Suppose, for a moment, that you are traveling through a small, landlocked sub-Saharan African country. One day you read in the newspaper that the President has declared a major policy reform—one that involves significant increases in financial support for community schools.[1] As mentioned in the last chapter, community schools are ones that, especially in African countries, local communities organize and build when parents find either that there are no public schools or that existing schools are wholly inadequate. Government support for these schools often amounts to a pro-poor policy change. Moreover, imagine for our case study that the President made this decision as a result of a nationwide movement that called for just such a change. Following your reading of this news story, you may hear at a local gathering that the National Assembly is debating the ramifications of the President's new policy initiative. Let us then assume that subsequently you learn that the essential legislation passed—and funding has even been promised.

People are now expectantly waiting for the action to begin. Most importantly, people living in rural communities at a distance from the capital look forward to the policy actually being implemented. Parents with access to news anticipate something will happen, but there is no word yet on what or when. They begin their wait. But then, in the past, they also waited for teachers to arrive, so they are accustomed to waiting. Meanwhile people in the capital even assume that the policy is already being implemented. But in fact, there is little evidence of anything much happening for those children in villages who continue to walk long distances to schools that lack books, chalk, blackboards, or, as happens, trained teachers.

Policy change is easier to declare than it is to implement. The major challenge comes in implementation. The first rule of implementation is that nothing is implemented automatically. Good will and commitment need nurturing to be sustained. The old aphorism, "well begun is half done" alludes to the importance of preparatory work—yet we all know that even a great menu plan does not mean dinner gets to the table. *Nothing is self-implementing.*

Staffing and funding need to be arranged and agencies need to act if policies are to be more than words on a page, or in speeches. Implementation is about putting legs under a policy so that its promises begin to be realized. Too often policy specialists focus on getting the "what" questions answered, without much focus on the "hows." Yet most policies fail at this *how* stage—the operational steps that make or break policy reform. Especially in countries with limited institutional capacities, implementation gets neglected because there are hurdles that are hard to overcome. Policies require financial and human resources. Where financial resources are scarce, the fights over them are worse. There are few skilled managers and no extra resources.

Implementation requires assessing what institutions in place might be of help—and which ones are lacking, or, worse, may impede, the work to be done. In doing policy implementation work, for example, with African governments, it often becomes apparent that more government policy analytical capacity is needed—a cabinet committee or an Office of the Budget, or a Secretariat—to assist with functions that need enhanced performance. Institution building of that sort has happened repeatedly in development assistance programs. Remember that we talked about this factor in Chapter 3—precisely because it is so central to many aspects of poverty reduction work.

Implementation is about who does what, when, and how. In poverty reducing policies, programs, and projects these are tough questions of agency, responsibility, roles, and techniques. Thus, this chapter discusses a range of tools and techniques for engaging people and moving toward agreement. Strategic managerial skills, workshops, capacity building, organizational learning techniques, political mapping, and stakeholder assessments—all are techniques that have been refined further in the field of development management. And yes, all require sufficient budget and appropriate staffing.

Much has been learned in the field of development management in the past several decades as a result of the cumulative experience, field work, reflection, and writing of several scholar-practitioners. (For example, Tendler, 1975; 2000; Grindle, 1980; Lindenberg and Crosby, 1981; Bryant and White, 1982, 1984; White, 1987, 1990; Esman, 1991; Chambers, 1994a, 1994b, 1997; Krishna, Uphoff, and Esman, 1997; Brinkerhoff, 1997, 2002.) Hence we are mainly distilling—and drawing upon the work of these people—when talking about lessons learned.

Development management practitioners have been working on implementing policy reform, participatory development, project management, institutional development, and capacity building in countries around the world for decades. These practitioners get together at least once a year in the Development Management Network, or the more recent Development Policy Roundtable, and review and refine lessons learned from extensive field experience in northern, southern, and transitional countries.[2] In addition to that work, international development programs within academic institutions are increasingly emphasizing practical tools. For example, the Economic and Political Development Program at the School for International and Public Affairs at Columbia University has devised a Development Management Toolkit. Starting with a simple one-page listing of tools and sources, graduate students in the program assemble techniques and tools together in their own binders to enable them to invent and improve upon tools in the course of their own work. In short, there is more of a technical core to be used in reducing poverty than there was in the past. Some of the tools covered are discussed in this chapter.

Development management skills that make a difference in implementation have been refined through field testing and exchanges of lessons learned among practitioners, many of whom have had a keen commitment to—and years of experience with—participatory processes. We know from experience that increased public participation in all aspects from designing to implementing policies, programs, and projects makes a large difference in effectiveness.

The factors involved in implementation (e.g., the importance of incentives, capacity, and roles of institutions) are equally important whether implementing policies, programs, or projects. Where policies, programs, and projects are different is in the scale of the endeavor, the level of national attention, and hence the political pressures unleashed. Differences exist between implementing national policies affecting a range of very different communities and implementing a project within a specific region. However, note that a very large project—especially in a large country such as, for example, China, Brazil, or India—is considerably more complex than the policy reach of a major policy reform in, for example, Malawi or Chad.

On the one hand, scale makes a difference. It increases the pressure for structure, system, and procedures. Processes for quality control are more complex. Management information systems become more centrally important with larger programs or projects. On the other, many factors are essential no matter the scale: judgment, listening, ability to monitor, and negotiation skills. Thus, often we will discuss all three levels of policies, programs, and projects—and upon occasion try to make clear where there are salient differences.

This chapter will review the process involved in implementing effective policies, programs, and projects, using the case described above of community schools in a small country—a case distilled from several different, but very real experiences in order to highlight the types of tools that are applicable to a wide range of development activities. We focus on a range of workshop techniques that can be used in different stages to ensure engagement from a variety of actors and information sharing—all elements that contribute to effective implementation by deepening ownership.

REFLECTIONS ON DESIGN AND IMPLEMENTATION

All too often books on policy, program, or project implementation lay out a purely linear model: design comes first, implementation follows, and evaluation comes later. A colleague of ours when teaching development management would, while teaching, write the first letter of each on the board and exclaim afterwards—"Look, that spells DIE. And dead it is." His point was that the process was neither that tidy nor linear. In the real world, design, implementation, and evaluation processes interact over the life of any policy or program or project. Evaluation people tell us to build evaluation in from the beginning, implementation people say think through implementation during design, and design people will argue that great design solves all problems that matter, only to learn that those charged with implementation often end up redesigning the project while facilitating its implementation by a country team.

In reality, all three major processes interact over the life of a policy, program, or project. Long ago most of us moved away from thinking of program and project design as a definitive blueprint to conceiving of it as a learning process. Changes will have to be made as one goes along, adjusting to the changing context and participants' needs and preferences. Of course, some basics require more attention than others when initiating a new or reformed policy process. One of the essential ingredients of the early stages in policy development is achieving some minimal consensus among key actors about the goals and objectives to be achieved by the changed or new policy.

Agreement on objectives matters. In the process of getting agreement, it becomes obvious that there are often times quite different visions in people's minds about exactly what the policy initiative means. Core decision-makers may have different aspects they choose to focus upon; others may have different interpretations. Some degree of ambiguity may be needed in order to keep the stakeholders moving forward on the change itself. This may be referred to as functional ambiguity.

This is not to say that design has no integrity of its own. Of course, senior decision-makers must say what components go into a major policy reform. And, of course, development projects need some kind of initial design—core concepts and central activities that will begin to actualize them and affect the way in which subsequent work will be implemented must be detailed, appraised for feasibility, and in short, written up so that others can make use of the paper trail. But projects most often will be redesigned too as implementers find themselves rethinking that core design and listening and learning from the initial stakeholders and project participants about their needs and expectations. Thus redesign becomes a major step towards implementation. And yet in this family of design, implementation, and evaluation, it is implementation that is all too often the middle child that is squeezed or neglected while the others—each for different reasons—attract the most attention.

The part of the design process that warrants special attention is getting clarity about the core concept of the policy reform or program goal or project objectives. And all too often, in the rush to get minimal agreement, it is exactly the core goal that is left without great clarity. There is a reason for that absence of clarity. Getting agreement among very different stakeholders means addressing the fact that each of those stakeholders has their own vision of what is to be done. In this day and age of multifunded projects, different donors have different goals and expectations. They may appear to come to some coherent consensus, only to find as the activities actualizing the project evolve, that these are not exactly what they had in mind.

Sometimes even a single term may be agreed upon as the goal, but it may not be unpacked and disaggregated. The resulting degrees of ambiguity—functional for getting initial buy-in—become dysfunctional for implementation. Disagreements result, and other problems grow over time as a result. In Figure 5.1 below, the cartoon depicts a meeting of core leaders on a housing or shelter program. Even when we think a term is clear, people's interpretation or envisioning of the concept behind a term can vary significantly. And each dissimilar vision leads in directions poles apart from one another.

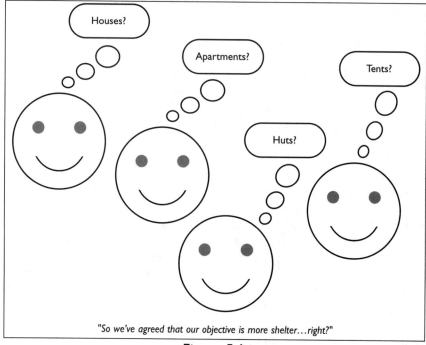

Figure 5.1
A False Consensus

PARTICIPATORY DEVELOPMENT

Maintaining a participatory process throughout the life of the policy, program, or project adds to the complexity but also helps ensure the value and validity of a design and implementation process. A widely participatory process can multiply the areas of ambiguity and thus increase the needs for communication, negotiation, and coordination. In short, participation increases the transaction costs. But it is clearly worth those costs, for with it, the foundation is laid for broadly shared commitment.

Participatory development requires attention to iterative problem solving, the careful unraveling of things that get snarled as programs are implemented. A participatory process multiplies the quantity (and hopefully the quality) of information traveling laterally and vertically. Managing those flows can become problematic—there can be "too many cooks in the kitchen." In poverty reduction work, each "cook" has his or her own needs and interests; these can conflict with those of others. An openness to work in a participatory way requires being willing to make tough choices and trade-offs and the ability to work with people, affirming their input as one goes along.

And, while managing information is hard, having more rather than less does reduce some uncertainty. Generally participatory processes generate local ownership and hence legitimacy. Legitimacy and credibility are part of the social capital that carries a project along over administrative hurdles. Legitimacy and credibility are also critical to ensuring that the policy or program will be carried forward over time, that is, that the program or project may be sustainable.

In short, process matters. It matters because people's beliefs, concerns, fears, and hopes shape their perceptions and actions—especially in regard to access to assets. Any intervention has to gain some acceptance among those who are to be engaged in either providing critical inputs, or receiving benefits, or paying costs. Processes to achieve "ownership" are inevitably central to moving a policy forward—and even more central for putting programs or projects into action.

Widespread experimentation with different ways of devising and constructing participatory processes among the urban and rural poor in the past 30 years has much to teach us about process. What has been learned is as rich and varied as people are diverse and knowledgeable. Much has been learned with regard to poverty reduction policies about ways to move forward through indifference, discord, or opposition. Public meetings, community meetings, leafleting, newspaper commentary, stakeholder conferences, Internet chat rooms, magazines, radio talk shows—all have a role to play in bringing people together and possibly in support of the program or project. More organized sessions, such as workshops, however, can help—especially when they are thoughtfully put together and allow for careful, in-depth discussions to take place. Hence workshops have come to have a special place in the world of participatory development.

Workshops are one of the techniques of choice because they can help achieve the shared perspectives necessary so that work processes can be agreed upon and implemented. Well-facilitated and documented workshops can ensure that everyone is on at least approximately the same page when implementing his or her part of the project.

Because the term workshop is widely used, often with very different meanings, we want to be clear that we are talking here about workshops as purposefully assembled groups of people to work through issues and objectives to meet specific purposes. This definition is important to keep in mind; we are not using the term workshops to mean what are really simply meetings or conferences. As useful as those other gatherings might be, they are not the same nor likely to be as productive as a well-prepared workshop in which participants come prepared to work through issues together in order to resolve issues or differences and to meet specific goals.

Those invited to a workshop need to know in advance that they will be asked to work—to actively participate in the discussions and breakout groups in order to reach new levels of agreement about next steps.

Workshops organized in this manner are a most useful technical tool for moving policies, programs, or projects forward. There are several different kinds of workshop modalities available for a variety of purposes. Indeed, it is centrally important to be clear about why one is organizing a workshop. Clarity about the purpose provides clarity about objectives, manner of facilitation, preparatory steps, and, most essentially, who needs to be there. Is the purpose to launch a project? Or to monitor one that is underway? Or to build support for a policy reform? Or to get agreement among stakeholders about next steps—whether for a project or for a policy reform? Or even to get some minimal agreement from hostile parties about what could be gained by working together? Workshops are useful tools for any of those purposes. But deciding which of these you are doing is critical to getting results. Indeed, blurring two or three of these purposes or conflating them usually results in an unsatisfactory workshop.

Clarity of purpose for the workshop being organized is the critical first step. As we can see in Table 5.1, there are several quite different types of workshops. There are Strategic Planning Workshops and Strategic Management Workshops; there are Stakeholder Assessment Workshops, which are held in order for stakeholders to provide their views on how effectively a program or project is unfolding. There is also another kind of workshop utilizing a different conceptual model altogether—the Acceptance, Influence, Control, or AIC workshop. There are also Participatory Appraisal Workshops, which have their own conceptual foundations.

The second step in preparing for a workshop is to decide on the line of inquiry that will guide the work toward the goals. Then the facilitation process, and identification of the actual facilitator, must be resolved. The *quality* of the facilitation is centrally important for it is through facilitation that participants come to trust that their views are respected, that differences can be safely discussed, and that through participation one gains support, not enemies.

Several different kinds and styles of facilitation, each with its own strengths, come to mind. Above all else, a facilitator must communicate the value of each participant's input and be able to ease the group forward when differences become intense or appear likely to derail.

BUILDING POLICY COALITIONS AND MOVING FORWARD ON IMPLEMENTATION

Getting back to our case study, we note that the President may have instructed the Ministry of Education to make this new education policy

Table 5.1
Workshop Types

TYPES	PURPOSES SERVED BY WORKSHOP
Strategic Planning Workshop	For centrally important actors to determine policy, program, or project goals and objectives.
Strategic Management Workshop	For operational managers in key organizations to determine who does what, when and how.
Stakeholder Assessment Workshop	For those with an interest in a policy, program or project in order to discern, or to generate, levels of commitment and relative roles.
Participatory Rural Appraisal	For those who are likely beneficiaries of a policy, program, or project to ascertain their perspectives on what they need, priorities, and possible roles in a policy, program, or project.
Participatory Monitoring or Evaluation	For beneficiaries of a policy, program, or project in order to monitor, or to evaluate, how performance to date has impacted them.
AIC Planning Workshop	For senior decision-makers in a sector or arena of activity to either consult with them, or to enlist their active engagement in a policy, program, or project.
AIC Monitoring or Troubleshooting Workshop	For those involved or impacted by a policy, program, or project to identify issues and concerns, and, if possible, address them

happen, but that only begins the process. Next, a Pandora's box of conflicting interests and competing agendas are unleashed.

The Ministry of Education is charged by the President to carry the policy out. But the Ministry of Community Affairs says it must have a role. And the Ministry of Finance has a major say in the flow of financing in order to make it work. The Teachers' Associations object, especially if they believe that communities are hiring teachers without adequate training, as certified by their association. And local District Councils want to know what roles they will have in deciding where community schools are to be built in their districts. Meanwhile parent associations vary in their strength and demand-making skills. Community groups and local NGOs come forward with their concerns in hand. In short, hosts of groups come forward to question what piece of the action they might look forward to having.

Assume a specific project has been funded to implement the policy in one area and that there are twenty schools in the project area reaching approximately 3200 children drawn from thirty-five villages. Participatory appraisal work indicated that the people in rural villages needed more primary schools within no more than three miles of their homes, with available water and basic supplies. The project manager—working out of the local office of an international NGO—also runs several other projects.

She works with partner agencies that in turn have made staff available to help with this project, but most of them also have other responsibilities. Funding for the project comes from both public and private sources representing private–public collaboration. Let us imagine that the donors include the Ministry of Education, District Councils, Mennonite Central Committee (based in the United States), Save the Children (UK), UNICEF, the Women's Council (a local voluntary association), and the Canadian International Development Agency (CIDA). Each of these donor agencies has principals and agents with differing goals and objectives, reporting requirements, and accountability issues. Each of these agencies or actors has policy initiatives that may be relevant to the impending policy reform. But each also has requirements to be met in order to be of assistance to the government.

Meanwhile, of course, those who opposed such a move in the first place now work more actively to undermine its being realized. But even for all those who support the policy, there are lots of issues to resolve: what the policy change means for different parts of the country, for different constituencies, and for different local groups. Hence the total range of players and issues grows—almost exponentially—and probably in inverse relation to the capacities of the government to manage the policy in the first place.

One way to get a handle on all this is to conduct an institutional assessment. As discussed in Chapter 3, institutional assessments provide deeper understanding of the context within which policies, programs, or projects must work. They allow you to see which functions need more support, and who might do what in the next phase of operations. They facilitate marshalling of human and financial resources to address the needs at hand, while ensuring the support needed for the future. But the tough question is: who does these things? Generally these tasks are shared among different levels and decision-makers—indeed, Dorothy, there is no magic Wizard of Oz. Titles like Task Manager, Chief of Operations, Director General, or Executive Manager hide more than they reveal about the density of overlapping tasks and responsibilities. Behind the magic curtain of titles must be real institutional capacity. What steps are most needed to build that capacity can be made clearer through the assessment itself. Sometimes the legal framework needs attention. In other cases, restructuring or reorganization—and/or the creation of new intermediary agencies—needs to be put in place.

The quality of results achieved by a policy change is determined by the incentives (social and political, as well as economic) motivating the policy change, and, as noted above, the institutional capacity (rules of the game, as well as organizations). The mortar holding these two structural pillars together is composed of leaders' attentiveness to process, investment in seeing the policy change through to results, and work through coalitions.

Why coalitions? Because the major characteristic of policy work is that no one individual is in charge. Multiple leaders—often from different organizations—are always working to build coalitions in order to move any given policy change forward. No matter how skillfully designed, policies require implementation by people acting together.

There have to be budgets, staff, and processes put in place in order to implement policies. And while we have talked throughout about the importance of participatory processes, we need to consider how to work when several decision-makers are working at different levels and have different needs, as well as some competing interests. The question then is what processes can be devised to find areas of agreement in order to move forward? There is no single answer, but what is clear is that the process itself matters. If the process is not managed by an authoritarian who chooses to have a few cronies on board and use force or violence to ensure enforcement, then leaders will need to use combinations of persuasion, negotiation, compromise, consensus-building—in short a great deal of discussion. The point is to reach an arena of shared perspectives.

Throughout the implementation of a major policy change, the question is how to bring on board all the other needed people in the puzzle—local councilors, competing political parties, the variety of NGOs, central government decision-makers, financial investors, local businesses—the list goes on. Yes, holding a workshop could help. But first, it is most useful to do at least a preliminary stakeholder assessment. Stakeholder assessments— closely akin to political mapping—are useful in order to depict the range of agencies and agents that have an interest in a policy change, or policy, program, or project implementation.

Stakeholder Assessments

It is not entirely clear how stakeholder assessments first came into development management practice. Ben Crosby and Marc Lindenberg talked about political mapping more than two decades ago. The approach they devised in the course of their work in Latin America was subsequently adopted for use in a large and long running successful project—the Implementing Policy Change Project (IPC)—funded by USAID (Lindenberg and Crosby, 1981; Crosby, 1992). Ben Crosby refined and utilized this technique for more than a decade with many useful results during his work on IPC. Often project leaders—or, at higher levels, those responsible for policy reform in central government ministries—had altogether less information than they needed about the range of stakeholders. What is needed is information not only about stakeholders' interest in a project or policy, but also about their capability to mobilize either in support or opposition to policy reform going forward.

The point of a stakeholder assessment is to depict in a summary manner four characteristics of stakeholders: the group's interest in the issue, its resources, its resource mobilization capacity, and its position on the issue (in support, or opposed). If one were to do a preliminary stakeholder assessment of the range of agents and agencies with an interest in this project, it might include village associations, community level NGOs, international NGOs, village and district councils—and councilors—as well as Ministry officials and donors. See, for example, Table 5.2 below, to see what a partial stakeholder assessment for such a project might look like.

The point of the stakeholder assessment is to provide the leaders who are trying to move the project or a policy reform forward with more insight into their support, or lack of support, as they go forward. Often leaders will claim that they already know about their support in their operational context. But when systematic stakeholder assessments based upon careful analysis, interviewing, and information checking are presented to clients, they find they had much to learn about their stakeholders. In the greatly abbreviated stakeholder assessment in Table 5.2, for example, it is apparent that feelings run high in favor and in opposition to community schools. Leaders may often hear from supporters who, like cheerleaders, encourage the program's leadership to carry on. But those opposed—like the Northern Districts' Teachers' Association with resources at its disposal and willingness to deploy them—are positioned to undermine the program. This is especially true if it teams up with those officials within the Ministry of Education that favor the more formal public system over the Community Schools movement.

Basically, achieving policy change—especially in countries with parties, parliaments, and local councils, an active press, etc.—means having to achieve agreement among leaders and decision-makers and public opinion that the change is acceptable. Getting this requires a great deal of listening, bargaining, discussion, adaptation, and compromise. In essence, part of what is going on during these processes is the airing of competing perspectives, surfacing of new or different information. The number, range, and proclivities of those with a stake in the outcome is going to vary significantly by the nature of the change proposed, its implications, and its trade-offs.

One can do a stakeholder assessment by hosting and facilitating a workshop in which one gathers some of the relevant data. Or one can gather data through interviews, observation, and document searches. Or one can do a preliminary stakeholder assessment through the latter approaches and then hold a stakeholder assessment workshop in which many of these agencies and groups are represented and revise and complete the assessment in light of additional information gathered or observed at the workshop itself. Usually, however, when holding a stakeholder assessment workshop, the prime objective is for stakeholders to assess a policy, program, or project. This makes assessing the stakeholders while they are assessing a program problematical. One needs to be clear about which

Table 5.2
A Sample—and Partial—Stakeholder Assessment

Group	Group's Interest in Issue	Resources	Resource Mobilization Capacity	Position on Policy, Program, or Project
District Council in Northern Region of the Country	Education and its delivery is a keen interest of the District Council	This District Council is nearly bankrupt due to civil unrest; major resources are its considerable social and political capital	Relatively able to mobilize its political capital	Originally opposed, the majority of the DC are now marginally in favor
Northern Church Women's League	Several key leaders in this Women's League helped organize the Community School Movement (CSM)	Meager financial resources; substantial grassroots credibility	Good capability to mobilize their supporters; organizational skills.	Strongly in favor
Northern Teachers Association	Interest in maintaining their teachers' certification	Some financial resources from dues	Both willing and able to marshal resources	Strongly opposed to community schools as teachers in the community schools need not be certified
Ministry of Education (MOE)—Community Affairs (CA) Section	Community Affairs section of ministry is keenly interested; rest of MOE is not.	CA section has no financial resources and little central political support within MOE	Little capacity to mobilize as internal politics is tying up all energies	Strongly in favor of community school movement in theory

objective is paramount—and also very sensitive to the fact that support, or lack of support, for a program or policy evolves and changes through any shared experience, including the workshop process itself. Workshops are powerful processes, especially when well facilitated. They engage people and lead to new insights and thus to new positions.

PARTICIPATORY RURAL APPRAISAL

Let us look at some of the components of a participatory process usually called Participatory Rural Appraisal (PRA). Participatory Rural Appraisal is really a large basket of different techniques for engaging the active involvement of people often ignored in project design, monitoring, and evaluation. While we cannot aspire to a complete review of the many techniques, a few can be considered. Most often PRA is conducted through workshops. These workshops are organized and facilitated with the goal of engaging local people in the appraisal of their own situation. The point is to listen to what they, themselves, can do toward resolving parts of the problem they have identified. Robert Chambers, Edward Jackson, Yusuf Kassam, Fran and David Korten, and Norman Uphoff have done much of the pioneering work in PRA. Fortunately, not only have they experimented with various ways of engaging people so that their voices and views are given primacy, but they have also documented many of these experiences so that others of us can learn from them (F. Korten, 1982; D. Korten, 1982; Uphoff, 1985; Chambers, 1994a; 1994b; 1997; Jackson and Kassam, 1998;).

PRA techniques are used to facilitate people telling their own views, experiences, and insights into what can or should be done to improve their well-being. This is done through all sorts of mapping and counting and recording exercises. In the project design stage, PRA can be effective in identifying and ranking problems, defining existing assets, and mapping out current and envisioned realities. Often participatory facilitators start with a simple walk around the village during which people point out and discuss their lives and livelihoods. During mapping, villagers use symbols to indicate water sources, housing patterns, roads, animal life and shelter, fields and crops, and storage arrangements in their map. Below we have two different photographs of communities engaged in PRA processes.

Below in Figure 5.2 we can see a typical kind of map that might have been drawn by villagers working toward selecting a location of a community school between two small villages.

Following the mapping are other group exercises, such as a problem identification diagram around an issue of their choosing. In the community school case, distance to the school was one such problem. It is linked to several other problems because that is their reality as they see it. Figure 5.3 is such a diagram.

And next they might well do a matrix (Figure 5.4) capturing the impact of the distance issue for different members of the community—along with their estimation of what they might do themselves and for what they might need external assistance. Later they could as readily be ranking their assets in order to begin the process of addressing their needs. This data not only is helpful for the community but also can be centrally important in project design and later in project monitoring.

The large body of experimentation and learning that has come out of the PRA movement is making a significant difference in communities in Asia, Africa, and Latin America. In short, participatory processes are not only important for reducing poverty but for the sustainability of that

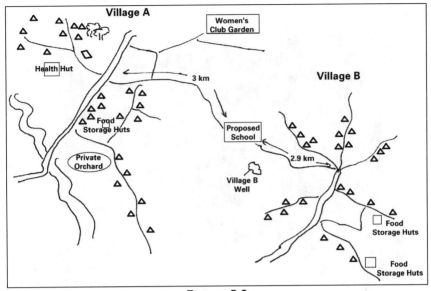

Figure 5.2
Village PRA Map: Community School Preferred Location

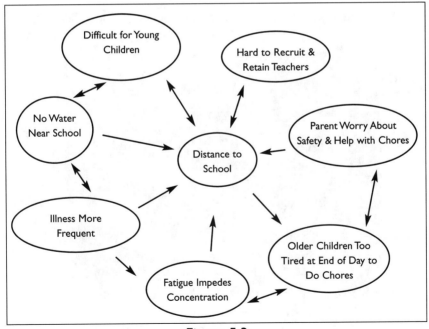

Figure 5.3
Participatory Problem Diagram

Photograph 5.1
A Ugandan Community Engaged in Problem Identification

Photograph 5.2
An Ecuadorian Community Engaged in Participatory
Evaluation of a Project

Family Members Impacted				Likelihood* We Can Solve Problem Ourselves	Chance We Can Get Outside Help
Problem ❧	Young Children	Older Children	Parents		
Distance To School	❧❧❧❧❧❧❧❧ ❧❧❧❧❧❧❧ ❧❧❧❧❧❧❧	❧ ❧ ❧ ❧ ❧ ❧	❧❧ ❧❧ ❧ ❧ ❧ ❧	❧❧❧ ❧ ❧ ❧ ❧❧❧ ❧	❧ ❧ ❧ ❧ ❧
Water Source Near School	❧❧❧ ❧❧❧❧❧ ❧❧❧❧❧❧❧	❧❧❧ ❧ ❧ ❧❧ ❧❧	❧❧❧❧ ❧ ❧ ❧	❧❧ ❧❧ ❧ ❧	❧ ❧ ❧ ❧ ❧ ❧
Supplies Chalk Boards Chalk	❧ ❧ ❧ ❧ ❧ ❧ ❧ ❧	❧❧❧❧❧❧❧❧ ❧❧❧❧❧❧❧❧ ❧❧❧❧❧❧ ❧❧❧❧❧❧	❧ ❧❧ ❧ ❧❧ ❧	❧ ❧ ❧ ❧ ❧ ❧ ❧ ❧	❧ ❧ ❧❧ ❧ ❧ ❧ ❧❧ ❧❧ ❧ ❧

❧ Beans used as counters.
* You may use different kinds of beans to reflect different estimations of community's ability to solve the problem themselves.

Figure 5.4
PRA Matrix for Problem Intensity and Possible Approaches

reduction as they enhance civic participation and people's awareness of their own problem solving capacities.

STRATEGIC PLANNING

As there was a participatory process that drove the identification and design of this project, there is local commitment that helps it move along towards implementation. Isn't that enough? No. Having a participatory process during the identification and design of a program or a project helps significantly because there are more people motivated to carry it along and more willingness to cooperate and negotiate the hard choices in implementation. But it does not solve all the aspects of implementation. Strategic planning is also going to be essential—not just at the beginning but at various times in the process. External events, governmental crises, international changes—all sorts of things can lead to a need for a major rethinking of where one is going, why, and also whether shifts, or major changes, are needed.

Strategic planning can be defined in multiple ways. One operational definition might be the process of discerning where one is heading given current data, scanning external and internal environments for opportunities, as well as threats, and setting goals and action steps for an improved future. When the leadership in an organization, sector, or project attempts this process, a strategic planning workshop is very helpful. A strategic plan helps to clarify goals and objectives and the means to reach them. Leaders organizing such a workshop need to clarify among themselves just what they need to have in hand at the end of the process—and that in turn helps to clarify who must be present and what information participants need to have beforehand.

Yet the critical part of this strategic planning workshop is the facilitation—what questions or issues are put up to breakout groups in what order and how they are presented. Working through a series of questions posed to all participants is one effective way to ensure that a variety of perspectives can be voiced. Conducting in-depth interviews with selected future participants before the workshop can help in the process of formulating questions. The questions should be sequenced so as to promote building upon shared views and moving discussion along toward consensus.

One of the most skillful interactive facilitators used interactive Power-Point throughout—catching views as they emerged and playing them back to the collected participants.[3] This has several advantages: it is a visual demonstration that the participants are working toward some shared views; it indicates that participants are being taken seriously; and overcomes the sense that everyone is just "whistling in the wind." This can be more effective than the older approach of catching ideas on a flipchart. Moreover, because of the versatility provided by the electronic form, a slide pack is available to all participants following the workshop so that they have the product of their labors in hand.

Senior leaders, as well as villagers need to know that their views—and time invested—are given weight and are being incorporated into the final product. Seeing their views on screen also affords them the chance to say— "Well, what I really mean is...." This helps to avert the serious threat that participants can walk away at the close of the workshop believing they are on the same page when they are not—as we had flagged as a danger above in Table 5.1. While this particular technique is limited to places with reliable electricity, elements from it can be used with other formats as well. Facilitators should always aim to capture participants' input visually in as accurate a form as possible. One technique for doing this is to have participants write their ideas out themselves. A method for doing this is described in the consensus workshop method below.

CONSENSUS WORKSHOP METHOD

The Consensus Workshop Method, developed by the Institute of Cultural Affairs (ICA), is highly flexible and adaptable to innumerable situations and applications.[4] It enables a group to reach a consensus quickly. And, because everyone in the group participates in the decisions reached in the workshop, they all see it as theirs and share ownership of it. This then makes it more likely that they will actually implement the agreed-upon decisions and plans. Such a workshop can be used to help a group make a decision, solve a problem, or create a plan. It is particularly appropriate in situations requiring imaginative and creative solutions, multidisciplinary team commitment, and urgent undertaking to design an action plan. The process can generate inventiveness and new dynamism in a short amount of time, infuse a group with a sense of accountability, catalyze integrated judgment (rational and intuitive), and fashion practical team agreement.

To be effective, the workshop should have one clear focus question that the group aims to answer. Generally the answer to the question entails five to seven elements; for example, the five to seven project priorities for a community or key outcomes from a project. In addition to a focus question, the workshop should have two stated objectives: a rational objective and an experiential objective. The rational objective is the result or product that you want to end the workshop with. It could be an action plan, a priority list of recommendations, etc. The experiential objective is the mood or emotional tone of the group that you hope will be occasioned in the workshop. Although this cannot be controlled, as a facilitator it is possible to influence it. It could be the sense of becoming a team or a buy-in to the next step of a change process.

The workshop has five basic steps: (1) opening that sets the context and defines the intent and parameters of the workshop; (2) brainstorming of data and ideas; (3) organizing or grouping of data into categories based on similarity of content; (4) naming or titling the categories; and (5) closing reflection that evaluates the work and its implications. The brainstorming process includes a combination of individual, small group, and full group work. The individual, silent brainstorming allows everyone in the room to generate ideas of their own. Working in small groups of two to three then gives everyone an opportunity to share their ideas. The small groups are charged with writing up on note cards the ten to fifteen ideas they agree on as a small group. This begins to build consensus and allows each team to write its ideas in its own words (using large cards and markers to get one idea per card). The cards from the small teams are then posted on the wall, taking a few from each team in waves, and then the full group is asked to suggest ways to group the cards. What emerges is five to nine groups of common themes from what can be 50–70 cards of distinct brainstormed ideas.

The grouping step shifts attention from individual reflection and team conversation to a conversation with the whole group. The purpose of this step is to order the chaos of the multiple responses generated in each team by giving form to new relationships. This is followed by the naming process, which is the task of discerning consensus. This step is the heart of the matter. Generally half of the workshop time will be spent in this step because it is only after the group sees all the options organized into a number of focused areas that it is ready to make decisions. The naming process is sometimes an "a ha!" experience as the group begins to see new ways to approach old problems. Or the group members may articulate new approaches on how they might act in the future in light of what they have learned from each other. The consensus that begins to emerge helps to focus the diverse perspectives so that the group feels empowered to move ahead.

CONSENSUS BUILDING THROUGH AN AIC PROCESS

Another specific type of workshop used in building consensus is the AIC, or Appreciate, Influence, and Control workshop. AIC workshops are grounded in a different conceptual foundation, one that was first developed by William Smith, a frequent consultant for the World Bank, and Turid Sato, a Bank staff member, in the 1980s. Through the AIC process, the subtleties and nuances of appreciating, influencing, and controlling are unpacked by participants iteratively throughout the workshop.

Behavioral psychology is behind most of the AIC material and informs the manner in which the workshop is conducted. Essentially one learns through the early initial exercises in which key decision-makers are asked to map out what areas they "control" in the problem under consideration. What emerges is just how little actual control any single actor has. This rather painful discovery has to be clear—and requires real skill on the part of the facilitator. Generally the timing is managed so that this awareness mounts toward the close of the first day. Then, the following day, what the participants can influence (in contrast to "control") is mapped out. By then, the members of the group are becoming more aware of how they need to work a little more together, or even collaboratively. Finally, the last exercises are about what they need "to appreciate" in the environment of their work—with emphasis on how reaching out to those other agencies and actors that should be appreciated leads to real possibilities for making change happen. That shift in view then fuels a growing sense of the need for collaborative work. These mapping exercises help to make transparent the interdependency that underpins effectiveness in any complex undertaking.

One of the successes of the AIC workshop method was first demonstrated by the Sato-Smith team when they were working on a World Bank financed sector-wide reform of the Colombia power sector. Major senior leaders in the sector saw one another as competitors—hence they instinctively did not trust one another, let alone think of working together. Moreover, as powerful people in their own right, they were not accustomed to thinking about their powerlessness in acting alone. But through the AIC workshops, they came to see the need for reform, and their complementary roles in that process, which greatly eased the implementation of the sector reform program, allowing them to get results.

This workshop type, however, requires exceptional skill in facilitation. Obviously, leading a process in which senior leaders come to terms with their limitations risks failure. Yet, well done, it can create subsequently a sense of shared purpose that can infuse considerable energy and commitment into implementation. The process of mapping out the different agents for any group that might be influenced, or should be appreciated even if they cannot be influenced, broadens participants' visions of what might be done. At its best, this can lead to strategic thinking, or, at least, tactical brainstorming. But the critical parts come in navigating through a tough first day in which egos are bruised and powerlessness is sensed, so that real movement toward collaboration can win out in subsequent days. Done well, this is a very powerful workshop technique. And it can be very empowering.

POLICY, PROGRAM, AND PROJECT MONITORING

Monitoring is one of the least discussed, yet potentially the most effective, means of enhancing implementation. First of all, it is through monitoring that problems can be caught and managed before they grow. Without program-wide monitoring, managers often see only the parts of the puzzle on which they are working—the "big picture" is seen only at the board room level, if there. (The demise of Enron and WorldCom brought home to millions in the United States the devastating consequences of inadequate auditing of financial records and inept monitoring.)

Monitoring and troubleshooting problems that crop up during implementation is one of the major requirements for ensuring results. Effective monitoring requires a management information system to capture both quantitative data—often already collected—and qualitative data—knowing how well or poorly performance is perceived by those impacted. Monitoring the quality of actual performance in the world of poverty reduction programs, projects, and policies is fraught with challenges. This is, however, where PRA workshops come back into our discussion—for these are pivotal in measuring impact by engaging in the monitoring process those for whom the project was intended.

If project evaluation is needed, PRA techniques can include using counters (stones or beans) and asking the participants, working in groups, to evaluate different aspects of a project. Those witnessing or facilitating these processes often report that the conversations among participants as they go through the exercise of deciding on quantities appropriate to reflect the value of an aspect of a project are also helpful in providing more information or insight into their qualitative data. (While we can consider much of PRA as providing qualitative data, some of this data can also be quantified and can be usefully depicted along with other, more traditional, quantitative data.)

Another technique of choice in participatory monitoring or evaluation is to use whatever measuring device is used locally—visiting the market can arm the evaluator with a culturally appropriate measuring device, prefer-ably one that is graduated. For example, in many Asian countries rice is measured in containers of four graduated sizes. Using these, the women in one project in Nepal could address several different aspects of their efforts in their local organization to manage changes. Each time they filled the dif-ferently sized containers in their self-assessment of what had worked well and what had not. Using differently sized containers affords the partici-pants a chance to indicate relative strengths.

WHAT'S SIMILAR, WHAT'S DIFFERENT IN NORTHERN INDUSTRIAL COUNTRIES?

Our focus in this chapter is on getting results and thus on implementation. Toward that end we have focused on a few of the processes—attention to stakeholders and the use of a variety of workshops—that have been proven to be effective in enhancing implementation. But we also want to remind you of the other theme that runs all through this book—the counterpart issues in northern industrial countries. How could poverty reduction policies get more, or better, results in, for example, the United States or the countries of the European Union?

There are some interesting ways in which lessons from the third world might be transferred to the first world. Participatory Rural Appraisal tech-niques are potentially as powerful in poor rural areas of the United States. One can well imagine that local community groups working from Appalachia to Baja California would do well to engage the rural poor in active dialogue about their needs, as well as their potentialities. It is the case, though, that federal programs and many state programs now have legal frameworks for public participation that have made what should be a lively exchange into a bureaucratic tangle. It is not that there should not be regulations—for the issue of who can speak for whom is challenging. But there are instances when the federal regulations inhibit more than they generate public engagement.

Church groups and local community organizations, as well as not-for-profit groups, can, and should, borrow from the experiences to date with PRA and utilize it in their work. It is more difficult in some of our cities to get the engagement and active participation that occurs in villages and towns in southern countries. There is more suspicion, more random vio-lence and criminality, which makes such work a bit more daunting. But it can be done. One successful experience has been that of the American Friends Service Committee's work in some inner city neighborhoods in Washington, D.C. Called the AFSC-DC project, this group of local residents working together focus on literacy, helping to increase the peace, and help-ing teenagers research and make a case for more attention to the poverty and environmental degradation in their neighborhoods—within the shadow of the Capitol.

In wealthier countries, pro-poor policies are often welfare policies for which poor people must apply and meet certain requirements. The Supplemental Food Program for Women, Infants and Children (WIC) or the Food Stamp program are programs that survived the welfare "reform" of the 1996 in the United States. These are prime examples of targeted assistance—and as such are highly vulnerable to cuts.

While the debates over targeting and its vulnerabilities continue, there are other modalities. One of the most significant poverty reduction programs in the United States is not a welfare program but part of the tax code: the Earned Income Tax Credit. However, it too relies upon individuals knowing their eligibility and how to apply for this benefit.

So targeting is vulnerable to cuts, and poverty projects are vulnerable to capture, and welfare programs can be hijacked by those who are not poor. These are the realities within which pro-poor work can and does get done. Arthur Okun in his classic, *Equity versus Equality*, told us about the likelihood of leaky buckets in any legislated welfare program. In part politics dictates that elected politicians are more likely to support programs benefiting many groups than ones benefiting one group—especially if that group has only a narrow, marginal political base. Politicians will always want to increase a program's political appeal by sharing some of the gains with groups that are less poor. If the pro-poor policies on the table are subsidies—as is often the case in education or health delivery programs—they are extremely vulnerable to cuts when austerity comes (Okun, 1975; Ravallion, 2002).

In the 1960s, the United States' "War on Poverty" was relatively short lived as a result of political pressures generated during implementation. When a careful exposition of that program is written, it will tell a more subtle and even convoluted story—for there were surprising successes along the way along with awful failures. Some failures were due to mismanagement. Others were due to a failure of political will. As John Gaventa points out, in some instances local participatory processes were seen as threatening by local elites (especially in Appalachia) (Gaventa, 1998). In other instances, as Pressman and Wildavsky documented in Oakland, California, local pressures exacerbated long-standing bureaucratic problems until implementation was hopelessly bogged down (Pressman and Wildavsky, 1973).

Reducing poverty in rich countries comes with its own challenges even where there is considerable capacity to deliver on policies. This is especially true for minorities subject to social exclusion who may also be concentrated in areas physically distant from assets that the majority enjoys.

While decentralization is often sought in order to strengthen local voices, it can, in some circumstances, actually add to the hurdles that the poor confront. This is equally true in either northern industrial countries or southern developing countries.

In Africa, for example, at the local level, village politics may be largely controlled by traditional elites long accustomed to their privileges. Mahmood Mamdani, writing about African polities, refers to decentralized despotism—especially the ruthless control by local chiefs over community affairs. The nature of face-to-face relationships in villages can mean that it is far more difficult to voice opinions or concerns that are at odds with dominant social or political belief and practice. Criticism or opposition, if voiced, can lead to being ostracized or further marginalized. For example, women in Afghanistan under the Taliban faced severe localized pressures for conformity with the strict Taliban strictures against their having any public voice.

The civil rights movement in the United States suffered from this problem of local elites controlling or subverting policy reform as well. The civil rights movement required firm federal level support—especially with regard to states that fought school integration, such as Mississippi, Georgia, and South Carolina. And, while the example we have returned to throughout this chapter is the Community Schools movement in an African country, there is much in that story that is comparable to the Charter School movement in the United States—families that are disadvantaged in the public system are struggling to find an alternative, one closer to meeting their needs and coterminous with their values.

CONCLUSION

Starting with what sounds like a straightforward policy change in an African country—a policy in support of the Community Schools movement—we moved on to cover a few, but key, parts in the "getting to results" puzzle. The point is that even seemingly straightforward policy changes require techniques for engaging people in the change process. Poverty reduction policies, programs, and projects are especially in need of such technical assistance. They are not self-implementing. Hence institutional assessments, stakeholder assessments, PRA workshops with their participatory processes for project design, implementation, and evaluation are essential. But so are other kinds of workshops—ones, for example, focusing on strategic planning, or strategic management. These are extremely useful techniques for building a firm foundation for implementing and monitoring policies, programs, and projects.

These are the processes and tools that help to achieve results by getting policies implemented, not just declared or legislated. While governance systems vary in the specific weights they attach to parts of that process, the underpinning determinant of success comes in devising a learning process about what works—and that in turn drives implementers back to engaging a wide and disparate audience so that they own the policy reform. Conceiving of these as parts of an ongoing learning process about effectiveness is a central part of the challenge for reducing poverty. Building up this technical core holds real potential for further development and for advancing institutional change—the very foundation for a less poor and more peaceful world.

NOTES

1. This case is constructed from several different country experiences and should not be attributed to any particular country. We opted for this approach because many different African countries are caught up in the various debates and issues related to their respective Community School movements. The point of the chapter is not to increase the reader's knowledge of the actual movements, but to consider what is essential for effective implementation of the generic issue of a pro-poor policy reform.

2. The Development Management Network has met each year since about 1973 to exchange views and insights derived from practice—often as consultants to major bilateral or international agencies. The meetings of the DVMN have been very useful for shared learning purposes. It meets in conjunction with the annual meetings of the American Society for Public Administration (ASPA), and is linked to the Section on International and Comparative Administration.

3. Marc Lindenberg used this PowerPoint technique to facilitate World Bank–UNDP meetings on evaluation at several sessions in Paris in 1999 and 2000. He also facilitated a series of highly interactive meetings Lindenberg and Bryant had jointly organized, financed, and prepared for the CEOs of major international relief and development NGOs (Oxfam, Save the Children, CARE, Médecins Sans Frontières, World Vision, Plan International, MercyCorps, International Rescue Committee, etc.) at Bellogio, Seattle, Oxford, and the Rockefeller estate, Pocantico, prior to his untimely death in May 2002. For more details of the results of those fertile and productive sessions, see Lindenberg and Bryant, 2001.

4. The Consensus Workshop Method as described here is a technique refined by partners at Millennia Consulting, a nonprofit and public sector consulting firm based in Chicago, Illinois. The method was developed by staff of the Institute of Cultural Affairs (ICA) initially for use in community development projects in the United States and globally, and adapted over the years to participatory group process in a wide range of settings. ICA continues to use and train others in the method, as part of their toolkit known as the Technology of Participation.

6

MEASURING RESULTS, LEARNING, AND BUILDING CAPACITY

"For all its simplicity, the concept of participatory evaluation contains a complex and wide-reaching promise for social justice."
—Jim Friedman, *Simplicities and Complexities of Participatory Evaluations*, 1998

INTRODUCTION

Few terms in the development field have generated so much heat, as well as light, as "results." In poverty reduction work at home or abroad, people want to know about results. While it is clear that results are wanted, it is by no means clear that anyone knows or agrees with what is meant by results. When the US Secretary of the Treasury visited Africa in 2002, he became aware of the water problem when villagers in Uganda pointed out their well to him. Few people in Africa have reliable access to water and wells are all too often merely holes in the ground. They often look like the one in the Photograph 6.1 below.

This well—while obviously inadequate—is not that different from millions like it in many African countries. But, new to Africa, the Secretary was stunned. He noted that here was something concrete the United States could do, and moreover that providing wells would show results. But in fact, most development professionals would say that building wells is not a result; it is only one step toward a result. Bceause the goal of a water project might be to increase access to water, just building wells is in reality an output, not a result. If wells run dry, or, worse, develop arsenic (as has tragically happened in millions of wells built in Bangladesh), the presence of the

Photograph 6.1
A Village Well in Uganda

wells themselves is neutral or negative. Hence this business of measuring results means much more than counting numbers of wells built.

Developing performance indicators, which facilitate problem solving and support project monitoring, help us to get at real results. While the physical sciences and economics have used indicators for decades, other social sciences were relatively late in adopting them. Serious work in this area, started in the early 1960s at places such as the Yale Political Data Center, paved the way forward. Multilateral development organizations picked up on their potential quickly—and before long several such organizations were collecting and publishing data sets: for example, the World Bank's World Development Report, UNICEF's State of the World's Children, and UNDP's Human Development Report. In many instances indicators have been combined to create development indexes.

Indicators are now so commonly used—and abused—that they have become a major part of efforts aimed at holding decision-makers accountable in both public and private sector work. In this chapter, we explore the use of indicators, starting with their use on a global scale with the Millennium Development Goals. Because indicators are essentially a tool for learning, and learning in turn is at the core of capacity building, we include as well a discussion of learning processes, accountability, and the complexities of building and measuring capacity.

MILLENNIUM DEVELOPMENT GOALS

In September 2000, 189 countries met at a summit in New York and adopted eight central goals they termed the Millennium Development Goals (MDGs). Among the accomplishments of the MDGs is that they were adopted at all. World leaders signed on to ambitious goals, pledging by 2015 to: eradicate extreme poverty and hunger; achieve universal primary education; promote gender equality; reduce child mortality; improve maternal health; combat HIV/AIDS, malaria, and other diseases; ensure environmental sustainability; and build a global partnership for development. Our colleague, Jeffrey Sachs, working for Secretary General Kofi Annan, has marshalled support for these goals in his book, *The End of Poverty: Economic Possibilities for Our Time* (Sachs, 2005).

While these development goals sound all too familiar, what set this agreement apart, and has given it impetus around the world, is that the heads of state went on to set up numerical and time-bound targets that are to be measured by specified performance indicators. In short, the governments committed to measuring the results of the Millennium Development process.

The UN Millennium Declaration, agreed to by 189 governments, states that they "will spare no effort to free our fellow men, women, and children from the abject and dehumanizing conditions of extreme poverty, to which more than a billion are currently subjected." The poverty goal's very ambitiousness makes many shake their head in disbelief. The goal is clarified by and becomes measurable as a result of its specific targets: between 1990 and 2015, to halve the proportion of people whose income is less than $1 a day and to halve the proportion of people who suffer from hunger. The

World Bank's statement of the target (which hangs on a banner in the atrium of its main building) provides additional specificity by noting that halving the proportion of people living on less than $1 a day means a reduction from 29% of all people living in low and middle income countries to 14.5%. Note that the target excludes countries not in the World Bank's mandate.

Now, if, as we argued earlier, people living on less than $10 a day (in, for example, Canada, the United States, England, or Italy) are experiencing extreme poverty or hunger, should they not be of concern as well? Living on less than $10 a day means homelessness in many US cities. Arguably, the lives of those living on less than $10 a day suffer as much from ill-being as those living on a $1 a day in, for example, Malawi, Chad, or Mozambique. Why should their poverty be overlooked by the MDGs? The answer of course is that the mandates of all of the specialized agencies of the UN system, including UNDP and the World Bank, are focused on low and middle income countries. The idea of holding wealthy countries accountable for poverty reduction in their own countries was never on the table at the Millennium Summit.

That said, the Millennium Development Goals are a breakthrough in terms of global attention to global problems—with poverty at the top of that list. The extent to which the goals are met will determine their longer term impact. That the MDGs actually specify indicators to monitor and measure progress is a step forward and represents a new role for the UN. As shown in Table 6.1, the goals are broken down into targets, and then again into measurable indicators.

Once the commitment to the MDGs was made, countries had to develop national strategies for addressing the challenges of meeting the goals. This process has drawn attention to the need for additional financing of official development assistance in order to fund the activities needed to meet the goals, resulting in a major summit in Monterrey, Mexico, in 2001 to identify pledges of support from donor countries. In fact, there is also an eighth goal in the MDGs, not featured in our Table 6.1 as it is not as closely focused on indicators. The eighth goal speaks of the need to develop a global partnership for development. One aspect of this multifaceted goal calls for donors to increase their levels of official development assistance. The pressure from those promoting this goal led in turn to President George W. Bush announcing that he would ask Congress for an increase of $5 billion for US development assistance, to be managed by the newly created Millennium Challenge Corporation. But, as often happens, the appropriations process resulted in a budget for the Millennium Challenge Corporation containing only a fraction of this amount.

The approach of President Bush in supporting the MDGs highlights another complexity in measuring effectiveness. He declared that countries

Table 6.1
Millennium Development Goals (MDGs)

Goal 1: Eradicating extreme poverty and hunger	Indicators
Target 1: Halve the proportion of people whose income is less than one dollar a day between 1990–2015 Target 2: Halve the proportion of people who suffer from hunger between 1990–2015	1. Proportion of population below $1 per day (PPP-values) 2. Poverty gap ratio [incidence x depth of poverty] 3. Share of poorest quintile in national consumption 4. Prevalence of underweight children (under five years of age) 5. Proportion of population below minimum level of dietary energy consumption

Goal 2: Achieve universal primary education	Indicators
Target 3: Ensure that by 2015, boys and girls alike will be able to complete a full course of primary schooling	6. Net enrollment ratio in primary education 7. Proportion of pupils starting grade 1 who reach grade 5 8. Literacy rate of 15–24 year olds

Goal 3: Promote gender equality and empower women	Indicators
Target 4: Eliminate gender disparity in primary and secondary education by 2015	9. Ratio of girls to boys in primary, secondary, and tertiary education 10. Ratio of literate females to males of 15–24 year olds 11. Share of women in wage employment in the nonagricultural sector 12. Proportion of seats held by women in national parliament

Goal 4: Reduce child mortality	Indicators
Target 5: Reduce by two-thirds the under-five mortality ratio between 1990–2015	13. Under-five mortality rate 14. Infant mortality rate 15. Proportion of 1 year old children immunized against measles

Goal 5: Improve maternal health	Indicators
Target 6: Reduce by three-quarters the maternal mortality ratio between 1990–2015	16. Maternal mortality ratio 17. Proportion of births attended by skilled health personnel

Goal 6: Combat HIV/AIDS, malaria and other diseases	Indicators
Target 7: Have halted by 2015 and begin to reverse the spread of HIV/AIDS Target 8: Have halted by 2015 and begin to reverse the incidence of malaria and other major diseases	18. HIV prevalence among 15–24 year old pregnant women 19. Contraceptive prevalence rate 20. Number of children orphaned by HIV/AIDS 21. Prevalence and death rates associated with malaria 22. Proportion of population in malaria risk areas using effective malaria prevention and treatment measures 23. Prevalence and death rates associated with tuberculosis 24. Proportion of TB cases detected and cured under DOTS (Directly Observed Treatment Short Course)

would be selected carefully for eligibility of funding under the Challenge Account, in order to maximize results obtained from the assistance. Countries will be selected for assistance according to criteria such as their having the "right" policy environment, open competitive elections, and some modicum of human rights. The argument for such selectivity is that these countries are better able to manage development assistance and achieve results. But this approach refueled arguments that have been at issue before in poverty reduction work. As we noted in Chapter 4, poverty reduction projects can be effective in hostile political environments, and may also have the positive externality of building capacity for grassroots collective action that leads over time to democratic reform. Eligibility requirements imply working with narrowly defined "winners" or governments that may be more politically adept at manipulating their political friendships. How fair is it to deny assistance to poor people who, by accident of birth, happen to be in the wrong countries at the wrong time?

The United Nations and the signatory governments around the globe are now gathering data to track and monitor progress on the implementation of the MDGs. Summary tables are available on the Web on the array of indicators listed in Table 6.1 above.[1] Among the many advantages of this global use of indicators is that it elicits more attention both from national and local governments and civil society on the progress, or lack thereof, in reducing poverty.

Let us now turn to looking at indicators and how they measure performance. Indicators are at the heart of many difficulties in measuring results and in the use, as well as abuse of results-oriented development.

PERFORMANCE INDICATORS: MEASURING INPUTS, OUTCOMES, AND RESULTS

Indicators are tools for measuring or predicting what has happened, or might happen, for any particular action or intervention. Checking the gas meter on the dashboard, using a thermometer when nursing a feverish child, or checking the interest rate when buying a mortgage are all common uses of indicators. They provide information about a problem and can be used to monitor whether an action taken has had intended results. But these examples are relatively linear and the singularity of actor and intervention makes the use of indicators straightforward. Poverty reduction projects, on the other hand, come with multiple interventions and lots of intervening variables.

In development work today, designs are expected to include indicators by which the project or program is to be monitored. Hence there are indicators measuring the delivery and effect of inputs, intervening steps or activities, outputs and immediate outcomes from that preceding work, and finally long term results. While there is variability in selection of terms with some practitioners talking about outcomes rather than results, the goal is the same—to build into project design a system of indicators in order to focus on implementation, monitor performance, and ultimately to know more about the impact of the project in the final analysis.

The current use of indicators is built upon several different bodies of thought and practice that coalesced in the late 1970s and 1980s. Mosse and Sontheimer point, for example, to results-oriented management, scientific method, systems analysis, and contract law (with its focus on deliverables in contracts) as the theories underlying the use of indicators (Mosse and Sontheimer, 1996). Their use in development projects was moved along significantly by the invention of the Logical Framework for Project Analysis, devised by consultants working on projects financed by official development assistance. The Log Frame, as it came to be called, provides a method for organizing the objectives, activities, inputs, outputs, outcomes, and impacts of a project. Once laid out, it allows the project team to devise indicators for every activity and ensure that every activity is directly related to a project objective. As in all such things, the Log Frame has had strong critics, as well as devoted followers. We are basically neutral in those competing views, but do point out that, as with any tool, it is only as effective as the quality of the processes used in implementing it. Alan Fowler, for example, reminds us that the linear thinking exemplified in the logical framework model imposes a presumed certainty that is not the reality at the village level (Fowler, 1996). Thus the efforts of donors to lay out the indicators and performance goals from the onset of a project may force upon a project a narrow window through which the work is viewed. The Log Frame can become a more dynamic tool when indicators are updated during implementation through a participatory process involving those engaged in, or affected by, a project.

The Log Frame became widely used and even required by several institutions, but the way in which it was applied varied widely among agencies and among staff. It warrants mention here precisely because its use spread across the globe and is still prominent. Official development agencies from Germany (where it became known as the ZOPP) to Japan came to use this planning device. Until recently, it was required in all USAID projects. It continues to be required by the IDB, and by several bilateral assistance agencies in Europe. The World Bank drew heavily upon it, especially following the Wapenhans report in 1993, which called for more attention to implementation and to strengthening its measurement.

While official development agencies increased attention to results in the 1990s, in part due to external pressure from NGOs, those same NGOs came under criticism for having little to show for their efforts and expenditures.[2] In the late 1980s, many NGOs had less than adequate evaluation capacity. This remains a challenge, but dramatic improvements have been made, in particular among large international NGOs, many of whom are now doing noteworthy work on measuring results and using indicators. They are also writing about their approaches and sharing their learning readily. For example, Chris Roche, a senior staff member in Oxfam Great Britain, has written a useful text entitled *Impact Assessment for Development Agencies*. He defines impact assessment as "the systematic analysis of the lasting or significant changes...in people's lives brought about by a given action or series of actions" (Roche, 1999, p. 21).

In analyzing impact (or long term results) of, for example, a legal rights program, Oxfam staff looked at whether an output such as participants' increased awareness of rights led to the desired outcome of people actually using the legal system, and if so, how this had led to improvements in their quality of life. Later Roche adds, however, that the distinction between outputs and impact, although useful, can be very blurred. He notes that distinguishing between outputs and impact "can ignore the fact that a person who is now sufficiently aware and confident to use the legal system may consider this a significant change in his or her life, even if it does not immediately lead to a positive legal result or demonstrable change in their quality of life" (Roche, 1999, p. 23). Similarly, training projects have sometimes been found to have minimal impact in terms of increased jobs and income for participants, but the output of increased skills and knowledge could have other significant impacts on participants' lives or lead to greater employment options in the longer term (an impact not yet measurable).

Developing indicators of results requires a clear focus on what one plans to achieve. That in turn means thinking through what can be achieved, the requisites that need to be in place, and asking, "how will we know when we get there?" Indicators need to be measurable and as objective as possible. But there are always judgments to be made. The larger the concept embedded in the project's goals, the more daunting the process of measuring it. Moreover, getting agreement among all those central to either collecting the data or using it requires careful attention.

It is important to distinguish between types of indicators, which can be differentiated along a continuum, as noted in Table 6.2. Note that the project goal is disaggregated into several objectives. Achieving these objectives requires a variety of inputs to produce activities that are intended to produce the desired results. In order to assess a project's effectiveness, one looks at indicators at various levels. *Input indicators* measure the quantity and sometimes the quality of resources, including financial, human, and physical resources (e.g., funding, consultants and staff, equipment and materials). *Output indicators* look at the goods or services provided with those inputs (e.g., community meetings held, people vaccinated, participants trained, etc.). *Outcome indicators* refer to the immediate results of a project, as compared to specific objectives. *Impact or result indicators* look at the

Table 6.2
Impact Chain and Continuum of Indicators

Inputs
Resources and activities used to actualize the project

Outputs
Products or processes or services produced with inputs

Outcomes
Immediate or short term results generated by project outputs
(compare with project's specific objectives)

Impact
Sustained or longer term change as a result of the project
(compare with project's overall goal/development objective)

extent to which the overall project goal is achieved.

An assessment of input and output indicators alone will demonstrate whether a project has carried out its intended activities but will not tell you whether or not the implementation of these activities succeeded in meeting specific objectives and project goals. For this we must look at the outcome and impact indicators. Although sometimes used interchangeably, outcome and impact are distinguished in that impact is generally longer term and farther reaching than outcome. For example, in a training project, an outcome indicator could be job placement whereas impact would be increased income and improved livelihood that resulted from job placement. Furthermore, impact assessments look at the question of whether or not these changes would have been achieved without the intervention of the project. This generally requires the study of a control group, as well as project participants.

While doing the work to get the indicators right from the beginning of a project is essential to enable monitoring and ensure that the project design is appropriate to meet the objectives, projects must maintain flexibility to adapt to changing realities. In some instances the external environment or the learning that occurs during the project requires that objectives or activities be reassessed. When this occurs, indicators must be adapted accordingly. One area of work where this flexibility is crucial is emergency relief. In complex emergencies, the measurement of the impact on project beneficiaries' livelihoods and welfare often calls for the continuous integration of new impact indicators during the project implementation period. In these contexts, tracking of impact indicators is important, as is careful attention to differentiated impacts on specific groups, particularly related to gender, minority status, and age. Specific indicators need to be developed for each particular context, but four areas of change that should be evaluated in every emergency situation emerged from an Oxfam study of impact assessments in emergencies: mortality and morbidity rates, coverage and differential impact, protection and security, and sustainability or connectedness with longer term development issues (Roche, 1999, pp. 184–185).

HOW IS "CAPACITY" MEASURED?

The complexity of measuring effectiveness appropriately can be illustrated through the case of capacity building projects. Endless numbers of projects are called "capacity building," but sadly many projects use that label without much to show for the investment. Building capacity is difficult and often elusive. Measuring success in this area is a thorny task.

An important starting point in assessing capacity building projects is distinguishing between personal capacity and organizational capacity, which are quite different both in level and scope. Table 6.3 highlights some of the key elements of each that can be strengthened through project work. These elements can build off each other but it is important to distinguish between the two for designing projects and measuring impact. For example, an organizational goal could be improvement of the learning process across administrative boundaries, while a goal for personnel would be to enhance the ability of staff members to learn, recognize, and correct errors.

Capacity building projects often have as outputs activities such as frequency and use made of training, establishing merit criteria for promotions, incentive programs, enhanced technology, better equipment used effectively, management information systems, and use of better information. Creative capacity building activities can include staff exchanges across borders or between public and private sector entities; establishing professional associations for standards of performance; building learning networks among staff who would otherwise be relatively isolated in their work; and experiential learning by engaging staff in programs using new techniques. Organizations can also gain capacities

Table 6.3
Elements of Human Capacity and of Organizational Capacity

ELEMENTS OF HUMAN CAPACITY
• Ability to learn, recognize, and correct errors
• Adaptability in changing contexts
• Problem-solving skills and behaviors
• Team work or collective action capabilities

ELEMENTS OF ORGANIZATIONAL CAPACITY
• Learning processes across administrative boundaries
• Ability to recognize, acknowledge, and correct errors
• Motivated staff with performance goals
• Budgets and records for financial accountability
• Products and policies of organization are valued

through structural changes or legislative actions to update mandates, add enforcement, or shift their arenas of activity. Just as private sector mergers can add capacity, so public sector mergers or restructuring can sometimes add capacity to agencies or organizations.

When turning to assess the impact of strengthened capacity, however, one has to look at how peer agencies view the capacities of the agency, whether and how beneficiaries indicate they have experienced improved service delivery from the agency, and broader public perceptions of improved service. If evaluating a capacity building project focused on an environmental agency, one could, when assessing impact, interview the users and enforcers of, for example, environmental assessments issued by the agency to discern how seriously those assessments were taken by peers, or by lawyers involved in enforcement of environmental assessments. Court documents, as well as other public sources reveal much about the effectiveness of environmental assessments.

All the way through project design there is the question, if that, then what? If X is the objective, then what, Y, is to be done? If Y is done, what will indicate that there were results? Devising result or impact indicators requires asking that question of every major input and output of a project. Then, the next step is to look at the objectives, and ask how one can know whether those objectives have been achieved and had an impact on the core goal of the project.

We struggled with this, for example, while working on a project that aimed at strengthening the capacity of state level environmental agencies in Brazil's Amazonian states. The severe poverty in this region means any efforts at environmental protection are under real stress as very poor people feel forced to mine natural resources to stay alive. But if they are to have a future, environmental protection is essential. In devising impact indicators, we had to ask what could one reasonably expect to see happen differently if state level environmental agencies did develop more capacity? Reduced illegal logging? More enforcement of environmental regulations? More local community support for environmental enforcement? The problem, of course, with impact indicators is that there are lots of other intervening variables that can undermine the achievement of results.

Staff charged with project responsibilities are wary of indicators that might be used to accuse them of failure when, in fact, there are political or other external factors that may undermine what the agency is trying to achieve. Adding to the challenge in this case were the local level political forces that had many Brazilian state political leaders beholden to those profiting from extractive enterprises without regard to their environmental damage—a problem not unique to Brazil.

So how does one devise result or impact indicators? It is clearly too sweeping to say that strengthening state level environmental agencies would mean that air, water, and forest environments would be less depleted. Unpacking impact measurements of capacity requires thinking in more detail about what is wanted from the agencies whose capacity will be strengthened. For example, if our concern with increasing capacity is related to the agency's impact on the policy context, how would we know when an environmental agency has more clout? One way would be to determine through focus groups and in-depth interviews of all the peer agencies upstream and downstream from an agency's work whether they have found the work of agency X more or less useful. Questions to get at this answer could include: have they taken its reports and products more seriously or have they seen that its environmental impact assessments command more respect? A sample of some plausible indicators for this project are presented in Table 6.4 below.

The identification of appropriate indicators can be done through discussions with those who are inside the agencies, those related to the agencies, and those in civil society who use the agency's goods and services. A cautionary note: sometimes these groups, or individuals, are so delighted to be asked, that they provide impact indicators that are idealized but not necessarily measurable or realizable.

Indicators have to be useful and realistic. If indicators, especially result indicators, are too high, too lofty, and most likely unreachable, they will not be helpful for project monitoring. In worst cases, they become dangerous. Defeated expectations, frustration, or attack by critics who use them destructively may undermine the useful things that have happened over the life of the project. Inappropriate results indicators can also be a sign of problems in project design. A well-designed project should be clear on what results it aims to achieve and what inputs and tasks will lead to achievement of those goals.

Results indicators, widely owned and further unpacked by communities, can energize motivation and movement toward shared goals. Moreover, the communities are then likely to be monitoring the project naturally as it goes along. At the international level, the explicit targets and indicators of the Millennium Development Goals have increased the attention to the goals themselves. One result of these explicit indicators is that literally thousands of actors and agencies around the globe feel a sense of ownership of the MDGs and therefore monitor the progress, or lack of progress, in widely different places and settings. The MDGs lend themselves to community level benchmarking so that local communities can see their links to these international targets.[3]

EVALUATION AS A LEARNING PROCESS: PARTICIPATORY APPROACHES

The obvious, though often unstated assumption, behind the use of indicators and evaluation, is that they allow for learning about what has worked

Table 6.4
Sample Project Indicators: Strengthening State Environmental Capacities in Brazil's Amazonian States
PROJECT GOAL: PROTECT THE AMAZON'S NATURAL RESOURCES

OBJECTIVES	INPUTS	OUTPUTS	OUTCOMES	IMPACT
To strengthen nine Amazonian states' environmental agencies' managerial and organizational capacities for protecting natural resources.	• Contract firms to undertake diagnostic assessments and assistance to each state environmental agency to improve their personnel systems. • Contract with auditing firms for assistance to each state agency to improve financial management, records and database, and their use. • Contract facilitators to prepare and facilitate stakeholder workshops to gather qualitative data, and develop database for future agency outreach.	• Reports on diagnostics—personnel systems—received, widely discussed by senior staff, and accepted. • Initial steps taken toward implementing new recruitment and promotion processes and reducing patronage appointments. • First steps taken to install new financial management system, records collected into electronic database; auditing routinized. • Staff training and exchange programs organized. • Several major stakeholder workshops completed. Reports circulated.	• 75% of staff, recruited and promoted through merit process, are producing more professional environmental assessments as measured through peer focus group interviews. • Reputation of the state environmental agencies improved. Surveys of top public and private sector leaders indicate that a majority find their environmental agency is more timely with reports, has better quality data, and regulatory enforcement has improved. • State environmental agencies greater professionalism is indicated by staff being sought after for advice by other Brazilian states planning to strengthen their state environmental agency. • Stakeholders have grown in number and in support of the work program of the agencies as measured by frequency and attendance at meetings.	• Illegal logging as measured by the Forest Police in the Amazonian states is 30% below its level at the start of the project. Illegal mining has also declined due to improved enforcement. • Protection of biodiversity has become widely accepted by citizens as a goal within the Amazonian states, indicated by new civic associations and local community organizations organized to protect natural resources. • Three sample ecologically damaged areas singled out for close scientific observation are recuperating. • Media coverage of environmental issues and the work of the state environmental agencies increases. • The state environmental agencies have significantly more resources as indicated by (a) increased budgetary support from state legislatures (b) external donors, and (c) more effective fee and fine collection. • The state environmental agencies have more influence as indicated by the seriousness with which their recommendations are taken by state leaders measured through focus groups and in-depth interviews.

and not worked within a project. This can influence the design of future projects, as well as ensuring continuous learning and improvement within an existing project. However, even with all the attention given to results and the use of indicators over the last decade, there has not been enough attention to the issue of learning. More emphasis has been given to final evaluation of end-results than to monitoring throughout the life of the project. Monitoring systems that have been developed by donors are often complex data-driven information systems that can become burdensome to project executors and develop into a formal reporting tool rather than a monitoring and learning mechanism. Many donors still focus primarily on external project evaluations carried out upon project completion and sometimes at the mid-point of execution.

But these static project evaluations, usually carried out by external consultants and often contracted directly by the donor rather than project executor, can simply result in reports that fulfill a contractual obligation, but do not lead to much learning. The findings of reports do not always get channeled back to projects. Many donors do not have a systematic means of collecting evaluations or tracking that they have been done—let alone pulling together evaluations for cross-learning. In some instances, the evaluation reports are even difficult to locate. Project executing agencies often lack a connection to the evaluation when it is contracted externally, or fear its results, viewing it as an audit of their work rather than a learning tool. Furthermore, the report of an external evaluator will contain his or her own analysis, usually based on data and qualitative feedback obtained during a relatively limited period of time.

Historically the evaluation departments of large multinational donors have worked quite independently of operations departments—for good reasons related to objectivity—but the learning from evaluations has also remained isolated, with few feedback loops back to the teams designing projects. Where donors do take advantage of the evaluation reports, it is often for their own benefit and not the benefit of the project itself. (For example, USAID may require as part of contract compliance that an NGO under contract to implement a project must agree to have an independent, USAID-chosen group evaluate that project. Then USAID staff read the report, but do not necessarily share it either with the NGO or with others doing comparable projects.)

Many private foundations funding projects in developed, as well as developing countries face similar problems. The World Bank has attempted to address this problem by requiring all new project documents to contain a section that discusses how the project addresses lessons learned from evaluations of similar projects. Donors also facilitate workshops or seminars to disseminate and discuss evaluation findings.

But for evaluation to be an effective learning tool, there are two essential practices that should be used: ongoing project monitoring systems that provide continuous feedback and learning and participatory evaluation. These can be utilized together. Effective project monitoring allows a project to have regular feedback. Information systems where data on key indicators and project progress are maintained can be useful, particularly if created in user-friendly formats that permit frequent reports on the status of different variables. However, these can be very data-intensive and time-consuming and tend to focus on quantitative data only. Monitoring systems that are effective in providing continuous learning also incorporate qualitative, more informal means of collecting data on project progress.

On one level, evaluation is always occurring within a project: as staff interact with beneficiaries and carry out projects, they are seeing reactions to projects, attitudes of clients, participation rates, etc. Several tools exist that assist projects in capturing these observations and reflecting on them in a way that allows for more learning. These include journaling for staff and clients and periodic meetings to share feedback. In order for monitoring to be effective, the indicators that are being monitored must be clear from the onset of the project. In this way, projects are continually evaluating the extent to which they are on track in meeting those indicators. When this is not done, a project can get caught up in the day-to-day implementation, losing track of objectives until an evaluation comes along at some point down the road.

Just as we have argued for other stages of the development process, evaluation of project results requires a participatory approach that engages all stakeholders and especially the end-beneficiaries. Note the definition provided by Jackson and Kassam:

> Participatory evaluation is a process of self-assessment, collective knowledge production, and cooperative action in which the stakeholders in a development intervention participate in the identification of the evaluation issues, the design of the evaluation, the collection and analysis of data, and the action taken as a result of the evaluation findings....This approach to evaluation employs a wide range of data collection and analysis techniques, both qualitative and quantitative, involving fieldwork, workshops, and movement building (Jackson and Kassam, 1998, p. 3).

Whereas traditional approaches to evaluation use an external "expert" to assess project impacts, participatory approaches place greater importance on the project beneficiaries themselves. Such approaches can improve the means by which local communities and development agencies share knowledge with outside specialists. The quality of knowledge that emerges from this process of shared knowledge tends to be higher than when the process is top-down or externally driven.

In order to achieve serious participation from as many groups of stake-holders as possible, one must always be conscious of how each person's voice is being heard and who is speaking for whom. Even at the very local level, community leaders are not likely to speak for all members of their community. In complex emergencies, the sensitivity of this issue is extremely critical as projects need to be accountable to the people in the camps, the burnt-out villages, and the ruins (Roche, 1999, p. 182, citing Christopolos, 1998). Ensuring proper sampling and participation from a range of stakeholders is important in the process of establishing indicators, as well as in gathering evaluation data for the project.

Resistance to participatory evaluation sometimes comes because of a perception that the process is more time-consuming and costly than a tra-ditional expert-led evaluation. But participatory approaches can lead to long term cost savings, not only in ensuring more accurate project analysis, but also in building consensus among stakeholders for a post-evaluation action plan through the evaluation process itself (Jackson and Kassam, 1998, p. 14). Because the tools and techniques used in participatory evalu-ation lend themselves to strategic planning and project management, they can be used in an integrated way to meet all of these objectives, thus becoming more cost effective. This was demonstrated, for example in a health development project in Nepal that utilized a participatory process evaluation, documented by Robinson and Cox (Jackson and Kassam, 1998, pp. 122–149).

The process evaluation utilized in the case of the Nepal health devel-opment project provides a good illustration of the participatory evalua-tion approach. The project's objective was to strengthen the capacity of government health-related institutions and rural communities to meet health needs through community participatory development, management strategies, and the training of physicians. The process evaluation looked at the extent to which the project met its capacity building objective and how these efforts had improved the health system in the district in question. The evaluation used a core team of evaluators composed of Nepalis and international experts that worked together with a team of counterpart evaluators composed of twenty-two Nepalis from eighteen different vil-lages, the district health system, and the Ministry of Health. Evaluators used a variation of participatory appraisal techniques including focus groups, community mapping, and community walkabouts to obtain infor-mation. Through this process, the key stakeholders—those impacted by the project and those responsible for carrying it out—had the main say in which indicators would be measured and in reporting on progress toward those indicators. Findings were presented in feedback assemblies.

In analyzing the Nepali case, Robinson and Cox found several bene-fits of the methodology, including the following: the methodology covered outcomes and impacts, rather than only outputs, it is flexible enough to be used in short and long term processes, it can inform operational issues and strategic issues, it is sensitive to outputs, as well as human dynamics that influence those outputs, and it facilitates consensus-building around the evaluation results during the process, thus facilitating the learning and application of learning within the project (Jackson and Kassam, 1998, p. 148).

Other approaches to participatory monitoring and evaluation place the emphasis on the project beneficiaries' perceptions of change throughout a project, without the use of predetermined indicators. As argued by Terry Bergdall, traditional approaches that focus on indicators and impact assessment can become complex and burdensome and do not easily lend themselves to learning, particularly at the community level (Bergdall, 2001). In Bergdall's alternative approach, a project's progress and achievements are monitored and eventually evaluated through a series of participatory meetings in which project participants review what has been done under the project and what "significant changes" have occurred in their communities as a result of the project. The information generated within communities is then shared with stakeholders at other levels, but the end beneficiaries drive the monitoring process.

This model utilizes an inductive approach in which indicative events become the basis for drawing conclusions about results. Such an approach is particularly valuable for community development projects with objectives that are difficult to evaluate such as increased participation, self-confidence, local responsibility, capacity for problem solving, or transparency. As argued by Bergdall, "rather than being confined to a narrow range of predetermined indicators, this alternative approach is flexible and adaptive to changing circumstances" (Bergdall, 2001, p. 8). Furthermore, he notes that the retelling of stories about change can have a modeling effect within the communities and tends to focus on positive results rather than negative shortcomings.

INCORPORATING MONITORING AND EVALUATION INTO PROJECT DESIGN AND BUDGETS

A challenge in monitoring and evaluation, especially if done using participatory processes, is that it is a complex task that requires significant resources—financial and human—that are often not available to fund monitoring, despite the increased emphasis on performance. Donors talk a lot about indicators and measurement, but resources must be dedicated to achieve this. Budgets are critical if many of the activities and tools we are advocating are to be utilized. A major problem in project budgets is that process activities are often not costed out carefully. Participatory activities *do* require financing—for space, equipment, logistics, facilitators, and follow-up data collection, documentation, and dissemination. Therefore it is critically important that there be line item support within budgets for this work to be done.

Measuring results often requires looking beyond the official termination point of projects, since impacts are not likely to be achieved immediately. Once a project has provided beneficiaries with tools, time is needed for beneficiaries to apply those tools and reap the benefits expected. Conducting ex-post evaluation 6 months to 2 years after project services have been provided can be complicated by donor disbursement cycles. Budgeting for ex-post evaluations needs to be coordinated and designed with those knowledgeable about donor disbursement processes.

An important component of measuring project impact is to determine not only the specific outcomes for project participants, but also the impact the project had on achieving those outcomes. So, for example, if a project provides training for a specific group of beneficiaries and a high number of those gain employment following training, measurement of the impact of that training requires looking at whether those participants would likely have achieved the same outcome without the project. To do this most often requires a control group designed with appropriate methodologies. Finding and tracking the right control group can be very difficult. Imagine, for example, in a community development context, the number of diverse factors influencing development, of which a particular development project is but one piece. Yet, without such impact assessments, it is difficult to determine the most effective means of investing limited resources.

In human resource development, significant resources have been channeled to training projects with employment generation in mind—in OECD countries, as well as the developing world. While these are seen primarily as part of a poverty alleviation strategy, they are also increasingly for enhancing company competitiveness and economic performance. Impact studies, however, are beginning to show that other types of interventions may be more effective than training. One such example is labor intermediation that helps link the unemployed more directly with jobs.

Another issue is who owns the evaluation, as this has a role in influencing its learning impact. Although transparency and objectivity are important, it is essential that those people most immediately engaged in making a project work have input into the evaluation process, and access to the final report. This was discussed briefly above but is underscored here given its salience. A review of an IDB-managed grant fund suggests that projects had less ownership and less learning when the IDB was responsible for contracting the evaluation, rather than the executing agency contracting it as part of the project budget.

Donors argue that objectivity is too easily lost if the donor does not control the contractual relationship for the evaluation. Yet if donors have major input into the terms of reference and selection of evaluation consultants, that already goes a long way toward ensuring objectivity. These questions admittedly take on more dimensions in participatory monitoring and evaluation approaches. But donors need to be very sensitive to who drives the identification of project outcomes. Those most immediately involved in the project are better positioned to identify outcomes and clarify why they came about. For real learning to occur, the evaluative process needs to be dynamic with multiple stakeholders engaged in an ongoing dialogue—usually over a series of workshops—about what a project is achieving, what is working effectively, and what needs improvement.

DIAGNOSTIC TOOLS: QUALITATIVE AND QUANTITATIVE DATA GATHERING

Collecting and analyzing data are centrally important for effective learning. But data is not always in numbers and statistics, though these clearly also matter. Validity is to be found in combining both qualitative and quantitative methodologies.[4] Some researchers argue strongly in favor of one method over the other, but we favor the integration of both qualitative and quantitative methods. That provides the most comprehensive approach, particularly when working on poverty issues, which require data on sensitive topics reflecting complex realities.[5] As noted by Hentschel, the analysis of data collection techniques needs to go beyond the simple quantitative/qualitative divide to examine "whether investigative methods are *contextual*, i.e., whether they attempt to understand human behavior within the social, cultural, economic, and political environment of a locality, or not" (Hentschel, 1998, p. 4). Whether quantitative or qualitative in nature, each data collection instrument must be designed to ensure it is contextual. A brief summary of some of the common qualitative and quantitative methods used helps illustrate ways in which data can be integrated for greatest effectiveness.

Quantitative data often provides larger data samples and systematic data that can be analyzed with relative objectivity and with some consistency across data sets. Common quantitative methods include closed-ended survey questionnaires, computerized statistical analysis, and statistical modeling. In poverty research, much quantitative data is based on standardized household surveys implemented across large population groups. The main strengths of a quantitative approach are that it allows statistical aggregation of data based on sampling, provides results that are measurable, and allows simulation of various policy options.

Weaknesses include the possibility of sampling error (drawing inferences for a whole population from a subset) and nonsampling error arising especially from either coverage (i.e., omission because of recall error, purposeful omission, lack of comfort or a variety of other reasons) or from content problems (falsification, misunderstanding, or incompetence on the part of interviewer or respondent) (Carvalho and White, 1997, p. 11). Other weaknesses include the possibility of missing information that is not easily quantifiable. As Chambers says, "what is measurable and measured then becomes what is real and what matters, standardizing the diverse and excluding the divergent and different" (Chambers, 1997, p. 8).

Qualitative data on the other hand involves more in-depth analysis, usually of a smaller sample, facilitating the capture of more detailed information from subjects than can be obtained through quantitative methods. Qualitative methods include conversational techniques, observation, workshop-based techniques, and self-assessment tools. Conversational techniques include open-ended interviews, focus groups, community meetings, and case studies. All of these provide an opportunity for open discussion in which participants' responses are not limited by the parameters of a rigid questionnaire. Each allows for a different level of analysis—from individual interviews to small groups of eight to twelve participants of similar characteristics brought together in a focus group to large community meetings. Case studies that follow individuals, households, or other units of analysis over an extended period of time provide in-depth insight, which, though limited in sample size, can be very revealing.

A range of self-assessment tools have been developed to facilitate communities' creation of their own indices for development that can be used for planning and impact assessment. For example, in Ghana, a North–South monitoring team for a rural development project developed a tool they called the Village Development Capacity Index, which was designed to rank communities involved in the project in terms of their performance on poverty indicators and village development capacity indicators (Jackson and Kassam, 1998, p. 55). Various stakeholders participated in the process of allocating scores to the villages for each indicator, and then results were discussed in workshops that not only allowed for feedback on the index and scoring but also on plans for addressing project weaknesses.

The strengths of the qualitative approach include the ability to identify richer definitions and concepts, explain causal processes, and obtain more accurate and in-depth information, while its weaknesses include the inability to generalize beyond the research area because of the often small sample size and difficulties in verifying information due to the subjectivity of the process (Carvalho and White, 1997, p. 14).

Qualitative data collection can also be used to develop measurable indicators and ultimately collect quantitative data. As noted in the examples in

Table 6.5, the description provided in an interview about water collection suggests specific indicators of the quality of the water. Such responses across several interviewees can provide data that can be translated into quantitative measurements.

Often the comparative advantages of various methods work together to create an effective approach. As noted by Carvalho and White in a study on the use of the two approaches for poverty work, "policy recommendations based on both quantitative and qualitative information as opposed to those based on only one of these two types of information will have obvious merits" (Carvalho and White 1997, p. 23).

As noted above, both quantitative and qualitative data have strengths and weaknesses. The relative value of each for various research objectives is summarized in Table 6.6, taken from an integration of the two approaches. We note, however, that we disagree with the statement that analysis of causality is higher with quantitative rather than qualitative data. Others argue the reverse—that rich descriptive data obtained through qualitative methods can often provide more insight into why certain things happened than can quantitative data.

The limitations of quantitative data, particularly when gathered through closed-ended questions, are particularly apparent when attempting to gather sensitive information. For example, in a study of interhousehold transfers in a squatter settlement on the coast of Colombia, we used both in-depth case studies of five households and a questionnaire of 150 residents in the same neighborhoods (Kappaz et al., 2000). In the course of interviewing and in home visits for the case studies, additional information on income level and support emerged over time, largely through participant observation. Additional information provided by case studies of particular families after trust levels with interviewers increased brought forth much more information. In one instance, a significant source of support to one of the female-headed households under review was discovered when a provider of support arrived with a supply of food while the researchers were present. The food might never have been mentioned, as it had not been so previously, and would most likely have been omitted in the questionnaire. Furthermore, interviewers found that the ability of subjects to quantify the scale and frequency of support was limited. The questionnaires, which were conducted simultaneously with case studies and participant observation, were thus considered to be of limited value, or, at least, to be treated with caution, as the likelihood of accurate information on such personal subjects being provided in a one-hour interview was questionable.

Often qualitative data is used to support or illustrate findings from quantitative data. But experience such as that in the Colombia interhousehold transfers study suggests that the opposite should be the case—qualitative data should be used to capture a more accurate understanding of the

Table 6.5
Converting Qualitative Data into Quantitative Indicators

Actual Quotation from Interviews	Qualitative Factors in the Quote	Moving to Quantitative Indicators
"The river is usually dry. We scoop out the little water left. It smells of urine and excretion…After digging, the water is dirty. We have to wait until it is clearer."	• Presence of odor • Bad taste • Insects in water • Animal matter in water • Excrement in water • Sediment in water	• Count number of factors in water, simply counting each factor as one point. Devise scale 1 to 6. Could then compare different communities' relative seriousness of water quality. • Using water gathering device—e.g. 25 liter container—ask respondents about quantities of each factor likely to be found in a single liter.
"In those places where there are hand pumps, I collect water twice a day. The queue starts at 3 am. I take four 25 liter containers. Two for drinking and two for cleaning. I have to go before 4 am or there is no water left. Then, we go again, after 4 pm to collect more."	• Limited quantity of water • Arduous queuing process to get it • Multiple collections every day	• % of water collected versus WHO standards for households • % of time devoted to collecting water • Number of family members engaged in water collection • Incidence of illness traceable to water shortage • Incidence of illness traceable to water quality issues • Gender implications of water collection • Impact of water collection work as it impacts on children's school attendance
"Since I am older, I cannot go and collect 35 liters. I have to hire a young person from the area who might take three hours to retrieve the water for me"	• Age differences in abilities to collect water • Increased costs of water collection for vulnerable groups	• Cost of hiring assistance to acquire water as % of income • Social costs (dependency) to acquire water • Vulnerability indicated by age or disability

issues under investigation, and then, based on those findings, quantitative instruments can be designed to test certain hypotheses or gather additional data on a larger scale. The benefits of integrated research methods and approaches are now widely supported by other researchers as well. The strengths and weaknesses of quantitative and qualitative data to complement one another and thus deepen the quality of the findings is increasingly accepted as being the state of the art in research (Miles and Huberman,

Table 6.6
Comparing Quantitative and Qualitative Methods

	Quantitative	Qualitative
Representative	High	Low
Analysis of causality	High	Medium
Understanding processes	Low	High
Intrahousehold dynamics	Low	High
Beneficiary perspective	Medium	High
Rapid feedback	Low	High

Source: Michael Bamberger, Presentation at World Bank Seminar, June 1998

1994; Bamberger, 2000, p. 145). On a practical level, the use of both methods has implications for costs and time. However, the benefits of integration suggest that relative benefits outweigh additional costs.

BUILDING CAPACITY FOR LEARNING

We now turn to the problem of *building capacity for learning* from projects and programs. At several points above we have discussed this big concept—capacity (either organizational or personal). But briefly here, we want to add an explicit focus on a specific kind of capacity—capacity for learning. Our interest in looking for results, in caring about evaluation, in concern for participatory projects—all of these are building blocks for greater effectiveness in reducing poverty. But the underlying process adding value to these endeavors is about learning—that uncanny process that happens when one recognizes errors and goes to work thinking, not defensively, but constructively, in search of the opportunity offered by errors to learn.

But learning, especially organizational learning, is about even more than that (Argyris and Schon, 1996). It is rewiring internal networks in order to process information better, differently, and with more effectiveness. Learning is intrinsically exciting—for individuals, for groups, and for organizations. The problem is that the capacity for learning can get lost at all levels. And the related tragic problem is that most places and people undertake evaluation without much attention to learning, with the result that the potential for excitement is lost and evaluation becomes tedious, or worse, is used to punish.

Much is being written and learned about what it takes to be a "learning" organization. Peter Senge, leading a part of this growing field, writes that a learning organization is one that is continually expanding its "capacity to create its future" and that organizations need learning that "enhances our capacity to create" (Senge, 1990, p. 14). What does this mean operationally for agencies, association, organizations, or individuals?

People and organizations need a sense of mission about their work. Senior leadership has the major task of embedding a sense of mission as a major motivator within an organization. Conceiving of evaluation as an integral part of a learning system changes the dynamic of the process. It is about discovery, not about punitive action when errors are uncovered. It is about discovering what works, why, and how to build on that insight in order to be more effective in achieving the mission of the work underway. It means searching through what has worked, and what has not, to get to a place where one can envision how to create ways forward. Notice that Senge uses that concept—create—twice in the quotation above. What enhances creativity is not just skill, or insight, or even wisdom, but a combination of all of those factors coupled with a drive toward a preferred outcome and a working context that rewards creativity.

When we were working on the issues around evaluation and accountability as part of a discovery process with six major international NGOs, we were reminded again and again how much staff want a learning system (Lindenberg and Bryant, 2001; Beckwith, Glenzer, and Fowler, 2002). In part, NGO staff are keen about learning because they also want to have more opportunities to share what they have discovered, to convey their information about what they have individually seen, experienced, and conceived of as possible ways forward. Too often top management, besieged by its own problems, does not have, or take, enough time to listen, or to learn from those in the trenches. The energy evoked through listening thus is usually not tapped. This lies at the heart of the need for agencies to develop learning capacities. Building these capacities is a real challenge for the leaders and managers working on either policy or project implementation. It is desperately needed in poverty reduction programs. The world of development practice is full of hardworking staff often fighting off burnout and wondering why they feel almost as marginalized as the people they are trying to help.

Even the term "evaluation systems" conveys not excitement but a sense of tedious postmortems on why programs did not work as planned. Staff are filled with apprehension about who will be punished for what others cite as failures. What a learning system brings to this scene is a sense of how one can look at errors with objectivity, not apprehension, and use them as laboratories for discovering better ways forward. Listening, evaluating, measuring, backing up to look at the big picture, adapting in light of new information, rewiring how one approaches problems—all these processes are intrinsic to learning.

How can we put these processes in place inside organizations so that there is an organizational capacity to learn? Much work is focusing on this question (Senge, Roberts, Ross, Smith, and Kleiner, 1994). Rather than try to summarize it here, we want to call readers' attentions to this important field and suggest that a starting point is development of a program and project evaluation process that starts with, and values, learning, discovery, and finding creative ways forward. Replacing old bad habits with better ones is undeniably difficult. But the sense that it can be done is the key. ̃hat is a step forward in eliciting capacity for learning and beginning to ̃te the culture needed to do it.

̃USION

̃o monitor and evaluate performance effectively are critical to ̃ the impact of poverty work. Monitoring and evaluation ̃ to learning so that there is ongoing progress, and contin- ̃n design of future policies, programs, and projects. Calls ̃ave produced significant progress in the monitoring ̃formance, but challenges remain. One must be clear ̃t one is measuring and acknowledge that there are ̃aluation work. This brings us back once again to ̃patory approaches that engage stakeholders at

̃imensional problem intertwined with larger ecõ   forces, the question of measuring results also rã   ̃ternal factors that negatively impact project effectivẽ   ̃eduction policies, programs, and projects are operating ̃   ̃er framework. There are broader economic, politi- cal, and sociã ̃ems and actors that contribute to the perpetuation of poverty and influence the direction of poverty reduction work. The global character of poverty means that accountability must be applied across countries and institutions. Global institutions play a key role in poverty work—from the World Bank, UN agencies and the WTO to international NGOs and multinational foundations. The way in which these institutions are held accountable, and by whom, impacts the quality of their poverty reduction work. As the world works toward meeting the historic Millennium Development Goals, careful attention needs to be paid to the indicators that will be used to track progress and measure success.

NOTES

1.   To view the United Nations reports on progress in implementing the MDGs, see www.un.org./millenniumgoals, see "Statistics on the Achievement of the Millenium Goals."

2.   See, for example, Roger Riddell and Mark Robinson, *Non-Governmental Organisations and Rural Poverty Alleviation* (London: Clarendon Press, 1995) and Michael Edwards and David Hulme, *Beyond the Magic Bullet: NGO Performance and Accountability in the Post-Cold War World* (West Hartford, Conn.: Kumarian Press, 1996).

3.   As part of the Applied International Development Workshop in the School of International and Public Affairs, Columbia University, a team worked for UNDP in the Republic of Altai and in Bulgaria to develop community benchmarking workshops, which are indicators related to the MDGs that can be used to focus public attention on critical needs.

4.   For a good source on this complex issue, see the work of Michael Bamberger, a sociologist whose work in the World Bank on integrating qualitative and quantitative data has achieved a level of excellence. See endnote below.

5.   For reviews of the core elements of the debate see, for example, Jesko Hentschel, "Distinguishing Between Types of Data and Methods of Collecting Them," *Policy Research Working Paper 1914* (Washington, D.C.: The World Bank, 1998) and Michael Bamberger, editor, *Integrating Quantitative and Qualitative Research in Development Projects* (Washington, D.C.: The World Bank, 2000).

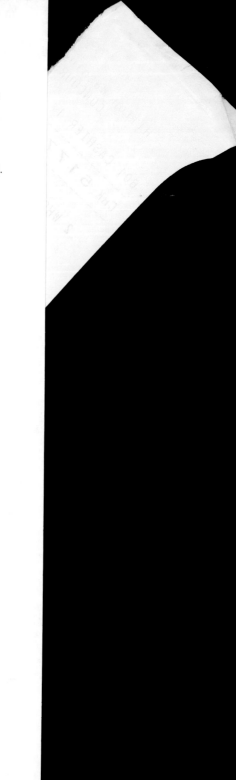

7

POLICY COHERENCE: REDUCING POVERTY AS POSITIVE PEACE BUILDING

"No man is an island, entire of itself. Every man is a piece of the Continent, a part of the main. If a clod be washed away by the sea, Europe is the less...as if thine own were. Any man's death diminishes us, because we are involved in Mankind."

—John Donne, "Meditation 17"

SUMMING UP

Poverty, stunting and shortening individual lives, diminishes us all. As we know how to redress it, we are more implicated in its impact. Chronic poverty undermines our shared humanity. The consequences wash over borders and erode prospects for peace and security. This, in spite of the fact that "development can be an effective instrument for conflict prevention," as Paul Collier points out. And in regard to how reducing poverty can open up space and opportunities for peace, he adds "civil war reflects not just a problem *for* development, but a failure *of* development" (Collier, 2003, p. ix).

Often, while waiting, with inestimable patience, for us to finish this work, our publisher, Krishna Sondhi, aware of the growing literature on poverty, asked, "What makes this book on poverty different from all the others?" Our answer has been first, the focus on poverty as a *global* problem given its cross-border implications; second, the argument that poverty, inequality, and social exclusion create circumstances that lead to or abet violence, even war; and third, the contention that it is no longer justifiable, if it ever was, to argue that we do not know how to reduce poverty, because

159

in fact much has been learned about effectiveness. These all invite debate, which we welcome.

We flew over the landscape of these three central topics and pointed out major features on the ground below, with special attention to what can be done. Throughout this book we have drawn heavily on the growing field of development management, as well as political economy, in both of which much has been learned about how to reduce poverty. We strived to balance technical issues with a view of the larger context in which they are embedded. This was done because we wanted to reach new readers who had not thought in these terms before. For others, already at work in development management or in poverty analysis, we hope to add to their perspective and indicate the wider potential for their fields of inquiry. Working, as many of them are, close to the problems, there is a tendency to become too focused on narrow development assistance mandated goals. That is a mistake. The field of development, with poverty reduction at its core, has come to mean, and do, much more.

And to point to that potential, we have emphasized that poverty must be seen as global in nature given the cross-border causes and implications of poverty. This poses a challenge for donors and, in particular, multilateral development agencies whose mandate is currently restricted to working in poor countries. The need for more global capacity to address global poverty is a large, unresolved question. In light of the current fierce criticism from both the far right and the far left about the roles and impact of the World Bank, it is unlikely that we will see much movement toward greater, more effective, and more responsible global governance for development. Yet, consider these questions: why is it unreasonable for the World Bank to ask each of its members to prepare a Poverty Reduction Strategy Paper? Are these unneeded in northern industrial countries? Why is it unreasonable for the UNDP to request a Human Development Report for each of its member countries? Several countries have come forward to do one of these reports on their own—but the silence of European and North American countries about their own internal poverty is stunning. Both the World Bank and UNDP are knowledge institutions—their research into serious poverty issues is far reaching—but right now their research is focused narrowly on a limited set of countries. They are not *global* knowledge institutions; nor is their poverty work *global*.

The absolute numbers of people living in poverty is increasing. Lasting solutions for moving people out of poverty need to be conceptualized and designed with attention to the multidimensional aspects of their problems. A key focus must be on increasing the access of poor people to assets. Access to assets is determined by the institutional frameworks within which they live and work. If a poor farmer cannot get credit because he lacks a clear title to his land, or a small business owner cannot get through the local bureaucratic labyrinth, or the peddler cannot get the license she needs, prospects for their working their way out of penury are dim. Strategic change can be moved forward by sensible projects just as attention to legal frameworks can move forward the prospects for increases in productivity. Sturdy participatory processes building local ownership best inform these institutional changes.

Institutional change (which includes policy change) and collective action are central to long term progress. Too often, however, one uses the term institutional change without considering how to analyze the existing institutional context, or how to interact with that context in order to facilitate change. We have argued for the importance of disaggregating the content of this oft-used and rarely unpacked term—institutional development—to identify possible program or project possibilities.

Our perspective on reducing poverty also requires a discussion of the roles and relationships among policies, programs, and projects. Choosing to address the impact of poverty through a focus on policy change, and therefore advocacy work, or through programs and projects raises trade-offs. For entering professionals, these are tough choices of when to undertake advocacy work, or when to work on projects in the villages, squatter settlements, or with minority groups on collective action to gain access to assets. Fortunately, however, there are increasing numbers of young people going into development studies programs and then on to development work thinking about these trade-offs.

The heart of getting results in reducing poverty comes through improved, effective, people-centered implementation, the orphan topic in most discussions of poverty reduction. Effective implementation is treated as uninteresting, inevitably messy, stuff. That view must change. The iterative puzzle solving required in implementation is intrinsically intellectually challenging. Moreover, it is where the action is in the development process. The process needed for effectiveness and getting to results happens on the ground. (Moreover, what passes for "innovative design" in program or project work not grounded in implementation often simply leads to unicorns: lovely to look at, but the essence of unreality.) Among many other things, this perspective means that large, complex organizations working to reduce poverty need to provide incentives for those skilled at, and devoted to, implementation.

Implementing social and economic change on the ground with people is complicated as interests conflict and honest differences surface. Resolving these takes talent and time. As large industrial countries become ever more capital intensive, there are real pressures toward looking for capital-intensive solutions in lieu of labor-intensive problem solving. Nonetheless, the real work when people are the central concern requires people working with people to achieve change. Well designed and facilitated participatory workshops can support these processes in a range of situations.

Achieving results is central to our arguments throughout all the foregoing chapters. Learning—social learning about effectiveness—is furthered through paying attention to results. Building capacity for learning in community groups, or local NGOs, or in larger, complex organizations also means paying attention to processes of communication and negotiation, given the inevitability of competing interests, cultural diversity, and the ease with which miscommunication occurs.

"Capacity building" is used too loosely in most official documents. It is rather as if it is an option on a menu drop-down box for terms to be inserted into development documents. The budgets for the resulting projects reveal how little analysis is involved in using the term "capacity." All too often, in capacity building work, the budgeted items are computers and training. Financial officers have trouble imagining how to budget for processes; objects like computers or other equipment are, on the other hand, easy to insert into a budget. But what is needed is more attention to facilitating a learning process—an openness to recognizing and correcting errors as they emerge.

Process changes do require considerable funding for (1) skilled people to guide those processes over time with (2) qualitative and quantitative data collection to measure change along the way to ascertain what has been absorbed and what remains to be done in terms of remedial work, (3) workshops, and (4) focus groups and other qualitative data analysis. All of these components need staff and logistical support if they are to be translated into realities. If they are not financed, they will not happen.

ELEPHANTS IN THE ROOM

Even though we have flown over a wide territory, other major problems germane to the issue have not yet been addressed. While a final chapter is meant to be a conclusion that integrates and sums up all that went before, these other factors of central importance have been present throughout—but in the background. It is rather like meetings in which everyone knows of an omnipresent concern casting a shadow over the deliberations—but no one is comfortable directly addressing it. Colloquially, such problems are referred to as "the elephant in the room." We have decided to address three of these "elephants in the room" in this final chapter. *The three major contextual issues are policy incoherence—military expenditures as they interact with or even undermine economic development assistance; lack of support for financing development—again in contrast with military expenditures; and the need for more effective and democratic global governance for development.* Each of these major problems plays its own part in worsening the problems of global poverty. Yet, we have argued throughout that much has been learned, especially in the field, about increasing the effectiveness of development projects. Is it possible that any of this learning will "trickle up" and lead to some breakthroughs in international politics? Is there, in short, a way forward on the problem of global poverty?

POLICY INCOHERENCE: MILITARY EXPENDITURES, ARMS TRADE, AND DEVELOPMENT

Policy coherence, and the current state of incoherence, is beginning to get some attention. Citizens and political leaders are asking, in effect, that the right hand pay some attention to what the left hand is doing. As sensible as this sounds, it is devilishly difficult to do. Tough political interests compete fiercely at this moment in history; there is little shared consensus about what kind of coherence is needed. The greatest incoherence given our focus on the need to reduce poverty is between ever rising military expenditures and the much lower levels of investment in human development. These two arenas pull directly against one another. Military expenditures often undermine economic growth, shifting investment into equipment and personnel that, by definition, one hopes will not be used. But even more devastating is the growth in military power that results from military investments. It is this military power that will deepen and further policy incoherence in the future.

In the political trade-off between defense expenditures and economic development expenditures, defense invariably wins, in small poor countries and in large powerful ones. The result is policy incoherence—on the one hand, defense expenditures adversely affect economic growth, while on the other, policies are intended to encourage economic development. Few development professionals look at this big picture policy incoherence, either in the donor countries or in the receiving countries that experience the conflicting impacts. In each place the military and development policy institutions have different organizational imperatives, bureaucratic politics, and constituencies. Most discussions of development assistance make no mention whatsoever of comparisons with military expenditures. (For example, when criticizing donor-funded development workers for not having been able to avert civil wars, few analysts also implicate the arms trade, military training, and military investments that were simultaneously taking place under the aegis of the same foreign power.)

Interestingly, decades ago one of the leaders who spoke out against ever-rising military expenditures was Robert McNamara, a former Secretary of Defense, who subsequently was the President of the World Bank. Speaking at the University of Chicago on May 22, 1979, he said:

> I had of course to wrestle with the problem of the fundamental nature of international security during my tenure as US Secretary

of Defense, and I spoke publicly about it....My central point was that the concept of security itself had become dangerously over-simplified. There had long been an almost universal tendency to think of the security problem as being exclusively a military problem, and to think of the military problem as being primarily a weapons system or hardware problem...but a nation can reach a point at which it does not buy more security for itself by buying more military hardware...excessive military spending can reduce security rather than strengthen it. In the matter of military force—as in many other matters in life—more is not necessarily better. Beyond a prudent limit, more can turn out to be very much worse (World Bank, 1979, p. 1).[1]

In the rough and tough competition for shares of national budgets, financing wars invariably wins out over financing investments in human capital or human well-being. The multiple competing currents drown out positive possibilities such as development. Large public organizations charged with allocating the limited flow of official development assistance (ODA) find that assistance undermined by the military training, military export credits, or military assistance going to (along with the arms trade) those same countries. A taxpayer revolt in rich countries could usefully ask why taxpayers fund the building of schools in poor countries and then pay for the military assistance that bombs that school. Or why they should pay when the army of that country turns on its own people using weapons stamped "Made in the USA." Of course, rich country taxpayers pay a third time—for the rebuilding of bombed facilities after the fighting stops—or for the peacekeepers sent to stop the fighting.

When countries are already entangled in conflict, military spending is prioritized even more readily over other expenditures, usually regardless of the extent of poverty and exclusion in the country that may be perpetuating the conflict. For example, as a means of support to the government of Colombia in combating drug traffickers and long-term guerilla insurgents, the United States provided Colombia with $1.2 billion in assistance in 2000 through a program known as Plan Colombia, with $1 billion of that funding going to the military and only the remaining $0.2 billion going to social development programs. Putting aside the question of whether or not the military expenditures are useful or needed in advancing the military campaign to bring an end to the conflict, it is compelling to consider for a moment what the impact might have been in Colombia, or any country, of $1 billion invested in human development. Such figures are commonplace for the military but unheard of for investments in human development.

The guns versus butter battles of the budget are worse in poor countries. Financing military interests wins out over investments in poverty reduction, economic development more generally, and peace building because military spending is perceived as conveying power. Rich countries vying for allies as colonies became independent financed much of the build-up of armies and defense expenditures, especially in sub-Saharan Africa. The intensity of this competition grew in direct relationship with the intensity of the Cold War. The Soviet Union, the United States, France, and the United Kingdom became major arms exporters in the 1970s and 1980s. China joined them in the 1980s with its arms shipments to the Middle East and South Asia (Grimmett, 1990, pp. 1–10). The share of developing country military expenditure in world military expenditure grew from 6% to 18% in the mid-1980s (Somnath Sen, 1991, p. 1).[2]

By the 1990s, these heavily armed poor countries were ten times more likely to experience civil war than international war (Degger, 1991, p.43).[3] Research on military expenditures and their implications has improved in technical sophistication, for example, through the development of carefully specified simultaneous equations that look at the interaction of several factors over time. Thus, more can be said about both the implications of military expenditures on economic growth and the economic factors that put a country at risk for civil war. On the former—we now know that military expenditures have negative implications for economic growth. In a study commissioned by the World Bank in 1991 for a conference on the implications of military expenditures, Saadet Degger wrote:

> As soon as one considers more complex models and looks at both direct and indirect effects, it becomes clear that military expenditure is a major economic burden and liability. The empirical and econometrics evidence for simple models is rather ambiguous. But the message from more complex models seems to be clear: defense spending tends to reduce growth—and in significant fashion (Degger, 1991, p. 45).

The adverse and costly environmental impacts of defense expenditures—storing toxic wastes, chemicals, heavy metal, equipment with little or no alternative use—is not currently factored into any of the economic equations, but it is a reality on the ground. Even sophisticated economic models on impacts of military expenditures have yet to incorporate environmental costs. In any event, in light of their deliberations about the impacts of military expenditures within poor countries, the IMF and World Bank agreed in 1992 to denote certain levels of military expenditures as "unproductive" when reviewing those countries' public expenditures.

Since the civil wars broke out in Africa and in the Balkans following the end of the Cold War, the situation has only worsened. Moreover, as we now know, the presence of valuable natural resources—oil, gold, precious gems, especially diamonds—worsened the situation in Africa. Collier points to greed or grievance or both interacting as drivers of civil wars. Lootable goods finance rebel troops and can, over time, facilitate the

development of a war economy, entrenching the conflict so that it continues for decades (Collier, 1999).[4] The burgeoning amount of new research
on violence and the new wars calls attention to the need for a better and
more accurate analytical framework than either the older ones or the
recent popular ones found often in the press that blame the victim (usually by pointing to ethnic tensions as ancient hence implying immutable)
rather than searching for underlying causes. Often there are real economic
causes fueling conflict.[5]

The wars in Guatemala, Nicaragua, and El Salvador preceded those of
the 1990s. The political economy of those wars, while different, share at
least one factor: arms sales and military training from wealthy countries
that kept the region caught in war and detracted from economic development. Moreover, as McElhinny and Seligson have documented, El Salvador,
for example, went from civil war to civil violence as a result of the unresolved problems not addressed by a peace settlement that did not resolve
the underlying economic problems. Skills learned in the war, and guns,
were used by mostly young men ineptly demobilized, as they turned to
gang membership and often criminal violence to earn their living (McElhinny and Seligson, 2000).

FINANCING DEVELOPMENT: OFFICIAL DEVELOPMENT ASSISTANCE

Official development assistance is one of the major sources of funding for
investment in poverty reduction abroad. There are other sources of funding such as national investment strategies, locally generated and hence
self-financed strategies, private sector investments, and the whole large
arena of nongovernmental organizations, faith-based initiatives, foundations, and public–private partnerships. But, official development assistance plays a critical role. And the levels of such assistance are
barometers of the commitment to poverty reduction more generally.

In this regard, US levels of development assistance, while large in
absolute terms, are very low in proportion to its GNP in international comparisons. Once the largest donor of development assistance, the United
States is now ranked twenty-second among middle and upper income countries, allocating less than one-tenth of 1% of its GNP for international
development. Further examination of the "150 account"—the part of the
US budget that funds international organizations, Peace Corps, and
USAID—reveals that a very small percentage of the total development
budget goes to reduce poverty and improve human well-being. The largest
share of US development assistance goes to Israel and Egypt as part of the
Camp David accords. Also, as USAID often points out to Congress, a significant share of the development assistance is actually spent to purchase
US goods—hence it returns to the United States.

More recently, the European Union has significantly overtaken all other donors. The European Union with its EUR 36 billion development assistance budget provides more than half of all development assistance. (That figure overshadows the World Bank's lending in recent years—which has been approximately $11 billion.) Moreover, the EU member states have pledged to increase their support until they provide 0.39% (up from 0.33% in 2001) of national income as Official Development Assistance by 2006 (Annual Report 2003 From the Commission to the Council).[6] Their programs reach 160 countries in eight regions and are not closely tied to foreign policy goals.

That the United States is now ranked twenty-second among contributing nations would be surprising to most people in the United States. Polls regularly indicate that it is popularly believed that a far higher percentage of GNP is committed to development assistance than is in fact the reality. That said, following September 11, 2001, there began to be increasing public awareness and support in the US Congress of the importance of development assistance to more general international security goals.

There was some encouragement among development workers with President Bush's announcement of $5 billion in new money for the Millennium Challenge Corporation at the Monterrey Conference in Mexico in 2001 to indicate US support for the Millennium Development Goals. But contrast that $5 billion with the $800 billion appropriated for rebuilding Iraq. Meanwhile as the costs of rebuilding Iraq increase, those costs and all the related problems have overshadowed other international events in the first years of this new millennium.

Of course the commitment of any given country to reducing poverty abroad should be evaluated by looking at other factors in addition to ODA. Trade policy, immigration policy, environmental policies all matter, as well as domestic agricultural policies. Producing one of the more innovative indicators of both the reach and the implications of development, the Washington, D.C.–based Center on Global Development has developed a "Commitment to Development Index" that incorporates measures of a country's behavior along six dimensions: aid, trade, investment, migration, peacekeeping, and environment.[7] The Center's look at the performance of twenty-one rich countries on how they help or hinder development of poorer countries along these dimensions produced several surprises. In sum, the members of the powerful Group of Seven countries scored low on their commitment to development, while smaller countries invariably were more open and supportive. Even more useful than the scoring, however, was the Center on Global Development's emphasis on the multidimensional work needed in order to reduce poverty.

In our view, it would have been very helpful if the Center on Global Development had scored countries on the effectiveness of these countries in redressing poverty within their own borders in addition to looking at their commitment to reduce poverty abroad. This would help to test the hypothesis that there is a relationship between effectiveness in addressing poverty at home and effectiveness in reducing poverty abroad. (Notably, several of the countries that give the largest percentage of their GNP to development assistance are also ones with substantial redistributive policies at home as reflected in their low domestic inequality rates.)

While throughout this book we often mention the larger array of actors in poverty reduction work, highlighting, for example, the important role of civil society, this does not mean that ODA is not important. On the contrary, ODA has a wider impact than is commonly appreciated. And yet, conflicting interests generated by military assistance and development assistance results in policy incoherence. Within recipient countries, each of these kinds of foreign assistance creates interests and organizations that compete for shares of investment from the public sector. But military leaders and their contractors amount to ever more powerful constituencies that crowd out the voices for development.

Writing after serious reflection on his 20 years as a senior staff member of USAID, Steven W. Sinding wrote, "I regretted that the agency's ability to focus its resources on economic and social development was consistently undermined by short-term political considerations that overrode longer term development investments" (Sinding, 2001, p. iii). This problem is all too well-known by anyone who has worked directly or indirectly for USAID. While Cold War policies reinforced this disconnect for decades, it was ironic and tragic that the atmosphere did not improve at the close of the Cold War, but worsened. After September 11, 2001, the lead bilateral agency, USAID, has become more affected by short term political goals then ever before. For example, NGOs were scolded at major public forums by the head of the agency for not properly acknowledging the major role of USAID support in their work and hence their implicit support of US foreign policy.

MORE DEMOCRATIC AND EFFECTIVE INTERNATIONAL GOVERNANCE FOR DEVELOPMENT

Of our three major issues detailed at the beginning of this chapter, this one—democratic and effective global governance for development—is the knottiest. Entangled, indeed snarled, by international politics and their even more daunting local roots in different political cultures, this goal is a long way off. Moreover, you might well ask how essential is strengthened international governance to reducing global poverty? Must not national governments be first and foremost responsible for addressing poverty within their borders? Is effective and responsible global governance—affected through an array of international organizations—needed in order to address global poverty? If it is, how do we get from where we are to where we need to be?

Today we are nowhere near a consensus within any of the major Group of Seven industrial powers on any of those central questions. If the circle is widened to include the 191 members of the UN system, the cacophony of differences is our modern equivalent of the Biblical Tower of Babel. But to address directly the first tough question over the relative responsibilities of national versus international organizations, let us be clear: All levels of governance, local, national, and global, have major roles to play in the battle against poverty. The global roles are, however, more important at this point than they have been in the past because of the increased interdependence of nations. There are more cross-border effects of national policies. Therefore more international agreement on the rules of the game is essential for lasting progress to be made on reducing poverty.

Global poverty is a global bad. It often results from national decisions that can both impoverish people within their own borders and also export poverty problems to other countries as well. (Ill-conceived agricultural subsidies, environmental abuse, inadequate public health management of infectious diseases are but a few of the instances that come to mind.) Just as late nineteenth century nations had to devise an international postal authority to address the need for a global public good—the ability to send goods and letters across national borders—today's world has need for more such global public goods.

Achieving international agreement on harmonizing postal regulations is taken for granted by all of us. That is the precursor for the kinds of harmonization now needed in several other areas. Our generation needs to tackle this work, to multiply the kinds of international policy harmonization needed in order to arrive at a less poor, less war-torn world, with protections for a depleted and degraded environment. The carefully argued book by Inge Kaul and others on *Global Public Goods* (Kaul et al., 2001) and the follow-up volume on *Providing Global Public Goods* (Kaul et al., 2003) provide helpful insight and guidance in this direction. While the first book made the case for global public goods, in the follow-up volume, the authors turn to addressing what and how these public goods might be provided.

But in all of these discussions, the serious imbalance between the tasks assigned to international organizations and their resources are made more apparent. The United Nations has far too many unfunded mandates, inviting further charges of incompetence, without addressing the central problem. Yes, much more remains to be done in tightening up parts of the bureaucracy, but the fact is that the United Nations has a modest budget given its workload. The total UN staff budget in 2002–2003 is only $2.97 billion (compare once again, for example, to the billions the United States budgeted for reconstruction of Iraq).[8] Yet, many countries fall into arrears in meeting their financial obligations to the United Nations. For example in 2000–2001, only forty-three of the then 181 members of the United Nations had paid their dues. Generally about fifteen member states contribute around 85% of the budget.

The prevalence of war and terrorism and the scale of civilian deaths have added to the push for more global capacity to manage issues of terrorism and insecurity as global public goods. So have the ongoing debates over globalization, with some arguing for either abolishing or reforming the Bretton Woods organizations and the World Trade Organization. The salience of the roles played by these organizations has become more apparent to millions of people. While his record as a unilateralist is well documented, it was still something of a first that President George W. Bush went to the Security Council before announcing his decision to attack Iraq in March 2003. He knew he had at least to ask for their support, though clearly he was going to proceed even if he did not get it. Large and powerful bodies of public opinion in the United States, as well as in other Security Council member states, have come to believe that the Security Council matters as a major part of global governance for development. Importantly, as this book goes to press, the High-level Panel Report on Threats, Challenges, and Change has gone to member governments so that its serious reform recommendations can be widely discussed, and hopefully adopted.

Some incremental progress has taken place toward more effective global governance on other fronts. For example, the increased awareness of the need for greater transparency in order to prevent the further growth of illegal markets in drugs or to counter money laundering in the lucrative and illegal market in small arms trade has led to measures improving international financial regulation. The Organization for Economic Cooperation and Development, the United Nations, and the European Union have, with the assistance of the Basel Committee on Banking Supervision, drawn up standards to improve financial transparency. Thus far they are relying on "naming and shaming" for enforcement—but at least the principle is accepted that the international community will no longer stand idly by while money laundering contributes to horrific loss of human life (R. Bryant, 2003). Increasingly, former political leaders are being tried for crimes committed against humanity in the War Crimes Tribunal, despite the lack of US support for the court.

The growing power of the WTO reflects the potential of international governance—when such efforts are supported by political will. This instance of international governance is functional because it fulfills the needs of economic powers to influence international trade in a way that meets their interests. Political will is needed to strengthen international governance in instances where global public goods are upheld—to meet the interests of all nations.

A multitude of other positive initiatives has also come from the large array of international organizations. These include increasing international awareness of issues—for example, through the Global Fund for AIDS—and adding to international law through international treaties. That said, the fact remains that several international organizations have not been nearly as effective, or as accountable, as they were intended to be. Interestingly, for example, the World Bank makes most of its project documents available to the public. The United Nations, UNDP, and UNICEF, on the other hand, do not make program or project documents public. Nevertheless, the increased transparency of many organizations has facilitated the advocacy efforts of civil society groups that monitor development assistance and seek to hold international organizations accountable—often to the organizations' own stated governance practices.

But this ongoing debate over how to increase the effectiveness of international bodies has also seen another debate; this one on the implications of the United States' hegemonic power and resurgent unilateralism. In his book, *Empire: The Rise and Demise of the British World Order and the Lessons for Global Power*, Niall Ferguson argues for the advantages of empire and bemoans the fact that the United States will probably not have the staying power that the British Empire did and hence will miss achieving all the good that the United States could do as an imperial power (Ferguson, 2002).

This paean to colonialism seems oddly out of touch with the large body of carefully researched critical scholarship on colonialism. (Perhaps Ferguson would argue that the bad stuff happened in other country's colonies—so King Leopold's Ghost does not tell anyone about the broader genus of colonialism. But then perhaps he has not read, for example, Packenham's *Scramble for Africa* or Rotberg and Mazrui's *Protest and Power in Black Africa* or Mamdani's *Citizen and Subject*.) But as Brian Urquhart, a renowned authority on the UN system, says succinctly, "this thoroughly British conclusion perhaps underestimates the basic fact that Americans don't want to be Romans, let alone Britons, and in any case powerful new anti-imperial forces have emerged since Britannia ruled the waves."[9]

Multilateral cooperation, like democracy—flawed, messy, and erratic—still trumps the alternatives. In thinking about the global poverty problem and its relationships to violence, we need to remember that total global population over the next 50 years is projected to be nine billion people—and the vast majority of those people will be poor. How can we expect this world in which the gaps between rich and poor grow ever more severe and the poor ever more numerous to lead to a stable and secure future? The major related problems of environmental degradation, global warming, and shortages of basic resources—such as water—indicate a future riddled with serious and far reaching threats to any concept of global security, let alone sustainable development.

Not only are there likely to be nine billion people on the globe by 2045, but an ever shrinking proportion of those people will be in Europe and North America. The aging phenomena occurring in several northern industrial countries is already leading to complicated policy issues for social security systems, labor, and immigration policy. It is entirely possible that one scenario could be that over time the countries in the Group of Seven will face a struggle to maintain their international political power when they are a far smaller proportion of total global population and have burdened economies. With inherited fiscal policy problems, mounting social security expenditures, and a smaller percentage of their population in their productive years, these countries will have trouble contending that they have inherent rights to maintain control of international organizations. Power will shift. And as power diffuses, countries with younger populations, and growing economies, will rightfully claim their rights to opportunities for greater influence in international organizations.

Is it not better to shape the change, rather than wait for it to be forced by events? More institutional imagination, akin to C. Wright Mill's sociological imagination, is needed now so that we might find a way forward in strengthening international institutions to govern ourselves (Mills, 1959). While an increasing number of problems are recognized as global in their reach, from global warming to the AIDS pandemic, our capacity to address these problems collectively lags far behind.

The capacity of the United Nations was shaken in 2003 by attacks on the UN offices in Baghdad that killed 15 UN staff including the Chief of Mission and the attack a week later on UN facilities and personnel in Afghanistan. These attacks underscore the fact that the United Nations is no longer viewed as a neutral party. Speaking after these tragic events, Secretary General Kofi Annan said that the United Nations "has come to a fork in the road" and must address more of the fundamental weaknesses in the institution. While some see the major threat to be terrorism, others feel that the "persistence of extreme poverty and growing disparity of income, the spread of infectious diseases, or climate change and environmental degradation are the major threats." And, the Secretary General added, "In fact all these struggles are linked" (*New York Times*, 2003, p. A11).

The United Nations is at a critical turning point. Criticized on many sides, weakened by resurgent US unilateralism, and bombed by terrorists who see it as a tool of the West, it now must revise its mission and refurbish the role it needs to play in building and keeping peace. But it clearly needs more support from civil societies, their networks, and the member countries in order to move forward on these agendas. The national members are too entrenched in their own power struggles and current perquisites (in the case of the core members of the Security Council) to bring much political-sociological imagination or managerial skill to the table.

The intricate, but enduring, relationships among security, reducing poverty, and building a more peaceful world can best be furthered by greatly strengthened international organizations. International financial stability, environmental sustainability, improved global health—none of these major endeavors can be achieved by nation-states acting independently of one another.

Security issues have stressed the parts of the UN system that are least able to foster collective action among states. Several valid issues and deeply conflicting responses to those issues underlie the inability of states to work more collaboratively. They can be summed up as power struggles and financial headaches. Who will pay for what they will not control? And who will cede some power in order to resolve the stalemates crippling the UN system, as well as the Bretton Woods organizations? Will civil societies work across borders to insist upon a stronger and greatly refurbished United Nations?

One central part of the governance puzzle is how to arrive at voting processes that reflect relative weights of population, wealth generation, and political influence. Each of the current international organizations has variants of these factors at play in voting and decision-making, with only the United Nation's General Assembly having a one nation, one vote regime. For all the calls for greater democracy in international organizations, no one has found a way to improve the current flawed and messy voting systems. The "consensus" models used by the IMF and WTO are cloaks for an unfair process in which powerful countries dominate the decision-making process. Yet it is impossible to move forward without crafting awkward compromises given the stark unevenness in national populations and economic productivity in a world of serious and increasing inequalities among people.

REASONS FOR HOPE?

Yes, there are reasons for hope. We are purposefully borrowing a book title used by Norman Uphoff and his coauthors, Anirudh Krishna and Milton Esman, not only because of the intrinsic relevance of that book with its accounts of surprising leadership and citizen-based collective action that made and continues to make real differences in the lives of poor people,[10] but also because of Uphoff's central argument that often development workers in the field find things that work that their social science colleagues would predict could not work (Uphoff, 1997).

But, the critic could say, those are simply the exceptions that prove the rule. But what if they are far more than that? Perhaps they are new fragile experiments that, if given half a chance, show us a path forward to real breakthroughs? Social innovation does happen all the time. As researchers focus attention more on documenting success and communications technology makes it easier to spread those stories, the pool of public knowledge on exciting innovations happening worldwide will grow. As Frances Moore Lappé and Anna Lappé point out in their book titled *Hope's Edge*, the success stories at the local level often involve people breaking away from systems that say they cannot succeed, and their stories provide insight for all of us on the possibilities for breaking away from traditional thought traps and embracing new mind maps that allow us to mobilize to create a better world (Lappé and Lappé, 2002).

Politicians do not lead so much as follow, as they scan the environment for potential public support. Most generally astute political leaders catch the scent or feel of shifting public opinion and discern how to ride its wave to further their ambitions. Public opinion moves and shifts with tides of feeling evoked by changing circumstances and information flows.

We saw far reaching and historic changes in whole political systems in the 15 years following the fall of the Berlin Wall, as evidenced by the "velvet" revolutions in Eastern Europe, the unraveling of the Soviet Union, and growing popular support for democracy around the world. While most social scientists predicted a bloodbath as the endgame for apartheid South Africa, negotiations behind walls were underway—due in large part to the growing sense that the change in Eastern Europe was reducing tolerance worldwide for undemocratic governance with widespread human rights violations. The release of Nelson Mandela and the toppling of the apartheid states in South Africa were the result. Few predicted it. But it happened. The steadily growing sense among people about the need for change is like the heavy consistent flow of water over a rock, wearing it down particle by particle, eroding its support, and finally shifting its structure. We live in just such a period of change.

The information revolution and the speed with which new voices enter into dialogue with one another across continents, through growing networks of community-based organizations—these are new forces to be reckoned with in our times (Weiss and Gordenker, 1996; Keck and Sikkink, 1998; Clark, 1999; Lindenberg and Bryant, 2001). The increase in literacy globally abets this change and will continue to fuel it. We have seen the changing views evidenced in more and larger public demonstrations against either war or mindless commercial globalization—or both.

Along with these new voices—and the technology that makes them possible—another major development is the emergence of transnational advocacy networks bringing nonstate actors into global diplomacy. These large national networks of NGOs include InterAction in the United States, which provides a platform for NGOs all across the United States; Coordination Sud (Coordination of French NGOs); CIVICUS (a large Asian network); VANI (Voluntary Action Network India); and ABONG (Brazilian Association of NGOs). Assuredly there are others. When, as often happens, these large platforms share common views on, for example, agricultural trade policy, or debt relief, or another such pro-poor position, they can make their weight felt at WTO meetings or other international negotiations.

They represent this century's counterpart to earlier, comparable efforts. What is different now is the speed with which they can, and do, communicate and their additional skill in researching their positions. They are part of the vanguard advocating more attention to poverty reduction. Two leaders of these groups, Henri Rouille d'Orfueil and Jorge Eduardo Durao, are arguing for a special kind of NGO diplomacy. Locally grounded and informed by work with people in the field, the goal of this diplomacy is to encourage "the emergence of a socially responsible global awareness, to push negotiators toward decisions that support equitable regulation and international solidarity" (Rouille d'Orfueil and Durao, 2004, p.2).

The interdependence of people and the growing disparities in human well-being around the world are drawing more attention. In the course of working on this book we found significantly more research and writing—articles, journal publications, electronic Web sources, news accounts, and, of course, books—on poverty than were available even as recently as a decade ago. That alone is a reason for hope. More voters are seized by the salience of poverty. First, because of the moral implications of living in a world with ever increasing numbers of poor people living shortened lives with so little opportunity. Their degradation diminishes us all. And, second, because the lethal combination of growing numbers of poor people and increasing inequality and social exclusion bodes ill for our future security. It could lead to ever increasing violence of all different kinds—crime, terrorism, kidnapping, state-sponsored violence, and war.

And there is a great deal more focus on the leadership possibilities of the growing civil society organizations around the globe. John Clark's powerful book, *Worlds Apart, Civil Society and the Battle for Ethical Globalization*, not only documents the growing role of civil society organizations but their potential for bringing about further change (Clark, 2003). Michael Edwards rightfully raises cautionary notes as he asks us to think carefully about the theory and practice of civil society organizations (Edwards, 2004). That said, there is growing awareness that citizens are acting beyond borders, and working collaboratively on a wide variety of issues, to achieve greater fairness in our time. Ann Florini lays out a paradigm for transnational governance (Florini, 2003). Much work is underway on many aspects of this complex phenomena—growing transnational advocacy from civil society (Smith, Chatfield, and Pagnucco, 1997; Anheier, 2004). One need only look to the website of the Center for Civil Society at the London School of Economics as their Annual Reports are a goldmine of information about this growing sector.

KEY POINTS TO REMEMBER

1. We can reduce poverty. We have learned a great deal in the past two decades about effectiveness and hence about getting results. Yes, there were mistakes along the way. (Most everyone in the field has a story of a failed project, program, or policy.) What matters is trying, learning, and then improving approaches. The critical issue for further progress on poverty is refocusing political will and increasing determination to continue development work.

2. Past failures in political will have resulted in resource constraints that crippled progress in the past and jeopardize current work on reducing poverty. Even a small fraction of the investments made by the Group of Seven Industrial Nations in war production could, if devoted to peace production, make a large difference to this work.

3. Cultural diversity is as intrinsic a value as biological diversity, thus policies to encourage social inclusion or solidarity are valuable for people, for peace, and for future productivity. Often minorities account for a large share of a country's poor. Reducing poverty, while respecting the rights of people to be different, is fundamentally important as part of long run peace building. Participatory development is central in this process.

4. Poverty reduction contributes to positive peace building. To get there we need more focus on inclusive development, on peace and well-being as basic human rights, and far more capacity building for conflict management. This implies working on problems generated by inequalities—it does not mean policy edicts or heavy-handed governmentally imposed egalitarianism. It does mean research and hence monitoring when inequalities slow down growth. And it also means we need more investment in effective human development programs.

5. Most poverty reduction work—especially that done by official donor agencies—has not actively incorporated attention

to peace building. For example, little attention has been paid to the ways in which policy changes or programs and projects can inadvertently worsen ethnic tensions.

6. The need for policy coherence warrants more attention. Paying heed to the political and social implications of military assistance to countries, which increases the power of local armies, is important. If the relative weights of military assistance and development assistance are out of balance, then we must confront the fact that development assistance and its goals—for example, building civil society—is being undermined by military interests. Given real differences in the amount of money and clout, the military factor will most often, with tragic consequences, trump development. This must change.

7. Economic policy coherence must also be addressed. Pro-poor programs will not be effective if they are implemented side-by-side with economic policies that exacerbate poverty and inequality. Fair trade policies that establish a level playing field for rich and poor countries are needed.

8. Last, but clearly not least, there is a serious need for far greater international organizational capacities to work toward reducing global poverty. Our current international agencies are encumbered with restrictions, underfunded, and inadequately enabled to do the multiple tasks assigned them. And they must be more accountable. We need global development agencies, where "global" means the ability to review and critique national poverty problems in all countries, not just the so-called "developing" countries. We all live in "developing" countries. Also needed are better funded bilateral development agencies more suited to the needs and problems of the twenty-first century.

CAN POLITICAL WILL BE CREATED?

Resoundingly, yes. Political will can be created. We live in an epoch characterized by more local level community organizing than ever before. The NGO and community-based organizations in the 200 members of the United Nations are robust, in touch with counterparts across borders, talking to one another through the Internet, and organizing more coalitions than at any other point in human history. Yes, there are many disagreements among these groups. That is, after all, to be expected in a very diverse world with competing interests. And the building of joint action will require a great deal more work at resolving differences. Generally, it requires working on all the hard details, in order to craft reasonable and thoughtful compromises. But it is possible. We have already seen more cross-border discussion and even some cross-border civil society political activism at work.

It is easy to think of the negative tensions that weaken international NGOs. But it is far more likely that we will be hearing more from them in the future than we ever have in the past. Moreover, many of these groups are mobilized to address the relationships between human degradation and violence. Many of the NGOs were established in reaction to wars or state-led violence in the first place. Sometimes the shifts in public opinion happen so incrementally that it is only after a certain point, or critical event, that it is obvious that the tide has shifted. But tides do shift.

The human rights and the civil rights movements are instances when the political tide shifted in response to public opinion.[11] There are other such examples—in the campaigns for debt relief and for ending the use landmines. The current campaign on poverty organized by a coalition of leading NGOs, called Toward a Better, Safer World, is working toward this goal of generating increased political will for fighting poverty. Public opinion about what is acceptable does change. Small drops of water together make a stream, and streams, rivers. As John Clark reminds us, these streams when combined can become torrents that change the contours of mountains.

In the first annual Center for Global Development's Commitment to Development Index, the analysts point out that "what the rich countries do to, and for, the rest of the world comes back to affect them—poverty and instability do not respect borders....Call it trickle up economics. When the poor become better off, so do the rich" (*Foreign Policy*, 2003, pp. 56–66). We would add to this statement that addressing poverty within borders, as well as across borders reinforces a virtuous cycle. Abetting inequality within a country by neglecting equitable policy positions comes back to slow down growth, and hence slows down trade and immigration policies that make for better neighbors. The European Union has decided, rightly, that it is in its own best interest, as well as the right thing to do, to address the poverty and social exclusion in the transition states of Eastern Europe. They also see this policy as equally applicable in the long run to the western Balkans.

Political will is, and has been, generated to move in new directions when large numbers of people—ordinary citizens—come to believe that a dominant widely practiced institution is wrong and not in their long term best interest. The concerted pressure of citizens, organizations, press, unions, schools, the media, and community groups moves the center of gravity on issues. As in all fields of endeavor, the steps needed for effectiveness begin with awareness, then acceptance of the problem, technical skill, organizational capacity, and knowledge about what works. So we do know how—and we know more about what needs to be done. We now have to muster the will to move toward a concerted effort—collective action through transnational advocacy—to put global poverty on the public agenda at every level of governance. Increasing fairness is central if we are to increase the chances for peace.

NOTES

1. It must be noted that, in 2002, the UN Commission on Human Security, led largely by Amartya Sen, proclaimed the importance of human security with development conceived of in these terms.

2. Sub-Saharan African countries had only small standing armies at independence. Nigeria, for example, had 11,500 men in uniform; Zambia had 3,000; Tanzania, only 1,800. That changed rapidly—especially in Nigeria as it approached the Biafran War. But the other major source of expansion of the military budget for Nigeria was the discovery of oil—for by then the military had much more political power and was positioned to get ever increasing shares of public expenditures from oil revenues.

3. Paul Collier writes that the incidence of civil war has increased steadily over the past few decades. He adds that poor countries relying on the export of primary commodities face higher risks—as much as 15 times higher than OECD countries. This, and several other major new findings are written up in *Breaking the Conflict Trap* (Collier, Elliott, Hegre, Hoeffler, Reynal-Querol, and Sambanis, 2003, p. 5).

4. There is a growing body of research and work on the relationships between poverty and violence. See, for example, Mats Berdahl and David M. Malone (eds.), *Greed and Grievance: Economic Agendas in Civil Wars*, one of several books from a project of the International Peace Academy. The book is published by Lynne Rienner Publishers, 2000. Also from the IPA project, see Karen Ballentine and Jake Sherman (eds.), *The Political Economy of Armed Conflict* (Lynne Reinner Publishers, 2003).

5. See, for example, the work of Mark Duffield in *Global Governance and the New Wars*, (Duffield, 2001) or Mary Kaldor, *New and Old Wars* (Kaldor, 2001).

6. This report—available on-line at the European Union website—is 312 pages long. It is entitled *Annual Report 2003 from the Commission to the Council and the European Parliament on the E.C. Development Policies and Implementation of Development Assistance Flows*. The EU development assistance agency, EuroAid, was reorganized between 2001–2002. Speaking at the NGO Leaders' Meeting in Oxford, England, in 2001—one of the meetings leading up to the publication of *Going Global*—Rudd Lubbers spoke about the significant efforts underway at that time to strengthen the effectiveness of the EU's development work (Lindenberg and Bryant, 2001).

7. "Ranking the Rich," published in *Foreign Policy*, May/June 2003 (pp. 56–66), describes this interesting series of indices developed by the Center for Global Development. This first annual publication of the indices ranks twenty-one rich countries on whether their aid, trade, immigration, investment, peacekeeping, and environmental policies help or hurt other countries. The Center combines a series of indicators to construct the index. For example, in assessing the quality of development assistance, it "measure[s] foreign assistance as a percentage of the donors' GDP, but adjusted to reflect the quality of aid. Aid to poorer nations is rewarded; aid to corrupt regimes is discounted." The Netherlands receives the highest score ranking for its pro-poor aid, trade, investment, and environmental policies. The trade score is constructed by looking at barriers to goods from developing countries and rewards imports from the world's poorest countries. In short, each score is constructed from a range of indicators, although the score for peacekeeping is

based narrowly on the rich country's personnel and financial contributions to international peace-keeping efforts as a percentage of GDP.

8. This data comes from an excellent article by Alix Freedman and Bill Spindle, "Now at the Top of U.N.'s Agenda: How to Save Itself," *Wall Street Journal*, Friday, Dec. 19, 2003, starting on front page and completed on p. A8. There is an important and growing body of research and analysis on the need for strengthening international governance. See, for example, Dennis Dijkzeul and Yves Beigbeder (eds.), *Rethinking International Organizations* (NY & Oxford: Berghahn Books, 2003).

9. Brian Urquhart, "World Order & Mr. Bush," in *The New York Review of Books*, Vol. 50, Number 15, October 9, 2003. Also on-line in archives of *The New York Review of Books* at www.nybooks.com/articles/16591.

10. See Anirudh Krishna, Uphoff, and Esman's inspiring book, *Reasons for Hope, Instructive Experiences in Rural Development,* which details eighteen instances of outstanding rural development success stories from around the world (Bloomfield Conn., Kumarian Press, 1996).

11. The film, "A Force More Powerful," is a moving documentary of this process in India, the southern United States, and South Africa.

BIBLIOGRAPHY

——— "Africa Could Feed Itself. Should It?" *Wall Street Journal*. 3 December 2002.

——— "The Global Menace of Local Strife." *The Economist*, 23–25. 24 May 2003.

——— "Righting Wrongs: Special Report on Human Rights." *The Economist*, 18–20. 18 August 2001.

Adam, C. S., and J. W. Gunning. "Redesigning the Aid Contract: Donors' Use of Performance Indicators in Uganda." *World Development* 30, no. 12 (2002): 2045–56.

Adamolekun, Ladipo, and Coralie Bryant. *Governance Progress Report: The Africa Region Experience*. Washington, D.C.: World Bank, 1993.

Ames, Brian, Ward Brown, Shanta Devarajan, and Alejandro Izquierdo. "Macroeconomic Policy and Poverty Reduction." In *PRSP Sourcebook*, Washington, D.C.: World Bank, 2001.

Andreas, David. *The French Revolution and the People*. London: Hambeldon & London Publishers, 2004.

Anheier, Helmut. *Civil Society, Measurement, Evaluation, and Policy*. London: Earthscan, 2004.

Annan, Kofi. "An Increasing Vulnerability to Natural Disasters." *The International Herald Tribune*. 10 September 1999.

Atkinson, Tony. "European and European Union Experience in Advancing Social Inclusion: A Review and Lessons for Latin America and the Caribbean." Presented at Seminar on Social Inclusion at Annual Meetings of Inter-American Development Bank, Milan, Italy, 2003.

Ball, Nicole. *Pressing for Peace: Can Aid Induce Reform?* Washington D.C.: Overseas Development Council, 1992.

Balla, A. S. *Poverty and Exclusion in a Global World*. New York: St. Martin's Press, 1999.

Ballentine, Karen, and Jake Sherman (eds). *The Political Economy of Armed Conflict: Beyond Greed and Grievance*. Boulder, Colo.: Lynne Rienner Publishers, 2003.

Balogh, Thomas. *The Economics of Poverty*. London: Weidenfeld and Nicolson, 1955.

Bamberger, Michael, ed. *Integrating Quantitative and Qualitative Data Research in Development Projects*. Washington D.C.: World Bank, 2000.

Barnett, Richard, and Ronald Muller. *Global Reach*. New York: Simon & Schuster, 1974.

Bebbington, A. J., and D. H. Bebbington. "Development Alternatives: Practices, Dilemmas and Theory." *Area* 33, no. 1 (2001): 7–17.

Bebbington, Anthony. "Capital and Capabilities: A Framework for Analyzing Peasant Viability, Rural Livelihoods and Poverty." *World Development* 27, no. 12 (1999): 2021–44.

Beckwith, Carol, Kent Glenzer, and Alan Fowler. "Leading Leaning and Change in the Middle: Reconceptualising Strategy's Purpose, Content and Measures." *Development in Practice* 13, no. 3 and 4 (2002): 409–23.

Behrend, Heike. *Alice Lakwena and the Holy Spirits: War in Northern Uganda, 1985–1997*. Ohio: Ohio University Press, 2000.

Berdal, Mats, and David Malone (eds). *Greed and Grievance: Economic Agendas in Civil Wars*. Boulder, Colo.: Lynne Rienner Publishers, 2000.

Bergdall, Terry. "Application of Assets Based Community Development in International Development." Presented at Millennia Consulting, Chicago, Illinois, 2002.

————. "Facilitating Participatory Evaluation through Stories of Change." In *The IAF Handbook of Group Facilitation*, ed. Sandor Schuman. Indianapolis: Jossey-Bass, 2004.

Birdsall, Nancy, Carol Graham, and Stefano Pettinato. "Is Globalization Muddling the Middle Class?" Working Paper, no. 14. Washington, D.C.: Center on Social and Economic Dimensions, 2000.

Birdsall, Nancy, John Williamson, and Brian Deese. *Delivering on Debt Relief: From IMF Gold to a New Aid Architecture*. Washington, D.C.: Center for Global Development and the Institute for International Economics, 2002.

Blauert, Jutta A. S. Z. *Mediating Sustainability: Growing Policy from the Grassroots*. West Hartford, Conn.: Kumarian Press, 1998.

Blunt, Peter, and D. Michael Warren. *Indigenous Organizations and Development*. London: Intermediate Technology Publications, 1996.

Bourgois, Philippe. *In Search of Respect: Selling Crack in El Barrio*. Cambridge: Cambridge University Press, 1995.

Brainard, Lael, Carol Graham, Nigel Purvis, Steven Radelet, and Gayle E. Smith. *The Other War: Global Poverty and the Millennium Challenge Account*. Washington, D.C.: Brookings Institution Press, 2003.

Braudel, Fernand. *Civilization and Capitalism (Civilisation Materielle, Economie et Capitalisme: XVe–XVIIIe Siecle)*. Paris: A. Colin, 1979.

Brinkerhoff, Derick W. "Integrating Institutional and Implementation Issues into Policy decisions: An Introduction and Overview." In *Policy Analysis and Concepts and Methods: An Institutional and Implementation Focus*, ed. Derick W. Brinkerhoff. Greenwich, Conn.: JAI Press. Policy Studies in Developing Nations Series. Vol. 5, 1997.

———. "Using Workshops for Strategic Management of Policy Reform." In IPC Technical Note, no. 5. Washington, D.C.: Management Systems International, 1994.

Brinkerhoff, Derick W., and Ben Crosby. *Managing Policy Reform: Concepts and Tools for Decision Makers in Developing and Transitioning Countries*. Bloomfield, Conn.: Kumarian Press, 2002.

Brown, Dee A. *Bury My Heart at Wounded Knee: An Indian History of the American West*. Henry Holt & Co., Inc., 1988.

Brown, Michael K. *Race, Money and the American Welfare State*. Ithaca, NY: Cornell University Press, 1999.

Bruno, Michael, Martin Ravallion, and Lynn Squire. "Equity and Growth in Developing Countries: Old and New Perspectives on the Policy Issues." In Policy Research Working Paper, no. 1563. Washington, D.C.: World Bank, 1996.

Bryant, Coralie. "Culture, Management, and Institutional Assessment." In *Culture and Development in Africa*, eds. Ismail Serageldin and June Taboroff. Washington, D.C.: World Bank, 1992.

———. "Institutional Development and Institutional Assessment." In *Handbook on Technical Cooperation*. Washington, D.C.: World Bank, 1992.

———. "Market Assisted Land Reform: Private Property Rights for the Rural Poor." *American Society for Public Administration Occasional Paper Series*, 1997.

———, ed. *Poverty, Policy, and Food Security in Southern Africa*. Boulder, Colo.: Lynne Rienner Press, 1988.

———. "Property Rights for the Rural Poor: The Challenges of Landlessness." *Journal of International Affairs* 52, no. 1 (1998): 181–205.

———. "Strategic Change through Sensible Projects." *World Development* 24, no. 9 (1996): 1539–50.

Bryant, Coralie, and Louise G. White. *Managing Development in the Third World*. Boulder, Colo.: Westview Press, 1982.

———. *Managing Rural Development: Peasant Participation in Development Projects*. West Hartford, Conn.: Kumarian Press, 1980.

————. *Managing Rural Development with Small Farmer Participation.* West Hartford, Conn.: Kumarian Press, 1984.

Bryant, Ralph. *Turbulent Waters: Cross-Border Finance and International Governance.* Washington, D.C.: Brookings Institute, 2003.

Bueno de Mesquita, Bruce, and Hilton L. Root. "The Politics of Poverty." *The National Interest,* no. 68 (2002). Accessed on-line at www.nationalinterest.org.

Buvinic, Mayra. "Social Inclusion in Latin America and the Caribbean: Experience and Lessons." Presented at Social Inclusion Seminar at the Annual Meetings of the Inter-American Development Bank, Milan, Italy, 2003.

Carnegie Commission on Preventing Deadly Conflict. *Preventing deadly conflict: Final report.* New York: Carnegie Foundation, 1997.

Carroll, Thomas. *Intermediary NGOs.* Hartford, Conn.: Kumarian Press, 1992.

Carvalho, Sonya, and Howard White. *Combining the Quantitative and Qualitative Approaches to Poverty Measurement and Analysis: The Practice and Potential.* Washington, D.C.: World Bank, 1997.

Center for Economic and Social Rights. *Economic, Social and Cultural Rights: A Guide to the Legal Framework,* 2000. Accessed on-line at www.cesr.org.

Chambers, Robert. *Managing Rural Development.* New York: Holmes and Meier Publishers, Africana Publishing Co., 1974.

————. "The Origin and Practice of Participatory Rural Appraisal." *World Development* 22, no. 7 (1994): 953–69.

————. Participatory Rural Appraisal (PRA): Challenges, Potentials and Paradigm. World Development 22, no. 10 (1994): 1437–54.

————. *Whose Reality Counts?* Brighton, England: University of Sussex Press, 1997.

Champernowne, D. G., and F. A. Cowell. *Economic Inequality and Income Distribution.* Cambridge, UK: Cambridge University Press, 1998.

Cherlin, Andrew, Paula Fomby, Ronald Angel, and Jane Henrici. "Welfare, Children, and Families: A Three-City Study." Policy Brief 1–3. Johns Hopkins University, 2001. Accessed on-line at www.jhu.edu/~welfare.

Chua, Amy. *World on Fire.* New York: Doubleday, 2003.

Clark, John D. *Worlds Apart: Civil Society and the Battle for Ethical Globalization.* Bloomfield, Conn.: Kumarian Press, 2003.

Cohen, Roberta, and Francis M. Deng. *Masses in Flight: The Global Crisis of Internal Displacement.* Washington, D.C.: Brookings Institution Press, 1998.

Collier, Paul, and Anke Hoeffler. *Military Expenditure: Threats, Aid and Arms Races.* 2002. Unpublished draft.

Collier, Paul, V. L. Elliott, Havard Hegre, Anke Hoeffler, Marta Reynal-Querol, and Nicholas Sambanis. *Breaking the Conflict Trap: Civil War and Development Policy.* Oxford and Washington: Oxford University Press and World Bank, 2003.

Cottrol, Robert J., and Tanya Kateri Hernandez. "The Role of Law and Legal Institutions in Combating Social Exclusion in Latin American Countries: Afro-America Populations." Presented at Social Inclusion Conference at Inter-American Development Bank, Washington, D.C., June 18, 2001.

Crosby, Benjamin. "Stakeholder Analysis: A Vital Tool for Strategic Managers." In IPC Technical Note, no. 2. Washington, D.C.: Management Systems International, 1992.

Cross, Terry et al. *Toward a Culturally Competent System of Care.* Washington, D.C.: Georgetown University, 1989.

Daerdorff, Alan V., and Jon D. Haveman. "The Effects of Trade Laws on Poverty in America." Discussion Paper, no. 947–91. Wisconsin: Institute for Research on Poverty, 1991.

Dalaker, Joseph. *Poverty in the United States: 1998.* Washington, D.C.: US Bureau of the Census, 1999.

Danzinger, Sheldon H., and Robert Haveman, eds. *Understanding Poverty.* New York: Russel Sage Foundation, 2001.

Davies, Susanna, and Naomi Hossain. "Livelihood Adaptation, Public Action and Civil Society: A Review of the Literature." IDS Working Paper 57. Sussex: Institute for Development Studies, 2000.

de Haan, Arjan. "Social Exclusion: An Alternative Concept for the Study of Deprivation?" *IDS Bulletin* 29, no. 1 (1998): 10–19.

de Haan, Arjan and Simon Maxwell. "Poverty and Social Exclusion in North and South." *IDS Bulletin* 29, no. 1 (1998).

de Soto, Hernando. *The Mystery of Capital: Why Capitalism Works in the West and Fails Everywhere Else.* New York: Basic Books, 2000.

de Tocqueville, Alexis. *Democracy in America.* New York: Vintage Books, 1945.

Degger, Saadet. "Military Expenditure and Economic Development: Issues and Debates." Chapter 3 in *Military Expenditures and Economic Development.* Washington, D.C.: World Bank, 1991.

DeJanvry, Sadoulet, and Thorbecke. "State, Market and Civil Organizations: New Theories, New Practices and Their Implications for Rural Development." *World Development Special Edition* (April 1993): 565–75.

Dia, Mamadou. *Africa's Management in the 1990s and Beyond: Reconciling Indigenous and Transplanted Institutions.* Washington, D.C.: World Bank, 1996.

Diamond, Jared. *Guns, Germs and Steel: The Fates of Human Societies.* New York: W.W. Norton & Co., 1997.

Dijkzeul, Dennis, and Yves Beigbeder. *Rethinking International Organizations: Pathology and Promise.* UK: Oxford: Berghahn Books, 2003.

———, eds. *Rethinking International Organizations: Pathology & Promise.* New York: Berghahn Books, 2003.

Dinan, Alden K. *State Policy Choices: Assets and Access to Public Assistance.* New York: Columbia University National Center for Children in Poverty, 2003.

Douglas-Hall, Ayana, and Heather Koball. *Basic Facts About Low-Income Children in the United States.* New York: Columbia University National Center for Children in Poverty, 2005.

Dreze, Jean, and Amartya Sen. *Hunger and Public Action.* Oxford: Clarendon Press, 1989.

Dudwick, Nora, Elizabeth Gomart, Alexandre Marc, and Kathleen Kuehnast, eds. *When Things Fall Apart: Qualitative Studies of Poverty in the Former Soviet Union.* Washington, D.C.: World Bank, 2003.

Edwards, Michael. *Civil Society.* Oxford: Blackwell Publishers, 2004.

Edwards, Michael, and David Hulme. *Beyond the Magic Bullet: NGO Performance and Accountability in the Post-Cold War World.* West Hartford, Conn.: Kumarian Press, 1996.

Eggertsson, Thrainn. *Economic Behavior and Institutions.* New York: Cambridge University Press, 1990.

Epstein, William M. *The Dilemma of American Social Welfare.* New Brunswick: Transaction Publishers, 1993.

Esman, Milton J. "The Elements of Institution Building." In *Institution Building: From Concepts to Application,* ed. J. Eaton. Beverly Hills, CA: Sage Publications, 1972.

———. *Management Dimensions of Development.* West Hartford, Conn.: Kumarian Press, 1991.

Farbman, Michael, ed. *The Pisces Studies: Assisting the Smallest Economic Activities of the Urban Poor.* Washington, D.C.: US Agency for International Development, 1981.

Fearon, James, and David D. Laitin. "Ethnicity, Insurgency, and Civil War." *American Political Science Review* 97, no. 1 (2003): 75–89.

Ferguson, Niall. *Empire: The Rise and Demise of the British World Order and the Lessons for Global Power.* New York: Basic Books, 2003.

Fergusson, James. *The Anti-Politics Machine*. Minneapolis: University of Minnesota Press, 1994.

Firebaugh, Glenn. "Empirics of World Income Inequality." *American Journal of Sociology* 104 (1999):1597–630.

Fisher, Julie. *Non-Governments*. West Hartford, Connecticut: Kumarian Press, 1998.

Fix, Michael, and Wendy Zimmerman. "All Under One Roof: Mixed Status Families in an Era of Reform." Urban Institute, 1999. Accessed online at www.urbaninstitute.org/immig/all_under.html.

Florini, Ann. *The Coming Democracy: New Rules for Running a New World*. Washington, D.C.: Island Press, 2003.

Friedman, Jim. "Simplicities and Complexities of Participatory Evaluations." In *Knowledge Shared*, eds. Jackson and Kassam. Bloomfield, Conn.: Kumarian Press, 1998.

Friere, Paulo. *Education for Critical Consciousness*. New York: Simon & Schuster, 1973.

Galbraith, James K. "A Perfect Crime: Inequality in the Age of Globalization." *Dedalus* (Winter 2002).

Gaventa, John. "Poverty, Participation and Social Exclusion in North and South." *IDS Bulletin* 29, no. 1 (1998).

Gertler, Paul. "Insuring the Economic Costs of Illness." In *Shielding the Poor*, Washington, D.C.: Brookings Institution Press, 2001.

Goldberg, P. K., and Nina Pavcnik. "Trade, Inequality, and Poverty: What Do We Know?" Brookings Institution Trade Forum, May 13–14, 2004.

Goulet, Dennis. *The Cruel Choice*. New York: Atheneum, 1971.

Graham, Carol. "Assessing the Impact of Globalization on Poverty and Inequality: A New Lens on an Old Puzzle." Brookings Institution Trade Forum, May 13–14, 2004.

Grimmet, Richard F. *Trends in Conventional Arms Transfers to the Third World by Major Supplier, 1982–1989*. Washington, D.C.: Congressional Research Service. Library of Congress, 1990.

Grindle, Merilee, ed. *Politics and Policy Implementation in the Third World*. Princeton, NJ: Princeton University Press, 1980.

Grootaert, Christiaan, Ravi Kanbur, and Gi-Taik Ok. "The Dynamics of Poverty: Why Some People Escape from Poverty and Others Don't: An African Case Study." World Bank Policy Research Working Paper, no. 1499. Washington, D.C.: World Bank, 1995.

Guaqueta, Alexandra, Rapporteur. *Economic Agendas in Armed Conflict: Defining and Developing the Role of the UN*. New York: International Peace Academy, 2002.

Gurr, Ted. *Why Men Rebel*. Princeton, NJ: Princeton University Press, 1970.

Haveman, Robert, and Larry F. Buron. "Destitution in the United States, 1973–1988." Discussion Paper, no. 963–92. Wisconsin: Institute for Research on Poverty, 1992.

——. "Who Are the Truly Poor? Patterns of Official and Net Earnings Capacity Poverty: 1973–1988." Discussion Paper, no. 956–91. Madison, Wisconsin: Institute for Research on Poverty, 1991.

Helliwell, John F. *The Contribution of Human and Social Capital to Sustained Economic Growth and Well-Being*. Ottawa: HDRC, 2001.

——. *How Much Do National Borders Matter?* Washington, D.C.: Brookings Institution Press, 1998.

Hentschel, Jesko. *Distinguishing between Types of Data and Methods of Collecting Them*. Washington, D.C.: World Bank, 1998.

Hirschman, Albert O. *Getting Ahead Collectively: Grassroots Experiences in Latin America*. New York: Pergamon Press, 1984.

Hoy, Paula. *Players and Issues in International Aid*. West Hartford, Conn.: Kumarian Press, 1998.

Hulme, David, and Andrew Shepherd. "Conceptualizing Chronic Poverty." *World Development* 31, no. 3 (2003): 403–24.

IFAD. *Rural Poverty Report 2001: The Challenge of Ending Rural Poverty*. Oxford Univ Press, 2001.

Iglesias, Enrique. *Reflections on Economic Development: Toward a New Latin America Consensus*. Washington, D.C.: Inter-American Development Bank, 1992.

Imig, Douglas R. *Poverty and Power: The Political Representation of Poor Americans*. Lincoln and London: University of Nebraska Press, 1996.

Inter-American Development Bank. *Action Plan for Combating Social Exclusion Due to Race or Ethnic Background, June 2002–December 2003*. Washington, D.C.: Inter-American Development Bank, 2002.

International Federation of Red Cross and Red Crescent Societies. *World Disasters Report: 1999*. Geneva: IFRC, 1999.

——. *World Disasters Report: 2003*. Geneva: IFRC, 2003.

Jackson, Edward T., and Yusuf Kassam, eds. *Knowledge Shared: Participatory Evaluation in Development*. Bloomfield, Conn.: Kumarian Press, 1998.

Jeffrey Pressman, and Aaron Wildavsky. *Implementation: How Great Expectations in Washington Are Dashed in Oakland, or Why It's Amazing that Federal Programs Work at All*. Berkeley: University of California Press, 1973.

Jochnick, Chris. "The Human Rights Challenges to Global Poverty." Center for Economic and Social Rights, 2000. Accessed on-line at www.cesr.org.

Johnson, Craig A. "Rules, Norms and the Pursuit of Sustainable Livelihoods." IDS Working Paper, no. 52. Sussex: Institute for Development Studies, 1997.

Johnson, John J., ed. *The Role of the Military in Under-Developed Countries*. Princeton: Princeton University Press, 1962.

Joshi, Anuradha, and Mick Moore. "The Mobilising Potential of Anti-Poverty Programs." IDS Discussion Paper 374. Sussex: Institute for Development Studies, 2000.

Kaldor, Mary. *New and Old Wars: Organized Violence in a Global Era*. Cambridge, UK: Polity Press, 2001.

Kanbur, Ravi, and Lyn Squire. "The Evolution of Thinking about Poverty: Exploring the Interactions." World Bank, 1999. Accessed on-line at www.worldbank.org/povertynet.

Kanbur, Ravi, and Nora Lustig. "Why Is Inequality Back on the Agenda?" World Bank, 1999. Accessed on-line at www.worldbank.org/povertynet.

Kappaz, Christina. *Evaluation of the Human Resources Development Portfolio of the Multilateral Investment Fund*. Report prepared for the Office of Evaluation and Oversight of the Inter-American Development Bank, 2003.

Kaul, Inge, Isabelle Grunberg, and Marc A. Stern. *Global Public Goods: International Cooperation in the 21st Century*. New York: UNDP, 1999.

Keck, Margaret E., and Kathryn Sikkink. *Activists Beyond Borders*. Ithaca, New York: Cornell University Press, 1998.

Korten, David. "Community Organization and Rural Development: A Learning Process Approach." *Public Administration Review* 40, no. 5 (1980): 480–511.

———. "The Working Group as a Mechanism for Managing Bureaucratic Reorientation: Experience from the Philippines." NASPAA Working Paper, no. 4. Washington, D.C.: National Association of Schools of Public Affairs and Administration, 1982.

Korten, David, and R. Klauss. *People-Centered Development: Contributions toward Theory and Planning Frameworks*. Hartford, Conn.: Kumarian Press, 1984.

Korten, F. F. "Building National Capacity to Develop Water Users' Associations." World Bank Staff Working Paper, no. 58. Washington, D.C.: World Bank, 1982.

Kretzmann, John, and John McKnight. *Building Communities from the Inside Out*. Chicago: ACTA Publications, 1993.

Krishna, Anirudh, Norman Uphoff, and Milton J. Esman, Editors. *Reasons for Hope: Instructive Experiences in Rural Development*. West Hartford, Conn.: Kumarian Press, 1997.

Krugman, Paul. *The Great Unraveling: Losing Our Way in the New Century*. New York: W.W. Norton & Co., 2003.

Kuczynski, Pedro P., and John Williamson, eds. *After the Washington Consensus: Restarting Growth and Reform in Latin America*. Washington, D.C.: Institute of International Economics, 2003.

Lappé, Frances M., and Anna Lappé. *Hope's Edge: The Next Diet for a Small Planet*. New York: Tarcher/Putnam, 2002.

Lee, Ronald. "The Demographic Transition." *Journal of Economic Perspectives* 17, no. 4 (2003): 167–90.

Lenoir, Rene. *Les Exclus: Un Francais sur Dix*. Paris: Editions de Seuil, 1974–1989.

Levy, Frank. *The New Dollars and Dreams: American Incomes and Economic Change*. New York: Russel Sage Foundation, 1998.

Limerick, Patricia. *The Legacy of Conquest*. New York: W.W. Norton & Co., 1987.

Lindenberg, Marc. "Measuring Household Livelihood Security at the Family and Community Level in the Developing World." *World Development*, 2002.

Lindenberg, Marc, and Ben Crosby. *Managing Development: The Political Dimension*. West Hartford, Conn.: Kumarian Press, 1981.

Lindenberg, Marc, and Coralie Bryant. *Going Global: Transforming Relief and Development NGOs*. Bloomfield, Conn.: Kumarian Press, 2001.

Lindenberg, Marc M. *The Human Development Race: Improving the Quality of Life in Developing Countries*. San Francisco: ICS Press, 1993.

Lipton, Michael. 1993. "Land Reform as Commenced Business: The Evidence against Stopping." *World Development* 21, no. 4 (1993): 641–57.

———. *Successes in Anti-Poverty*. Geneva: International Labor Organization, 1998.

Lundberg, Marc, and B. Milanovic. *Globalization and Inequality: Are They Linked and How?* Washington, D.C.: World Bank, 2000.

Lundburg, Mattais, and Lyn Squire. "The Simultaneous Evolution of Growth and Inequality." *The Economic Journal* 113 (2003):326–344.

Lustig, Nora, ed. *Shielding the Poor: Social Protection in the Developing World*. Washington, D.C.: Inter-American Development Bank, 2001.

Mallikarjun, B. "Language(s) in the School Curriculum: Challenges of the New Millennium." *Language in India: Strength for Today and Bright Hope for Tomorrow* 1, no. 4 (2001). Accessed on-line at www.languageinindia.com/junjulaug2001/school.html.

Marris, Robin. *Ending Poverty*. New York: Thames & Hudson, Inc, 1999.

Martin, Gerard. "Observations on the Interrelations between Exclusion and Violent Conflict." Unpublished paper. 1999. Accessed on-line at

Marx, Karl. *The Eighteenth Brumaire of Louis Bonaparte. Selected Works of Karl Marx and Frederick Engels*. London: Lawrence and Wishart, 1968.

Maxwell, Simon. "Comparisons, Convergence and Connections: Development Studies in North and South." *IDS Bulletin* 29, no. 1 (1998): 20–31.

Mazur, Jay. "Globalization's Dark Side: Labor's New Internationalism." *Foreign Affairs* (January/February 2001): 79–93.

McElhinny, Vincent, and Mitchell A. Selgison. *From Civil Wars to Civil Violence: The Impact of Agrarian Inequality in El Salvador*. Pittsburgh: University of Pittsburgh, 2000.

McGee, Rosemary. *Analysis of Participatory Poverty Assessment (PPA) and Household Survey Findings on Poverty Trends in Uganda-IDS Mission Report*. Unpublished paper: Institute for Development Studies, 2000.

Meerman, Jacob. "Poverty and Mobility in Low-Status Minorities: The Cuban Case in International Perspective." *World Development* 29, no. 9 (2001): 1457–82.

Milanovic, Bruno. *Worlds Apart: The Twentieth Century Promise that Failed*. Washington, D.C.: World Bank, 2002.

Milanovich, Branko. *True World Income Distribution, 1988 and 1993: First Calculations Based on Household Surveys Alone*. Washington, D.C.: World Bank, 1999.

Miles, Matthew, and Michael Huberman. *Qualitative Data Analysis*. 2nd ed. London: Sage Publications, 1994.

Moore, Mick, and James Putzel. *Thinking Strategically about Politics and Poverty*. Sussex: Institute for Development Studies, 1999.

Moore, Mick, Jennifer Leavy, Peter Houtzager, and Howard White. *Polity Qualities: How Governance Affects Poverty*. Institute for Development Studies, 1999.

Morris, Mathew. "Social Capital and Poverty in India." IDS Working Paper 6. Sussex: Institute for Development Studies, 1999.

Moser, Carolyn. "The Asset Vulnerability Framework: Reassessing Poverty Reduction Strategies." *World Development* 26, no. 1 (1998): 1–19.

Mosse, Roberto, and Leigh Ellen Sontheimer. "Performance Monitoring Handbook." World Bank Technical Paper, no. 334. Washington, D.C.: World Bank, 1996.

Myrdhal, Gunnar. *Asian Drama: An Inquiry into the Poverty of Nations.* New York: Twentieth Century Fund, 1968.

Nafziger, Wayne E., and Rimo Vayrynen. *The Prevention of Humanitarian Emergencies.* New York: United Nations World Institute for Development Economics Research, 2002.

Narayan, Deepa. *Bonds and Bridges: Social Capital and Poverty.* Unpublished paper. 2000. Accessed on-line at www.worldbank.org: World Bank.

———. "Social Capital and the State: Complementarity and substitution." World Bank Policy Research Working Paper, no. 2167. Washington, D.C.: World Bank, 1999.

Narayan, Deepa, Robert Chambers, Meera K. Shah, and Patti Petesch. *Voices of the Poor: Crying Out for Change.* Washington, D.C.: World Bank and Oxford Univ Press, 2000.

Ndegwa, Stephen N. *The Two Faces of Civil Society: NGOs and Politics in Africa.* West Hartford, Conn.: Kumarian Press, 1996.

Nelson, Joan, ed. *Economic Crisis and Policy Choice.* Princeton, NJ: Princeton University Press, 1990.

Nelson, Joan M. *Poverty, Inequality, and Conflict in Developing Countries.* New York: Rockefeller Brothers Fund, Inc., 1998.

Nolan, Peter. *China's Rise, Russia's Fall.* London: MacMillan Press Ltd., 1995.

North, Douglas. *Institutions, Institutional Change and Economic Performance.* London: Cambridge University Press, 1990.

O'Brien, David, and Arjan de Haan. "Deprivation in the North and South: An Annotated Bibliography on Poverty and Social Exclusion." *Development Bibliography* 15, 1998.

O'Brien, David, Joanna Wilkes, Arjan de Haan, and Simon Maxwell. "Poverty and Social Exclusion in the North and South." IDS Working Paper, no. 55 (1997).

Oakley, Peter. "Social Exclusion and Afro Latinos." Presented at Social Inclusion Conference at the Inter-American Development Bank, Washington, D.C., 2001.

OECD. Development Cooperation Report 1999.

———. Development Cooperation Report 2004.

Okun, Arthur M. *Equality and Efficiency: The Big Tradeoff.* Washington, D.C.: Brookings Institution, 1975.

Ostrom, Elinor. *Crafting Institutions for Self-Governing Irrigation Systems*. San Francisco: Institute for Contemporary Studies, 1992.

———. *Governing the Commons: The Evolution of Institutions for Collective Action*. Cambridge: Cambridge University Press, 1990.

Oxfam International. "Education Charges: A Tax on Human Development." Oxfam Briefing Paper, no. 3. Oxford: Oxfam, 2001.

———. *Rigged Rules and Double Standards: Trade, Globalization, and the Fight against Poverty*. Oxford: Oxfam International, 2002.

Pigozzi, Mary J. *Implications of the Convention on the Rights of the Child for Education Activities*. New York: UNICEF Website, 2002.

Press, Eyal. "Rebel with a Cause." *The Nation*. 10 Jun 2002.

Pressman, Jeffrey, and Aaron Wildavsky. *Implementation: How Great Expectations in Washington Are Dashed in Oakland, or Why It's Amazing that Federal Programs Work at All*. Berkeley: University of California Press, 1973.

Pugh, Michael, and Neil Cooper with Jonathan Goodhand. *War Economies in a Regional Context*. Boulder, Colo.: Lynne Rienner Publishers, 2004.

Putnam, Robert D. *Bowling Alone*. New York: Simon & Schuster, 2000.

———. *Making Democracy Work*. Princeton, NJ: Princeton University Press, 1993.

Ravallion, Martin. *Competing Concepts in Inequality in the Globalization Debate*, 2004.

Ravallion, Martin. "Who Is Protected? On the Incidence of Fiscal Adjustment." World Bank, 2002. Accessed on-line at www.worldbank.org/poverty.

Ravallion, Martin, and Gaurav Datt. "When Is Growth Pro-Poor? Evidence from Diverse Experiences of India's States." World Bank Policy Research Working Paper, no. 2263. 1999.

Riddell, Roger, and Mark Robinson. "*Non-Governmental Organisations and Rural Poverty Alleviation*." London, Great Britain: Clarenden Press, 1995.

Roche, Chris. *Impact Assessment for Development Agencies: Learning to Value Change*. Oxford: Oxfam GB, 1999.

Rodrik, Dani. *Has Globalization Gone Too Far?* Washington, D.C.: Institute for International Economics, 1997.

———. "The New Global Economy and Developing Countries: Making Openness Work." Overseas Development Council Policy Essay, no. 24. Washington, D.C.: Johns Hopkins University Press for ODC, 1999.

Rouille d'Orfeuil, Henri, and Jorge Eduardo Durao. *The Role of NGOs in the Public Debate and International Relations: Elements for a Definition of Nongovernmental Diplomacy.* Unpublished manuscript. 2003.

Rubio, Francois. *A Quoi Servent Les ONG?* Paris: L'Hebe, 2003.

Sachs, Jeffrey D., *The Era of Poverty: Economic Possibilities for Our Times.* Penguin Press, 2005.

Sachs, Jeffrey D., John W. McArthur, Guido Schmidt-Traub, Margaret Kruk, Chandrika Bahadur, Michael Faye, and Gordon McCord. *Ending Africa's poverty trap.* Unpublished manuscript. 2004.

Sambanis, Nicholas. "Poverty and the Organization of Political Violence: A Review and Some Conjectures." Presented at Brookings Institution Trade Forum, May 13–14, 2004.

Schultz, T. P. "Inequality in the Distribution of Personal Income in the World; How It Is Changing and Why." *Journal of Population Economics* 11, no. 3 (1998): 307–44.

Schumpeter, Joseph A. *Capitalism, Socialism, and Democracy.* New York: Harper Torchbook, 1942.

Sen, Amartya. *On Economic Inequality.* Oxford: Clarendon Press, 1973.

Sen, Amartya K. *Choice, Welfare and Measurement.* Cambridge: Harvard University Press, 1997.

———. *Commodities and Capabilities.* New York: Elsevier Science Publishing, 1985.

———. *Development as Freedom.* New York: Knopf, 1999.

———. *Inequality Re-Examined.* Cambridge, MA: Harvard University Press, 1992.

———. *Resources, Values, and Development.* Cambridge, MA: Harvard University Press, 1984.

Sen, Somnath. "Military Expenditure Data for Developing Countries: Methods and Measurements." Chap. 1 in *Military Expenditure and Economic Development.* Washington, D.C.: World Bank, 1991.

Senge, Peter. *The Fifth Discipline.* New York: Doubleday/Currency, 1990.

———. *The Fifth Discipline Fieldbook.* New York: Currency Doubleday, 1994.

Siegel, Wendy, and Christina Kappaz. *Strengthening Illinois' Immigration Policy: Improving Health and Human Services for Immigrants and Refugees.* Chicago: Millennia Consulting for the Illinois Immigrant Policy Project, 2002.

Silver, Hilary. "European Policies to Promote the Social Inclusion of Disadvantaged Groups: Lessons for Latin America and the Caribbean." Presented at Social Inclusion Seminar at the Annual Meetings of the Inter-American Development Bank, Milan, Italy, 2003.

Sinding, Steven W. *Re-Engaging with the Developing World: The Aid Imperative.* New York: Columbia University Printing Services, 2002.

Skoufias, Emmanuel. "Economic Crises and Natural Disasters: Coping Strategies and Policy Implications." *World Development* 31, no. 7 (2003): 1087–102.

Smeeding, T. M., Gary Burtless, and L. Rainwater. "United States Poverty in a Cross National Context." In *Understanding Poverty*, Sheldon H. Danziger and Robert H. Haveman, eds. New York and Cambridge, MA: Russell Sage Foundation and Harvard University Press, 2002.

Smeeding, Timothy M., and Katherin Ross Phillips. "Social Protection for the Poor in the Developed World." In *Shielding the Poor*, Washington, D.C.: Brookings Institution Press, 2001.

Smith, Jackie, Charles Chatfield, and Ron Pagnucco, eds. *Transnational Social Movements and Global Politics: Solidarity Beyond the States.* Syracuse, NY: Syracuse University Press, 1997.

Stevens, Guy. "Welfare Reform and the Well-Being of America's Children." *Challenge* 45, no. 1 (2002): 6–46.

Stiglitz, Joseph. *Globalization and Its Discontents.* New York: W.W. Norton & Co., 2002.

Tendler, Judith. *Good Government in the Tropics.* 2000.

———. *Inside Foreign Aid.* Baltimore: Johns Hopkins University Press, 1975.

Thomas, Caroll. *Intermediary NGOs.* West Hartford, Conn.: Kumarian Press, 1992.

Thurow, Roger. "Makeshift 'Cuisinart' Makes A Lot Possible in Impoverished Mali." *Wall Street Journal.* 26 Jul 2002.

Tilly, Charles. "Violence, Terror, and Politics as Usual." *Boston Review* 27, no. 3–4 (2002): 21–24.

US Census Bureau. *Income, Poverty, and Health Insurance Estimates 1996.* Washington, D.C.: US Census Bureau, 1997.

Ul Haq, Mahbub. *The Poverty Curtain: Choices for the Third World.* New York: Columbia University Press, 1976.

UNCTAD. *World Economic Situation and Prospects for 1999.* New York: United Nations Conference on Trade and Development, 1999.

UNDP. *Human Development Report 1999.* New York: UNDP 1999.

———. *Human Development Report 2001.* New York: UNDP, 2001.

———. *Human Development Report 2002.* New York: UNDP, 2002.

———. *Human Development Report 2003. Millennium Development Goals.* New York: UNDP, 2003.

———. *Poverty in transition?* New York: UNDP, 1998.

Uphoff, Norman. *Learning from Gal Oya: Possibilities for Participatory Development and Post Newtonian Social Science.* London: Intermediate Technology Publications, 1996.

Uphoff, Norman, and C. M. Wijayaratna. "Demonstrated Benefits from Social Capital: The Productivity of Farmer Organizations in Gal Oya, Sri Lanka." *World Development* 28, no. 11 (1998): 1875–90.

Urquhart, Brian. "World Order and Mr. Bush." *The New York Times Review of Books* 50, no. 15 (2003).

Urquhart, Brian, and Erskine Childers. *Towards a More Effective United Nations.* Uppsala, Sweden: Motala Grafiska AB, 1992.

Uvin, Peter. *Aiding Violence.* West Hartford, Conn.: Kumarian Press, 1998.

van de Walle, Dominique. "Public Spending and the Poor: What We Know, What We Need to Know." World Bank Policy Research Working Paper, no. 147 (1995).

van Genugten, Willem, and Camilo Perez-Bustillo. *The Poverty of Rights: Human Rights and the Eradication of Poverty.* New York: Zed Books, 2001.

Wade, Robert H. *Globalization, Poverty and Income Distribution: Does the Liberal Argument Hold?* Unpublished draft. 2002.

Watkins, Kevin. *The Oxfam Poverty Report.* Oxford, UK: Oxfam, 2000.

Watts, Michael. *Silent Violence.* Berkeley and Los Angeles: University of California Press, 1983.

Weber, Max. *The Protestant Ethic and the Spirit of Capitalism.* New York: A. Knopf. 1958.

White, Louise G. *Creating Opportunities for Change: Approaches to Managing Development Programs.* Boulder, Colo.: Lynne Reinner Publishers, 1987.

———. *Implementing Policy Reforms in LDCs: A Strategy for Designing and Effecting Change.* Boulder, Colo.: Lynne Reinner Publishers, 1990.

Williamson, Oliver E. *The Economic Institutions of Capitalism.* London: The Free Press, 1985.

Winters, L. A. *Trade Liberalisation and Poverty.* London: Centre for Economic Policy Research and London School of Economics, 2000.

———. "Trade, Trade Policy and Poverty: What Are the Links?" Unpublished article for World Bank. 2001.

World Bank. *Development and Poverty: World Development Report 2000–2001.* Washington, D.C.: World Bank, 2001.

———. *Economic Causes of Civil Conflict and Their Implications for Policy.* Washington, D.C.: World Bank, 2000.

———. *Governance Policy Paper.* Washington, D.C.: World Bank, 1991.

————. *Poverty: World Development Report 1990.* Washington, D.C.: World Bank, 1990.

————. *Social Funds: Assessing Effectiveness.* Washington, D.C.: World Bank, 2002.

————. Speech of Robert McNamara delivered at the University of Chicago, 1979.

INDEX

ABOUT THE AUTHORS

CORALIE BRYANT, Professor and Director of the Economic and Political Development Program at the School for International and Public Affairs, Columbia University, is also currently assisting L'Institut des Estudes Politiques (Sciences-Po) in Paris with the development of their Atelier in Development. Both Coralie and Christina worked with Marc Lindenberg on a previous Kumarian book, *Going Global: Transforming International Relief and Development NGOs.* Prior to Columbia University, she was a senior staff member of the World Bank, where, among other work, in 1990–1991 she was one of the central authors and negotiators for the World Bank's first policy paper on governance. She was a senior institutional specialist working on strengthening environmental institutions in Brazil, and on civil service reform in Zambia. In the 1980s she was a senior fellow at the Overseas Development Council working on poverty and food policy in Southern Africa. While a professor at the American University in Washington, 1967–1987, she was the cofounder and codirector with Steven Arnold of their International Development Program. An active consultant working generally in Eastern and Southern Africa, with experience as well in Bangladesh and Brazil, she has captured some of the lessons learned in five books and dozens of articles and monographs. Her doctorate is from the London School of Economics.

CHRISTINA KAPPAZ is a consultant on economic development projects, currently based in Chicago and working with Millennia Consulting on a range of projects in the United States and throughout Latin America. Prior to beginning consulting work in 1996, Christina worked at the World Bank from 1991 to 1994 and at the Inter-American Development

Bank from 1994 to 1996. Her work has primarily focused on issues of labor market development including projects related to enhancing the effectiveness of training and job placement programs, including projects targeted at displaced workers, microenterprises, small and medium business, youth, and female headed households, as well as projects that specifically aim to advance policy reforms related to labor market development and the introduction of skill standards and certification. She has applied her practical project experience to project evaluation and has also conducted numerous policy studies on a range of policies related to economic and social development. Christina, fluent in Spanish, has worked primarily in Latin America but has also done project work in Central and Eastern Europe, as well as Africa and the Caribbean. Christina holds both a Master's of Business Administration and a Masters of International Affairs from Columbia University. Her B.A. in Government is from Dartmouth College.

Also from Kumarian Press...

International Development, Humanitarianism, Peacebuilding

Ethics and Global Politics: The Active Learning Sourcebook
Edited by April Morgan, Lucinda Joy Peach, and Colette Mazzucelli

Human Rights and Development
Peter Uvin

Nation-Building Unraveled? Aid, Peace and Justice in Afghanistan
Edited by Antonio Donini, Norah Niland and Karin Wermester

Ritual and Symbol in Peacebuilding
Lisa Schirch

Southern Exposure
International Development and the Global South in the Twenty-First Century
Barbara P. Thomas-Slayter

War and Intervention: Issues for Contemporary Peace Operations
Michael V. Bhatia

Global Development

Going Global: Transforming Relief and Developing NGOs
Marc Lindenberg and Coralie Bryant

A Civil Republic: Beyond Capitalism and Nationalism
Severyn T. Bruyn

Global Civil Society: Dimensions of the Nonprofit Sector, Volume One
Lester M. Salamon, Helmut K. Anheier, Regina List, Stefan Toepler, S. Wojciech Sokolowski and Associates

Global Civil Society: Dimensions of the Nonprofit Sector, Volume Two
Lester M. Salamon, S. Wojciech Sokolowski, and Associates

Globalization and Social Exclusion: A Transformationalist Perspective
Ronaldo Munck

The Charity of Nations: Humanitarian Action in a Calculating World
Ian Smillie and Larry Minear

When Corporations Rule the World, Second Edition
David C. Korten

Worlds Apart: Civil Society and the Battle for Ethical Globalization
John Clark

Visit Kumarian Press at **www.kpbooks.com** or
call toll-free **800.289.2664** for a complete catalog.

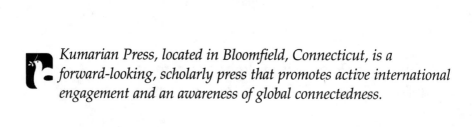
Kumarian Press, located in Bloomfield, Connecticut, is a forward-looking, scholarly press that promotes active international engagement and an awareness of global connectedness.